THE CLASSIC BEST-SELLER
OVER 500,000 IN PRINT

THE MEASURE OF A
MAN

20

ATTRIBUTES OF
A GODLY MAN

GENE A. GETZ

This book truly transcends culture. We are using it to help train over three thousand pastors here in Nigeria—who in turn can train other men in our churches throughout West Africa.

REV. MUSA NCHOCK ASAKA, DIRECTOR OF LEADERSHIP DEVELOPMENT
EVANGELICAL CHURCHES OF WEST AFRICA (ECWA)

Gene's "Measure of a Man" seminars and general assembly presentations have been a godsend to thousands of men at our Maximum Man Conferences. Gene also lives what he teaches. We heartily recommend *The Measure of a Man* for personal and small-group use.

KEITH BOYD, EXECUTIVE DIRECTOR, MINISTRY TO MEN FOUNDATION

This book has real substance!

TED MAXWELL, PRESIDENT AND FOUNDER, MEN ALIVE, CANADA

I know of no tool more biblical and practical than *The Measure of a Man*! It's excellent!

DAVID MCCOMBS, MEN'S MINISTRY, CAMPUS CRUSADE FOR CHRIST

I believe that this book is especially relevant as it relates to developing the character of Black men in the midst of the crisis we face in urban America. I pray that it will get wide distribution within the African-American community.

DR. JOHN M. PERKINS, PUBLISHER, *URBAN FAMILY* MAGAZINE

I'm excited about this new edition of *The Measure of a Man*. It's been a classic in men's literature. This new edition includes powerful illustrations that have grown out of Gene's own ministry to men.

BRIAN PETERSEN, EDITOR, *NEW MAN* MAGAZINE

I highly recommend *The Measure of a Man*. It is practical, biblical and filled with experience!

RON RAND, AUTHOR: *FOR FATHERS WHO AREN'T IN HEAVEN*

THE CLASSIC BEST-SELLER
OVER 500,000 IN PRINT

THE MEASURE OF A
MAN

20
ATTRIBUTES OF
A GODLY MAN

GENE A. GETZ

FOREWORD BY BILL McCARTNEY
FOUNDER, PROMISE KEEPERS

THE CLASSIC BEST-SELLER

OVER 500,000 IN PRINT

THE MEASURE OF A MAN

20

ATTRIBUTES OF
A GODLY MAN

GENE A. GETZ

Regal Books
A Division of Gospel Light
Ventura, California, U.S.A.

Published by Regal Books
A Division of Gospel Light
Ventura, California, U.S.A.
Printed in U.S.A.

Regal Books is a ministry of Gospel Light, an evangelical Christian publisher dedicated to serving the local church. We believe God's vision for Gospel Light is to provide church leaders with biblical, user-friendly materials that will help them evangelize, disciple and minister to children, youth and families.

It is our prayer that this Regal Book will help you discover biblical truth for your own life and help you meet the needs of others. May God richly bless you.

For a free catalog of resources from Regal Books/Gospel Light please contact your Christian supplier or call 1-800-4-GOSPEL.

Library of Congress Cataloging-in-Publication Data
Getz, Gene A.
    The measure of a man / Gene Getz.
        p. cm.
    ISBN 0-8307-1756-0 (trade)
    1. Men—Religious life. 2. Spiritual life—Christianity.
I. Title.
BV4843.G47 1995   95-6970
248.8'42—dc20   CIP

1 2 3 4 5 6 7 8 9 / 02 01 00 99 98 97 96 95

Rights for publishing this book in other languages are contracted by Gospel Literature International (GLINT). GLINT also provides technical help for the adaptation, translation and publishing of Bible study resources and books in scores of languages worldwide. For further information, contact GLINT, P.O. Box 4060, Ontario, CA 91761-1003, U.S.A., or the publisher.

CONTENTS

"FORGETTING WHAT LIES BEHIND ...I PRESS ON"

These are the words of Paul to the Philippians. He made it clear he had not "become perfect," but he said, "But one thing I do: forgetting what lies behind and reaching forward to what lies ahead, I press on toward the goal for the prize of the upward call of God in Christ Jesus" (Phil. 3:13,14).

This is what becoming a man of God is all about. Paul made it clear that he was in process. His journey toward maturity was still incomplete, and unfinished.

The true "measure of a man" is not that we're manifesting all the qualities Paul outlined as goals for himself and us, but whether or not we're taking significant steps to reach those goals. Each one of us is somewhere on that continuum. The important question relates to where we are on our spiritual journey in the light of our personal history—our past lives as non-Christians, our present environment now that we are Christians—and the difficulties we face, perhaps because of unfortunate decisions we've made over the years or even because of circumstances beyond our control. Are we pressing on? That's the question!

A PAINFUL JOURNEY

As I sat and read the article in *Sports Illustrated* entitled "Putting His

House in Order," I was deeply moved by Coach Bill McCartney's comments about why he resigned as head football coach at the University of Colorado—at a moment in his life when he was at the peak of his professional career. Bill's explanation for this decision reflected honesty, integrity, humility and courage. His statements also demonstrate what *becoming* a man of God is all about.

Early on in the article, the authors (Richard Hoffer and Shelley Smith) succinctly summarized the reason Bill gave for his decision: "He is quitting to spend time with his wife of thirty-two years, Lyndi, and he waves all other explanations aside."

Hey, Get Real!
As is always true, everyone tries to second-guess this kind of decision. After all, the world is filled with illustrations of people who sacrifice everything to achieve their own personal, selfish goals. But Bill McCartney made the opposite decision. By his own confession, he *was* motivated by selfish goals. But he decided to change all that—to put his family first, more specifically, his wife.

A Startling Reflection
Some of Bill's statements in this article from *Sports Illustrated* are powerful, and are convicting to any man who has been caught up in the demands and expectations of our culture.[1] Listen to this. Bill states:

> The glory of a man is his wife. Nothing tells you more about a man than what you see in his wife. When you look into the countenance of a man's wife, you will see everything he has invested or withheld. You will see what kind of character he has.

A Face Filled with Pain
Bill shared with me personally how and when this biblical truth first began to penetrate his soul. He was sitting in church with his wife, Lyndi. The visiting speaker was explaining Paul's statement to the Corinthians—what he meant when he said that "the woman is the glory of man" (1 Cor. 11:7). Sensing that the Holy Spirit was speaking to him personally, Bill glanced over at Lyndi. He was startled!

Her face reflected deep emotional pain. That experience, Bill reflected, was the moment that jolted him into reality—a moment that eventually led him to resign from one of the most prestigious positions in the world of college athletics.

A New Priority

When interviewed by the authors of the *Sports Illustrated* article, they asked Bill why he resigned. He stated further:

> I see an opportunity to put everything on a back burner and have a marriage become all it's capable of being. That's what's in my heart, and nothing else. I know it's almost un-American to quit your job, and I know it sounds arrogant, because not everybody can do it. But not everybody has a job as demanding or taxing as being head football coach. I recognize this is not conventional thinking, but it's very much my thinking. And I wasn't always in touch with that. But now that I am, it's the most compelling convicting thought that I have.
>
> Many of our best years are ahead of us. I don't want to be [spending time with her] as a result of some adversity, some catastrophe. I want to do this while we both have a lot of energy and excitement about our lives.

A Different Look

Once Bill made this decision, he knew he had made the right decision. He saw a different face. He explains:

> Over the last three weeks [since his resignation] I've seen a woman radiant. She knows I love her more than football. If you could just see the glow on Lyndi's face, you'd understand. Because it's real clear now what's more important. Lyndi's more important.

One of the most telling comments in this article comes from an old friend, Tom Versaci: "Mac has always put football first. Lyndi has had to contend with a lot of late meals, a lot of missed meals, and she's been hurt a lot....He could have written his own ticket to several big programs, but he has said, 'No, I want this time with my wife.' He's trying to play catch-up with his family, to make up for the last thirty years."

WHY THIS TRIBUTE?

As you read and study *The Measure of a Man*, I'm confident you'll understand why I want to dedicate this book to Coach Bill McCartney. But I think you'll also understand why I want to dedicate it to his wife, Lyndi. It's obvious she has faithfully stood in the shadows—watching, waiting, hoping and often suffering. But she hung in there through a lot of adversity, including some really tough family problems. A lesser woman would have bailed out, or issued an ultimatum years ago and said, "It's either me or football."

Lyndi did neither. She deserves tremendous credit for Bill's success as a winning football coach. The maxim is still true: Behind every successful man is a great woman—not a perfect one—for greatness is not measured by perfection. But one thing is certain. Had Lyndi not been so supportive during all these years, there may have been no winning football team and certainly no Promise Keepers. More importantly, Bill McCartney could not have come face-to-face with his blind spots—namely his neglect. Furthermore, he may never have been able to do something about it before he faced an irreversible crisis.

WHAT ABOUT YOU AND ME?

All of us as men—including those of us in full-time ministry—need this example. And I'm convinced that many of our wives *need* the results. This in itself is the most valuable aspect of this story.

And it's what becoming a man of God is all about. Again, it's not demonstrating perfection. Rather, it's admitting our mistakes and making decisions to correct those mistakes in the light of God's will for our lives.

Bill has made it clear that not everyone can quit his job and devote time to his wife. For most of us, this is totally unrealistic. But there *are* things most of us can do to make sure we're not neglecting one of our greatest gifts. Perhaps the *most important thing* we can do is to learn to listen.

So Lyndi—thanks for hanging in there. But thanks also for getting Bill's attention! It's a great example to us all. And Bill, thanks for listening, and thanks for your courage and vulnerability! You've marked my own life!

Gene A. Getz

Note

1. Richard Hoffer and Shelley Smith, "Putting His House in Order," *Sports Illustrated* 82, no. 2, 16 January 1995, 28-32.

FOREWORD

This book—*The Measure of a Man*—has become a classic! Though Gene Getz wrote it a number of years ago as a professor turned pastor, it has continued to be the basis of men's Bible studies, not only in America, but also all around the world. A multitude of pastors are using this book to equip dozens of men in their churches, using it as a discipling tool to prepare these men to be good husbands, good fathers and key leaders in the church. Thousands of men meet regularly—one-on-one or in small groups—and discuss this dynamic biblical material and work through the practical projects at the end of each chapter.

The reason this book has *never* gone out of print is simple to explain. The basic outline comes directly from the Word of God. Gene, himself, says, "I'm excited that over the years this book has continued to impact men spiritually. But I often remark that the apostle Paul is really the original author of *The Measure of a Man*. I simply took the qualities that he received directly from the Holy Spirit and brought these truths into the twentieth century with current illustrations and practical projects to help us develop these characteristics of maturity in our lives."

I'm delighted to write the foreword to *The Measure of a Man*. I recommend it. It's not just an "old book" with a "new cover" but it's completely rewritten. It's also a "Promise Keepers" kind of book since it reflects Gene's own experiences in working with men over the years. Fellowship Bible Church North—one of several churches Gene planted and the one he presently pastors—reflects his commitment to developing a strong men's ministry. Every year, hundreds of men retreat to a conference center to learn more about becoming mature men of God. At that time, every man is encouraged to find an accountability partner as well as to continue to meet in small groups to help one other maintain a high level of integrity in their Christian lives.

Those of you familiar with Promise Keepers are aware of how much I believe in accountability—especially among men. We all need it. This book provides an excellent means for all of us to develop this kind of relationship with other men. *The Measure of a Man* will give you an opportunity to become open and vulnerable in the context of scriptural truth. Will it be a stretching experience—perhaps even threatening? Yes, but as someone has said, "Where there is no pain, there's no gain." How well I know—on the football field—but more importantly, in my own spiritual journey. But the spiritual results outweigh the price you may pay for being honest before God and one another.

Bill McCartney

INTRODUCTION
A CRY FOR HELP

One day I received a call from D. D. Lewis, former linebacker with the Dallas Cowboys. "I'm in trouble," D. D. said, "and I need help! Will you help me?"

D. D.'s voice sounded desperate. "Sure," I replied. "Let's meet on Thursday morning at the Harvey House Hotel in Plano."

COULD THIS BE AN NFL SUPERSTAR?

While playing with the Cowboys, D. D. had attended the church I pastored. After earning five Super Bowl rings under Coach Tom Landry, he eventually retired and went into business for himself. At some point along the way, he had stopped attending church and I had lost contact with him.

Unfortunately, things didn't go well for D. D. after he left the Cowboys. He experienced two business failures and eventually went through a painful divorce that also left him alienated from his children. Although a professing Christian, D. D.'s life had deteriorated.

As we met that Thursday morning, this once powerful man on the football field poured out his sad story. By the time D. D. called me that day, he had already determined to change his life. He knew he needed more spiritual help and more accountability.

Getting Back on Track

As I sat with D. D. that day, I saw the desperation in his eyes. "I'll help you," I replied. "Let's meet once a week for breakfast, and then work through my book *The Measure of a Man*."

D. D. was grateful. He would read a chapter each week and then we would meet to talk, discuss and pray.

"You'll need to be honest with me," I said. "No secrets. If you fail in some area of your life, you'll need to admit it up front, and get back on track with the Lord."

Again, D. D. agreed and together we worked through the chapters in this book. Here is what this experience meant to him:

> Meeting with Gene and going through his book, *The Measure of a Man*, helped usher me back into renewed relationships with the family of God. The book showed me that God does have a design and standard for godly men to follow.
>
> I grew up in the church, but the Ten Commandments were as close as I got to any instructions on being a man of God. With Gene's loving encouragement, I got to see that God loves me in spite of my past behavior (Titus 3:3-7), and that my journey toward maturity is a process and not an overnight quick-fix emotional sensation.
>
> Our time together fostered in me a real thirst for God's Word. It has sustained me through some rough periods and trials. I have found out that most men have the same problems over the years, and that healing begins when we share ourselves with other godly men.

AN EXPERIENCE I WILL NEVER FORGET

As D. D. and I sat week after week, working through *The Measure of a Man*, my thoughts went back to a dynamic Bible study I had with a group of men in Dallas. We met on 20 successive Thursday mornings— from 6:45 to 7:45—in the Downtowner Motel conference room before we all went off to work for the day. We wanted to discover from Scripture and from each other how we could become better husbands, better fathers, better Christians—in short, more mature men of God. Today, we might say we wanted to become "Promise Keepers."

What made this time with D. D. Lewis so special was that the book we were using to study what God says about becoming a mature man of God grew out of that earlier group Bible study. You see, I was so excited about what was happening in all of our lives that

I began to duplicate the experience in writing. The end result was *The Measure of a Man.*

HOW DO WE MEASURE MATURITY?

The apostle Paul outlined in his two pastoral letters 20 dynamic qualities for measuring our maturity levels—his first letter to Timothy and the one he wrote to Titus. The group of men spent 20 weeks looking at these characteristics one by one. Each Thursday morning, one of us in the group took about 30 minutes to share what we could learn from Scripture about each particular quality. We then spent another 30 minutes in discussion and personal sharing, focusing primarily on how each one of us could develop each quality more adequately in our lives.

Our study together had a profound effect on all of us. As I helped lead some of these sessions, and as I simply listened and participated in others, my own life was influenced and changed in some profound ways. What was happening in all of our lives motivated me to share this experience with other men.

AN AMAZING DISCOVERY

As an official minister of the gospel, this Bible study experience also caused me to reflect back on my ordination evaluation questionnaire. I was asked many questions: to prove Christ's deity, to demonstrate why I believed the Bible was the inspired Word of God and many other doctrinal questions. I was also asked some practical questions: how to counsel divorced people, how to resolve other personal problems and so on. *But no one asked me if I measured up to the qualities in 1 Timothy 3 and Titus 1.*

This is amazing because this is where Paul began evaluating men for the ministry to determine if they were qualified to lead others. As I became more experienced in the ministry, I discovered that my ordination experience was not uncommon. Few ordination counsels ask this question. Needless to say, when serving in this capacity, this is one of the first questions I ask.

"Entrust to Faithful Men"

As you read through, study through and share this experience with others, you are one of these men. And I trust you will duplicate this experience in the lives of others, for if you do, you will be a part of a great dream that was implanted in the mind of the apostle Paul by the Holy Spirit nearly 2,000 years ago. Writing to Timothy shortly before he died a martyr's death at the hands of Nero, Paul penned these words:

> You therefore, my son, be strong in the grace that is in Christ Jesus. And the things which you have heard from me in the presence of many witnesses, these entrust to faithful men, who will be able to teach others also (2 Tim. 2:1,2).

Will you become one of these "faithful men"?

"THE MEASURE...OF CHRIST"

Those 20 weeks together in Bible study affected all of the men in the group. Each of these men ministered in a special way to me, and to one another. Our vocations differed. Our life goals varied. But we had one thing in common—our personal struggles as well as our victories in Jesus Christ. As we studied the Scriptures and shared our lives with each other, these experiences became a divine source for mutual encouragement and challenge to conform our lives "to the measure of the stature which belongs to the fulness of Christ" (Eph. 4:13).

For all of the men in the group, this was just the beginning. We are still on the journey. Won't you join us? Paul expressed it well:

> Not that I have already obtained it, or have already become perfect, but I press on in order that I may lay hold of that for which also I was laid hold of by Christ Jesus (Phil. 3:12).

As I sat that day and looked across the table at D. D. Lewis, I reminisced. *What we began several years ago is continuing,* I thought. This time, it was just the two of us. The difference was that we both had a copy of "the book" to help us understand and apply the truth in "God's Book." This is really what *The Measure of a Man* is all about.

CROSSING LANGUAGE BARRIERS

Through the years, I have been thrilled by hearing reports of men's groups that have used this study to repeat what we did originally at the Downtowner Motel—in small groups, in large groups and one-on-one.

An Experience in French-Speaking Quebec

One weekend my wife and I were ministering to a group of pastors and their wives in Quebec, Canada. Following one of the services, a pastor shared with me that he had been meeting with a large group of men on Saturday mornings. "We spend an hour working through a chapter in *The Measure of a Man*," he said, his eyes beaming. "We then spend another hour discussing how to develop these qualities in our lives. And then," he continued, "we spend a third hour in prayer, asking God to help us become more mature men of God." Frankly, I was overwhelmed. But what meant even more is that they were studying the French edition of the book.

A Current Experience

As I was putting the finishing touches on this introduction to this revised edition, I met a missionary couple who were ministering in Brazil. They had been there for several years and were back in the United States taking some courses in a Bible training school. I had never met them before. We had a wonderful conversation, but what amazed me the most was the husband's comment about *The Measure of a Man*. He had used the Portuguese translation to disciple a group of men. And then his wife added, "And I used *The Measure of a Woman* with a Brazilian woman, and it changed her life."[1] What an encouraging experience to motivate me to do this very extensive revision of this book. God's timing was perfect.

Pleasant Surprises and Unexpected Events

When I first wrote *The Measure of a Man*, it never entered my mind that this book would be translated into many languages and be used literally all over the world. You see, the eternal principles of the Word of God are transcultural. What Paul outlined nearly 2,000 years ago are God's standards for maturity for all time and in all cultures. When all is said and done, it is only God's Word that can penetrate our hearts and conform us to the image of Jesus Christ.

MULTIPLYING FAITHFUL MEN

Earlier, I referred to Paul's challenge to Timothy—to multiply himself by passing on to others what he had learned from Paul. But there is more. Paul wanted the process to go on and on as "faithful men" are "able to teach others also" (2 Tim. 2:2).

Following are some practical suggestions for multiplying "faithful men."

- Look for another man who will meet with you regularly and work through the 20 qualities described in the chapters to follow.
- Look for four or five men who will join you in this study. Several men meeting together will bring even greater enrichment to this experience.
- As a pastor, Sunday School teacher or Bible study leader, enlarge the circle by inviting a larger group to join you in this study. Our first time through, we had approximately 25 men attending the study.
- As a pastor, use this study with your church leadership—your elders, your deacons, your trustees, your Sunday School teachers—either one-on-one or in a group.

A PLAN OF ACTION

- Ideally, plan for 20 weeks of study—a week for each chapter. It is possible, of course, to cover two or more chapters at a time. You might also select certain chapters for the group to study. If you choose this suggestion, have the group vote on which chapters they would like to study together.
- As a leader, you can take the primary responsibility for guiding the group through this study. Or you can select men from the group who you believe are also qualified to participate as lead-

ers. If you choose this second suggestion, make sure you model how to lead in the first session.

SUGGESTED FORMAT

- Spend half the session (ideally 30 minutes) studying from the Scriptures the particular quality outlined in each chapter. Use *The Measure of a Man* as a springboard into the Word of God. For each quality, define the characteristic and then look for related passages where this quality is used and described.
- Spend the second half of each time discussing how to develop the particular chosen quality in each of your lives. Use the "Points of Action" in each chapter as a springboard into your discussion. The question section in "Thinking and Growing Together" is designed for interaction and application.
- As a leader, illustrate how you are developing these qualities in your own experiences. Model vulnerability. Share your weaknesses as well as your strengths. It is important to encourage the other men in the group to be open and candid as well.
- Conclude each discussion by encouraging the men to pray for each other.

THE NEXT ASSIGNMENT

- As you conclude each session, encourage each participant to read the next chapter in *The Measure of a Man* and to personally work through the "Points of Action."
- As a leader, you might call all the men in the study during the week to see if they have any questions about the assignment or if they have any suggestions for the next group study.

Note
1. See Gene A. Getz, *The Measure of a Woman* (Ventura, CA: Regal Books, 1977).

1
BECOMING FAITHFUL MEN

We are living in a day when instant formulas are applied to almost everything we do—from preparing microwave meals to trying to get rich in three simple steps. Our push-button society and computerized age have conditioned us to think this way. We want "presto-chango" solutions to all our problems.

Some Christians think this way about becoming spiritually mature. The facts are that it takes time to conform our lives to Jesus Christ. It is a lifetime process. No quick shortcuts are available to become a man of God. This is why Paul wrote to the Philippians:

> Not that I have already obtained it, or have already become perfect, but I press on in order that I may lay hold of that for which also I was laid hold of by Christ Jesus (Phil. 3:12).

BUILDING ON A SOLID FOUNDATION

All of us embark on our Christian journeys with a variety of backgrounds and experiences, which affect the progress we make in our spiritual lives. Some people who accept Jesus Christ as their personal Lord and Savior grow quickly, simply because they have had a good home environment and good role models. They have made good decisions in life. They have managed to sidestep the deterioration that comes with alcohol abuse, drug use and sexual promiscuity.

And that from Childhood

In this sense, these people are like Timothy, who learned the Scriptures from childhood. Although his father was not a believer (see Acts 16:1), Timothy had great role models in his mother, Eunice, and his grandmother, Lois (see 2 Tim. 1:5). When Timothy heard the gospel, he responded and became a follower of Jesus Christ. His spiritual growth was rapid, simply because he had a great foundation on which to build. Consequently, Paul wrote to Timothy and said:

> You, however, continue in the things you have learned and become convinced of, knowing from whom you have learned them; and that from childhood you have known the sacred writings which are able to give you the wisdom that leads to salvation through faith which is in Christ Jesus (3:14,15).

Equipped for Every Good Work

Timothy was fortunate. He had a good foundation in the Old Testament. When he heard Paul preach the gospel, his heart was open and he understood that Jesus Christ—the Messiah predicted by the prophets—had come. This wisdom led him to accept Christ as Lord and Savior.

When Timothy became a Christian, Paul built on that foundation with additional biblical truth—the New Testament Scriptures. Thus Paul wrote to Timothy:

> All Scripture is inspired by God and profitable for teaching, for reproof, for correction, for training in righteousness; that the man of God may be adequate, equipped for every good work (3:16,17).

Because of his foundation in the Scriptures, Timothy grew spiritually by leaps and bounds. Within a year or two—the time Paul returned to Lystra on the second missionary journey—Timothy was already mature enough in his faith to become Paul's missionary companion (see Acts 16:1-3).

NO BIBLICAL FOUNDATION

Today, many people who have not been as fortunate as Timothy become Christians. They have not had a good Christian heritage. In the twentieth-century American culture, some people have no biblical foundations whatsoever. They are more like the Ephesians and other Gentiles who came to Christ in the first century. They have grown up living a pagan—or irreligious—life. They have "walked according to the course of this world" (Eph. 2:2). And now as Christians, they need to learn to "lay aside the old self" (4:22)—their old ways of thinking and feeling that have been programmed to follow sinful patterns. In a special way, they need to "be renewed in the spirit" of their minds (v. 23). They need to "put on the new self" (v. 24).

Paul succinctly outlined this process of spiritual growth in his profound and powerful letter to the Romans:

> I urge you therefore, brethren, by the mercies of God, to present your bodies a living and holy sacrifice, acceptable to God, which is your spiritual service of worship. And do not be conformed to this world, but be transformed by the renewing of your mind, that you may prove what the will of God is, that which is good and acceptable and perfect (Rom. 12:1,2).

The background we bring to our conversion experience *does* make a difference in how quickly our spiritual growth occurs.

WHERE ARE YOU ON THE CONTINUUM?

A Positive Religious Background

I am reminded of a man in our church who was converted to Jesus Christ from a very religious background. In fact, he was an elder in a liberal church. And although he wasn't a born-again believer, he was a man of high moral and ethical character. He had been taught, and believed, that we are saved by good works. Consequently, he worked hard at being good.

One day this man heard that salvation "is the gift of God; not as a result of works, that no one should boast" (Eph. 2:8,9). When he understood this great truth, he received Jesus Christ as his personal Lord and Savior. Because of his religious heritage—wrong though it was in terms of the salvation message—he began to grow rapidly in his Christian life. And soon all the members of his family became Christians. Together, they began to grow rapidly in their Christian faith.

Once this man became a true believer, his spiritual growth was phenomenal. In that sense, he was like Timothy. In a short time period, all of us who knew this man encouraged him to become an elder in the first Fellowship Bible Church I launched in Dallas, Texas. Today, years later, he is serving as an elder with me at Fellowship Bible Church North. He is still growing in his Christian life and is a godly model for other men in the church.

A Negative Secular Background

I am thinking of another man in our church who became a Christian after living a sinful lifestyle. He came from an abusive home and his parental role models were anything but positive. Although he had a little knowledge of the Bible, he knew nothing of true Christianity.

When I first met this man, he had been married and divorced several times. In his own words, he was on the verge of becoming an alcoholic and was also a womanizer. He was so disillusioned with life that he was planning his suicide, when by God's grace, a friend of mine reached out to him and led him to Jesus Christ.

This man's life was dramatically changed. He then began a spiritual journey about which he knew nothing. He discovered he had problems from the past he never knew existed. Needless to say, he struggles daily but hasn't given up. The process of "laying aside the old self" and putting "on the new self" is a much more difficult process. But it is happening. He knows very well that becoming a man of God—the man he wants to become—will take time.

A LIFETIME PROCESS

What we bring to our conversion experience *does* make a difference in terms of our spiritual progress. When all is said and done, however, one thing is true of all of us. It still takes time to become a man of God, no matter what our spiritual and psychological heritage. Although we reach a certain level of maturity, conforming our lives to the image of Jesus Christ is an ongoing lifetime process until we meet Jesus Christ face-to-face. Paul testified to this in his own life when he wrote to the Corinthians:

> When I was a child, I used to speak as a child, think as a child, reason as a child; when I became a man, I did away with childish things. For now we see in a mirror dimly, but then face to face; now I know in part, but then I shall know fully just as I also have been fully known (1 Cor. 13:11,12).

DISCOVERING FAITHFUL MEN

When Paul wrote to Timothy, he referred to a "man of God" who is "equipped for every good work" (2 Tim. 3:17). This raises an important question. How do we recognize a "man of God"? What does he look like?

Timothy in Ephesus

These are not new questions; they were also going through Timothy's mind when Paul left him in Ephesus to establish the church. While he was in Ephesus, Timothy had to deal with men who wanted to be teachers and spiritual leaders.[1]

Paul commended these men in Ephesus. "It is a fine work he desires to do" he wrote to Timothy (1 Tim. 3:1). But he cautioned Timothy to make sure that each man who wanted to serve in a leadership role was a certain kind of man.

Titus in Crete

Titus faced the same challenge in his ministry. Paul left him in Crete to "appoint elders in every city" (Titus 1:5). Again, Paul cautioned Titus to make sure that men who emerged as leaders measured up to certain qualifications.

Apparently, Titus faced problems in Crete that were more difficult to resolve than those Timothy faced in Ephesus. Already, men who evidently claimed to be Christians had emerged and were "upsetting whole families, teaching things they should not teach" (1:11). Their motive was money. Titus not only faced the awesome task of discovering and training men to be godly, but also to silence those who were "empty talkers and deceivers" (1:10).

PAUL'S MATURITY PROFILE

The two paragraphs in Paul's letters to Timothy and Titus give us a powerful profile for testing our maturity levels in Christ (1 Tim. 3:1-7; Titus 1:5-10). The following is a combined list of these spiritual qualifications from both letters:

1. **Above reproach** (a man with a good reputation)
2. **Husband of one wife** (maintaining moral purity)
3. **Temperate** (exemplifying balance in words and actions)
4. **Prudent** (being wise and humble)
5. **Respectable** (serving as a good role model)
6. **Hospitable** (demonstrating unselfishness and generosity)
7. **Able to teach** (communicating sensitively in a nonthreatening and nondefensive manner)
8. **Not given to wine** (not being addicted to substances)
9. **Not self-willed** (not being a self-centered and controlling personality)
10. **Not quick-tempered** (void of anger that becomes sinful)
11. **Not pugnacious** (not an abusive person)
12. **Uncontentious** (nonargumentative and nondivisive)
13. **Gentle** (a sensitive, loving and kind person)
14. **Free from the love of money** (nonmaterialistic)
15. **One who manages his own household well** (a good husband and father)
16. **A good reputation with those outside the church** (a good testimony to unbelievers)
17. **Love what is good** (pursuing godly activities)
18. **Just** (wise, discerning, nonprejudiced and fair)
19. **Devout** (holy and righteous)
20. **Not a new convert** (not a new Christian)

PAUL'S PRAGMATICS

I had an interesting experience one day when I was conducting a "Measure of a Man" seminar in Chicago. Two men sitting near the front row were obviously interested in what I was sharing about this list of 20 qualities. They actually began giving me positive feedback, not only with body language, but also with words such as: "That's right, Gene." "That's true." "That's a good point."

Who's This Titus Guy?

Encouraged by these two men's responses, I went over and sat at their table during the next coffee break, hoping to get better acquainted. I discovered they were both in upper management in a large steel mill in Gary, Indiana. Furthermore, they were both brand-new Christians. One of the men said, "Gene, this is outstanding material. We've heard it before, but not from the Bible." The other agreed, and then added, "Yeah, I've heard of Timothy before, but this Titus guy, I've never heard of him."

This Is the Kind of Men We're Looking For

I then knew I was relating to two men who were not only new Christians, but who also knew little about the Bible. But I soon discovered these men were not new to the field of management. At that point, they made an observation I will never forget. "You know," they said, "this is the first time we've heard this list of qualifications from the Bible. But," they continued, "we've learned from experience in hiring people for middle-management positions that this is the kind of men we're looking for. We want men who have a good reputation. We don't want a man who is cheating on his wife or sleeping around, because chances are, he'll cheat the company. We certainly don't want a man who has all kinds of domestic problems. If he can't handle his own family, how in the world is he going to handle people in our steel mill?"

Characteristic by characteristic, these men outlined what they learned from experience, and had arrived at the same basic list of qualifications that closely paralleled Paul's list.

All Truth Is God's Truth

How fascinating, I thought. We had been looking at a list inspired by the Holy Spirit and outlined by Paul nearly 2,000 years ago. And here were two men who were new Christians and knew little about the Bible, but had learned by experience that this biblical profile is pragmatic and essential in selecting people who will be serving in responsible positions. This certainly verifies the statement popularized by Frank Gaebelein when he concluded that "all truth is God's truth." In other words, if it is true, it is true wherever you discover it, whether in the Bible or through personal experience. These two men were simply affirming that these qualities outlined by Paul were indeed a mature profile.

BUT, I'M NOT A LEADER

When you first look at the list of spiritual qualifications in Paul's two letters, you might conclude that Paul was exclusively outlining qualifications for men who serve in pastoral and teaching positions in the church. Paul *was* outlining a criteria for selecting men to occupy these ministry positions. But in essence he was saying, "Timothy, if a man wants to become a spiritual leader, that's great. Just make sure he's a mature man, and here's how you can determine if he measures up to God's standards as a Christian."

In other words, some men will possess these qualities and qualify to serve as spiritual leaders. Other men will possess these qualities but will not necessarily feel called to serve in this kind of spiritual capacity. The qualities, however, are *goals for every Christian man.* Paul simply pulled together several qualities he and other authors mentioned elsewhere in the New Testament and then compiled a marvelous profile for measuring our maturity levels in Christ.

THINKING AND GROWING TOGETHER

The following questions are designed for group discussion after reading and studying the content of this chapter:

1. Why do some men grow rapidly in their Christian faith once they become believers, and why do others struggle, seemingly taking as many steps backward as forward?
   Note: When you are finding the answers to this question, try to

add to the reasons already outlined in this chapter. Think of examples you can sensitively share. If you feel free, share your own personal experiences.

2. As you look at "Paul's Maturity Profile" on page 30, what would you consider to be your areas of strength?

3. As you look at the same profile, in what one specific area would you like to grow the most? Can you identify the factor or factors that are holding you back?

DON'T GET DISCOURAGED

As you evaluate your life, be on guard against becoming discouraged. See this as a great opportunity to become the man of God you really want to become. Remember that Satan may be looking over your shoulder and whispering in your ear, "You'll never become that kind of man. You've blown it too badly. There's no hope for you. You'll never break out of your old sin patterns."

When Satan tempts you with these thoughts, meditate on these words from James:

> Submit therefore to God. Resist the devil and he will flee from you. Draw near to God and He will draw near to you (Jas. 4:7,8).

Listen to God's voice, which is saying, "I love you no matter what you've done, no matter where you are in your spiritual growth, no matter what your feelings. I'm on your side. I have not rejected you. You are My child. You *can* become a man of God, and I'm here to help you."

SET A GOAL

Write out one goal you'd like to achieve as a result of this study:

_____

_____

_____

_____

_____

Note

1. Paul used two words to describe the pastoral leaders in the local church: "bishop" and "elder." These words are used interchangeably by several New Testament writers. For a fuller treatment of why this is done, see Gene A. Getz, *Sharpening the Focus of the Church* (Chicago: Moody Press, 1973).

2

BUILDING
A GOOD
REPUTATION

*An overseer, then, must be **above reproach**.*
—1 TIMOTHY 3:2

A number of years ago, Dale Carnegie wrote a book entitled *How to Win Friends and Influence People.* The book was filled with good practical advice based on good common sense. It had no biblical base, however, but much of what Carnegie suggested certainly reflects Christian values.

Is it proper for you as a Christian man to want others to like and respect you? More specifically, is it right and proper to take action to cause it to happen?

The answer to these questions is a decided yes. If we are going to have any positive Christian influence on others—our wives, our children, our friends (both Christians and non-Christians) and those we work for and with—we *must* be liked and respected. In other words, we must have a *good reputation.*

ABOVE REPROACH
(AN OVERARCHING QUALITY)

When Paul stated that a mature man is "above reproach," he was not referring to perfection. Rather, he was simply stating that we should strive to have a good reputation.

Paul listed this quality first in both his first letter to Timothy (see 3:2) and in the letter he wrote to Titus (see 1:6,7). He had a reason; it is an overarching characteristic. It is a summary quality—the result of living out the other qualities mentioned in these two lists.

FIND US SEVEN GOOD MEN

Having a "good reputation" is not a new idea in the New Testament. When the church faced its first organizational problem in Jerusalem, the apostles recommended that "seven men of good reputation" be selected to help solve the problem of food distribution (Acts 6:3).

The apostles knew that they would only make the problem worse if they delegated this task to men who had questionable reputations. People wouldn't trust the men. People would second-guess their every move. People would accuse the men of showing favoritism, even if they had no direct evidence. This is why the apostles asked the Grecians themselves to make this selection, because they alone would be aware of those men who had this kind of integrity.

TIMOTHY'S SPIRITUAL JOURNEY

Apparently Timothy became a Christian at some point during the time Paul and Barnabas visited the city of Lystra on their first missionary journey. Perhaps Timothy saw Paul heal the man who had been crippled from the time he was born (see 14:8). If Timothy had not witnessed the healing firsthand, he certainly would have seen this healed man leaping and jumping and shouting as he ran up and down the streets of Lystra (see 14:10).

Timothy's Personal Conversion
It is hard to imagine that Timothy had not seen the people in his city initially try to worship Paul and Barnabas, thinking they were gods who had "become like men" (14:11). But he most certainly heard Paul and Barnabas reject this kind of worship and declare that Jesus Christ was the true Son of God (see 14:14-17). Is this when Timothy and his mother became Christians? It is possible.

But the event that would have influenced Timothy the most would be the grand culmination—when the people who had tried to worship Paul and Barnabas turned against them because of Timothy's Jewish brothers who came from Antioch and Iconium (see 14:19). Timothy saw men in the crowd grab Paul—probably because he was the primary spokesman—and drag him out of the city and stone him, leaving him for dead. If Timothy had witnessed this event—and I believe he did—he would have been among "the disciples" who saw Paul miraculously healed as he arose from his bruised and battered position and turn and walk back into the city (14:20).

We are not told the exact moment when Timothy understood the gospel. But we can be sure that at some point during all of these events, Timothy came to the conclusion that the Christ that Paul and Barnabas were preaching was the true Messiah promised in the Old Testament. Consequently, Timothy put his faith in Jesus Christ and became a Christian (see 2 Tim. 3:15).

He Was Well Spoken Of
When Paul came to Lystra on his second missionary journey, he met Timothy—perhaps for the first time. But Paul had heard about Timothy before he met him because "he was **well spoken of** by the brethren who were in Lystra and Iconium" (Acts 16:2). In other words, Timothy had a good reputation, and Paul found out about it as soon as he arrived back in Timothy's hometown.

Note Three Things
First, people were *talking* about Timothy—not negatively, but positively. A good reputation creates this kind of conversation.

Second, *several key men* were talking about Timothy. This is another good test of whether a person has a good reputation. Not just one person, but more than one were saying these positive things.

Third, people were talking about Timothy in both Lystra and Iconium—that is, in *more than one location*. Timothy's reputation was good both at home and away from home. This is another test whether a man's reputation can be trusted.

All of this demonstrates how quickly Timothy matured in his Christian experience. The facts are that he had a good reputation as a good Jewish boy before he became a Christian (see 2 Tim. 3:15).

When he came to know Christ, it only added to the respect he already had.

A Goal for Every Christian Man

For most of us as Christian men, it takes time to build a good reputation. But whatever our background, this should be a goal for every one of us. It should happen naturally if we are growing and maturing in our Christian lives as we should be. Conversely, a Christian who has a poor reputation is obviously demonstrating traits that are not in harmony with Christian principles, nor is his lifestyle in harmony with what people naturally expect from a mature man.

This entire study is designed to help you develop a godly reputation. But a good place to start is to determine what people actually think of you right now.

A Question to Get You Started

- Do I get positive feedback from those *closest to me* that would indicate I have a good reputation—from my wife, my children, my friends?

Be Cautious

Remember, feedback from those who do not know you well is not necessarily a good test regarding your reputation. Their judgments can be superficial. They may be impressed with your physical appearance, your speaking ability, or with your "platform" or "public" personality, which may or may not represent what you really are as a person.

How Well Do You Know Me?

Merely reading this book will not necessarily give you a true reading about my reputation. You might be impressed with what I say, how I say it or what appears to be a commitment to godly living. But how do you know what I am *really* like? The facts are, you don't.

The same is true when I go out to speak, particularly to those I have never met before or have only met casually. You see, I could easily fake spirituality. It may surprise you that this is done all the time by well-known Christian personalities. It is easy to be impressed with a person's "public" personality, which may or may not be what the person is like in private.

I say this not to make you skeptical, but to help you to be cautious. If you really want to know what I am like, you have to talk to those who really know me. You will need to ask my wife—who has lived with me for nearly 40 years. You will need to talk to my children— who grew up in our home and now have homes of their own. You will want to talk to the elders in my church who have ministered with me for a number of years.

How Well Do You Know Yourself?

To personalize this study, you will need to do the same research about yourself. If you really want to know what kind of reputation you have—what people really think of you—ask your own wife, and then give her freedom to answer the question openly and objectively. Ask your children and then give them the freedom to do the same. Ask those who know you well in your church. You will be amazed at what you learn. Threatening? Yes. But it will be well worth it in terms of results.

ONE DAY, I ASKED MY DAUGHTER

I remember when my oldest daughter was only a youngster, perhaps about eight years old. I was preparing to speak on the subject of the family. Consequently, I asked her if she would mind listening to what I was planning to share with the congregation the following Sunday. I also asked her if she would give me feedback on whether my life as a father measured up to what I was going to share with the people in the church.

An Intimate Moment

I still remember Renee climbing up beside me on the couch in our living room. It was indeed an intimate moment. I began to share my message point by point. She listened intently, and then I noticed about halfway through she became tearful. I immediately asked her if something was wrong, if something in my life troubled her.

"Just one thing," she responded softly and gently.

"What's that, Honey?" I asked her.

"Well, Daddy, sometimes when I talk to you, you don't listen," she responded.

Renee Pinpointed My Weakness

Do you know what Renee was talking about? I do. I immediately got the message. You see, she was talking about one of my weaknesses — my tendency not to listen when my children are speaking. This was particularly true when they were young. In that special and vulnerable moment, my little girl was telling me that at times she tries to share with me some things that are important to her. But she was also saying she knows by the look in my eyes that my mind is a thousand miles away, solving a problem at the office, thinking through a message outline or simply concentrating on my own agenda, not realizing she has been waiting all day long to tell me something exciting that has happened in her own life.

I'll Never Forget That Experience

I wish I could say that Renee's comments that day totally changed me. Through the years, I have had to fight the temptation to not listen when my children are speaking. How easy it is to take those who are closest to us for granted. *They'll understand,* we conclude. For the most part, they *do* understand. But it still hurts them, and it is still a weakness in our personalities that also hurts our reputations. One thing is for certain — the experience with my little daughter made me aware of my weakness and helped me set some new goals that hopefully have changed me from that day forward. I have never forgotten that experience, and I have worked hard to be a better father.

SOME ADDITIONAL QUESTIONS

- Do more and more people select me as a person to share their lives with me? Do people trust me with confidential information?
- Do my relationships with people grow deeper and more significant the longer they know me and the closer they get to me? Or do my friendships grow strained and shallow as people learn to know what I am really like?
- Does my circle of friends grow continually wider and larger?

Do an increasing number of people admire and trust me?
- Do people recommend me for significant or difficult tasks without fear of my letting them down?

"STILL WATER" OR A "BUBBLY BROOK"?

One thing I have learned through the years is that we must be careful in judging people's maturity by the degree to which they project an outgoing personality. More often than not, I have discovered that "still water" runs deep, whereas a "bubbly brook" can be shallow. Some people who appear to have it all together in public are hurting terribly in private. Conversely, others who may be quiet and appear reserved have qualities that are enduring and represent a true measure of maturity.

This, of course, is not always true. But when it is true, the bubbly people don't wear well in the long haul. But the people who are more real—although perhaps reserved—become the people you truly want to have as close friends. They *do* wear well. And the more time you spend with these so-called reserved people, the more you realize what quality people they are.

TAKING THE PLUNGE

If you have difficulty in being objective about the answers to the previous questions, or in getting started, sit down with your spouse or a close male friend and ask him or her to help you honestly evaluate the answers.

I realize this is a threatening assignment. It is not easy to do. It is like standing on a cliff getting ready to dive into a pool you have never explored before. But I would like to encourage you to take the plunge. I assure you that it will change your life and how people feel about you. The fact that you are willing to go through this process will in itself build your reputation.

MY MOST REWARDING ASSIGNMENT

Although I am presently a full-time pastor, I still serve as a part-time professor at Dallas Theological Seminary. In the course I teach, I ask my students to read through *The Measure of a Man* with either their marital partners or a close friend. I suggest that they ask their partners or friends to help them evaluate their lives in the light of the qualities listed in the book. I then ask them to write a personal assignment outlining their strengths as well as the areas where they believe they need to improve. Invariably, these students report that this is the most significant and life-changing assignment they have ever completed. The reason? They have come face-to-face with what God says should be the true "measure of a man."

THINKING AND GROWING TOGETHER

The following questions are designed for group discussion after reading and studying the content of this chapter:

1. What is the first step we can take as men to determine what people really think of us?
2. Are there areas in our lives where we believe people have false views of us and have misjudged our attitudes and actions? Why has this happened? What can we do to correct this misperception without appearing to be defensive?
3. Are we aware of any attitudes and actions in our lives right now that are hurting our reputations? What steps can we take immediately to rebuild our reputations in those particular areas?
4. What one thing would you like to do immediately to begin to enhance your reputation as a Christian man?

SET A GOAL

Write out one goal you'd like to achieve as a result of this study:

_____

_____

_____

_____

MORAL PURITY

An overseer, then, must be above reproach,
the husband of one wife.
—1 TIMOTHY 3:2

This qualification for leadership—being the husband of one wife—
has puzzled a lot of people. What did Paul mean? Why did he say
this? Why did he specifically say that being "the husband of one
wife" is a qualification for men who want to be spiritual leaders? Let
me share with you a contemporary illustration that will help you
unravel the answers to these questions.

HIS FATHER INTRODUCED HIM TO A PROSTITUTE

I remember meeting a young family man several years ago when I
was ministering in a South American country. When he was just a
young boy—entering the age of puberty—his father took him to a
prostitute and offered her money to teach his son everything there
was to know about sex. In addition, the father put this woman on a
retainer so his son could visit her anytime he wished. Hard to imagine? Yes, but it is true, and is common in that particular culture.

The Power of Sexual Addiction

Needless to say, this young man became addicted to this kind of
lifestyle. Eventually, when he grew older, he decided to get married
and have children. Like so many of his friends who grew up in that
society, he continued to visit a prostitute regularly, including after he

was married. And like so many women in that culture, his wife knew about his extramarital activities. She accepted it, though reluctantly, as normal behavior among men.

Then It Happened

Then this man became a Christian. For the first time, he discovered the biblical standard for morality and marriage. To continue his association with the prostitute, or any other woman other than his wife, would be to continue to sin against God as well as his wife and family. Unfortunately, his addiction was so powerful that he struggled continually to measure up to this new standard.

The Key to Victory

When I met this young man, he had been victorious over his sin for several months, thanks to an accountability group. Through Bible study, prayer and the power of the Holy Spirit, as well as being accountable for his actions, he was finally able to conquer the temptation when he left his office after work. Rather than making his regular visits to a prostitute, he returned home and spent the evenings with his wife and family.

THIS BEHAVIOR ALSO HAPPENED 2,000 YEARS AGO

If you can understand the dynamics in the previous story, you can also understand more clearly what happened regularly in the New Testament culture, especially among Gentiles.

Three-Women Men

In New Testament culture, it was common for affluent men particularly to have at least three women in their lives, including their wives. One woman might be a *slave girl* who lived in the same house or compound who was always available to her master for sexual pleasure. Another woman might be a *prostitute* down at the pagan temple, which was considered a religious rite in the various pagan religions. The other woman would be the man's *wife*, the one who would help carry on the family name by giving birth to children and taking the primary responsibility for rearing them.

How Could This Be?

"Who could tolerate such behavior?" you ask. Good question. But the facts are that these women had little control or choice about these circumstances. Their very lives and sustenance depended on their full cooperation.

Value Systems Vary

Many of us who live in countries that have been deeply influenced by Hebrew-Christian morality find it difficult to comprehend these social dynamics. People who grow up in cultures that are guided by a different value system from ours, however, come to accept this kind of lifestyle—like it or not.

I remember talking to a young woman from an Eastern country. She related a story similar to the one I have just told. "How can this be?" I asked. She responded, "The women in our country are very tolerant of their husbands' extramarital behavior."

This is the kind of culture in which the apostle Paul preached the gospel. And it was in this kind of culture that men came to Christ. And for the first time in their lives, these new Christians heard God's message regarding moral purity: God's plan for them was to have only one woman in their lives—their wives.

GOD'S TRUTH PENETRATES CULTURE

Many of these New Testament men had the same problems and temptations in their lives as men who come to Christ in similar cultures today. Although these men hear and understand Christ's message of living morally, changes often come slowly. The power of sexual addiction often controls them, even after they have become believers.

Get the picture? Paul was concerned that a man who did not have victory over sexual immorality should never be appointed as a spiritual leader in the church. Therefore, Paul told Timothy that a spiritual leader must be "the husband of one wife"—or more literally, "a man of one woman."

Consider the Corinthians

If you have difficulty understanding such a cultural situation, look carefully at the Corinthians. They were tolerating as well as bragging about a man who was having a sexual relationship with his stepmother —an act of immorality that wasn't even practiced in the pagan community. Most of the non-Christians in Corinth were licentious and immoral people, but evidently they didn't engage in this kind of sexual relationship (see 1 Cor. 5:1). How the Corinthian Christians could rationalize this kind of behavior I haven't a clue, except I know our hearts can deceive us although we are believers. It also demonstrates the influence of a value system that is contrary to Christian morality.

If Christians in the New Testament church tolerated this kind of degeneracy, it is not surprising that Paul made sure all believers knew that a man of God—especially a Christian leader—should have only one woman in his life (his wife) and that he was faithful to her and to her alone.

What About Polygamy?

Polygamy was outlawed in the Roman Empire at the time Paul was writing this letter to Timothy. Consequently, I don't believe he was arguing against this practice when he said a man should be "the husband of one wife." Rightly interpreted, however, the principle Paul was outlining here certainly would exclude this practice. But it is amazing how men have rationalized this standard in God's scheme of things. For example, Joseph Smith—a leader and elder in a religious movement that began in the nineteenth century—contrived a way to make polygamy compatible with Christianity. The facts are that if it were not outlawed in the United States, thousands of Smith's followers would no doubt still be practicing this approach to marriage today, which would be a direct violation of God's standard.

A HIGHER STANDARD STILL

Christian morality extends its boundaries beyond the physical act of sexual intercourse. Jesus Christ spoke directly to this issue:

> "You have heard that it was said, 'You shall not commit adultery'; but I say to you, that everyone who looks on a woman to lust for her has committed adultery with her already in his heart" (Matt. 5:27, 28).

Lust Versus Temptation

"To lust for her" means to not only desire a woman in a sexual relationship, but also to think in terms of how to cause it to happen. This differentiates temptation from lust or sin.

I remember the highly publicized statement by former President Jimmy Carter when he occupied the White House. In essence, he stated that he "commits adultery in his heart every day." Knowing Mr. Carter's standard of morality, I am confident he was misinterpreting what Jesus meant. To be accurate, he should have said he was "sexually tempted every day." There is a big difference.

Living in a Sexually Oriented Culture

Most every man, married or single, is sexually tempted. No one can avoid completely the twentieth-century sensuous messages that emanate from magazine covers, movie ads and television commercials. Add to this the multitude of sensuously dressed women and female exhibitionists that permeate our culture, and it is not difficult to understand why many men are tempted every day of their lives.

But to be tempted is not a sin. Temptation, however, can quickly lead to sin. Any man who deliberately enjoys and pursues an illegitimate sexual relationship with a woman in his mind has, in God's sight, already committed an immoral act.

Men Also Differ

A fine line exists here, of course, which is not easy to describe for every person. Men also differ in their sexual needs and drives. Some men are able to handle provocative situations without much difficulty. Others are extremely vulnerable to any circumstances that are sexually stimulating.

Every Christian man must come to grips with his own inner struggles and concerns regarding moral purity. Far better to be too careful than to allow the subtle influences of the world to lead to mental adultery.

MAINTAINING MORAL PURITY

When the group of men I was initially involved with interacted with this quality for measuring spiritual maturity, we discussed some practical steps we could take to be men of high moral integrity. The following are some of our conclusions:

Maintain Good Communication

Husbands must develop good communication with their wives.
A married man who is able to keep his "moral house" in order and who is able to handle the normal temptations that arise in our contemporary culture is usually a man who has a satisfactory sex life.

Another Corinthian Problem
Paul spoke to this morality problem in 1 Corinthians 7:1-5. He instructed both wives and husbands to meet each other's sexual needs so that Satan would not lead one or the other into sexual immorality and unfaithfulness.

Many a married man has become involved with another woman, either mentally or physically, because of a wife who is insensitive to his sexual and psychological needs. She may be selfish or even hostile, using sex as a weapon. Or she may just be naive and unaware of the tremendous drives that can be triggered in a man who has faced temptation all day long in the office.

Men Are Also at Fault
Many men are also to blame. They often suffer in silence and do not communicate with their wives, or they may sin against their wives and then blame them for not meeting their needs.

The average Christian woman may know little of the inner problems of men, including her man. First, most women cannot identify internally with this problem because they, by creation, do not function in their sexual lives physically or psychologically the same as men. Second, if women are not instructed in the differences between the sexes, they may have no way of knowing how significant their role is in the sexual union. The couple must be in communication if the woman is to have understanding and sensitivity.

If He Were Mature, He Wouldn't Be Tempted
I remember talking with a woman one day who, along with her hus-

band, was involved in a Bible study with several other couples. The subject of sex surfaced. In the process, the men attempted to communicate their inner struggles because of the way they normally think and respond.

In my conversation with this woman, two things became apparent about her reactions to what the men had to say. *First*, she was highly threatened by the fact that her husband would be sexually stimulated by other women. How could he be? In her mind, for him to even have sexual thoughts would be sinful and mental adultery.

This woman obviously did not understand the difference between "temptation" and "lust." In our culture, men have little control of fleeting thoughts, unless they deliberately expose themselves to sexual stimuli. But regardless of the circumstances, we do have control of the kind of "lust" about which Jesus was talking.

Second, I noticed that this woman had no concept whatsoever of how she differed from men in terms of temptation and response to sexual stimuli. She interpreted everything they were trying to communicate in terms of her own psychological and physiological perspectives and reactions.

Considering this woman's tendency to be threatened by her incorrect perceptions, it is easy to see why she had difficulty relating to what the men in this group were trying to communicate. A wife who responds this way when her husband tries to communicate his struggles might close the door forever for any kind of communication to occur. When this happens, the marriage is in serious trouble.

Avoid Sexually Stimulating Situations

Men should not set up conflict situations by deliberately exposing themselves to temptation.

Several of the men in our study group traveled extensively, and it was their consensus that airport newsstands featuring *Playboy*, *Penthouse*, *Hustler* and a variety of other "girlie" magazines are not conducive to moral purity. Neither are video stores. Most of these places of business specialize in pornography of one sort or another. Furthermore, most sophisticated hotels are now equipped with in-house movies that feature sexually explicit activities.

Meet My Friend Jim

Most adult movies shown in major hotel chains are classified as "soft porn." Interestingly, I had the opportunity to lead the CEO of one of the largest producers and distributors of this kind of pornography to resign from his position and to redirect his life in living for Jesus Christ. While visiting with Jim in his office one day before he resigned, he pointed out the room (I didn't go in) in the large complex where they regularly edit X-rated movies to make them "acceptable" fare for viewing in thousands of hotels nationally and internationally.

An Embarrassing Moment

After he resigned, Jim shared with me an experience he had with a group of potential investors, all well-known businessmen. He was leading them on a tour of this multimillion-dollar porn-producing and distributing facility. They wanted to see the editing process, so he took them into a room that was filled with video monitors. On the screens were dozens of explicit hard-porn images. Sitting at the editing keyboard was a woman. The moment these men walked in, she pushed a button and everything went dark on the screens. "Go ahead and show us what you're editing," urged one of the bankers. Because of her embarrassment, she refused.

At the time, this company was doing more than 200 million dollars in business in thousands of sophisticated hotels across America, and in many other countries as well. Nearly 80 percent of its income was generated through adult movies.

Soft Porn Plays Hardball

Dr. Judith Reisman has written a powerful book entitled *Soft Porn Plays Hardball*, demonstrating the effects this kind of sexual stimuli has on men—the millions who are viewing this adult fare every night of the week as they travel on business. In her book, Dr. Reisman demonstrates why allegedly innocent "girlie" magazines have done more harm to children, women, men and the family than has hardcore, illegal entertainment. Reisman identifies the ideas of soft porn, which has filtered into advertising, TV, art, music, novels and sex education in schools. She documents how pornography bears an enormous responsibility for the spiraling rate of divorce, venereal disease, abortion, as well as new and deadly forms of sex crimes against women and children. The havoc wreaked on our culture is inestimable and the family has been the prime target.

Sadly, Christian men have become addicted to this kind of pornography, which has often led them into more explicit kinds of viewing. And sadder still, the Christian family is not exempt from the damage this inflicts on wives and children.

"Pursue Righteousness"

In the provocative society in which we live, and no matter what our spiritual maturity, we must guard against deliberately exposing ourselves to literature, movies, TV shows and activities of any kind that are designed to illegitimately excite and stimulate a person's sexual nature.

This advice is just as relevant for a single man, if not more so. As stated before, a married man has a legitimate means—the marriage bed—for maintaining his sexual equilibrium. But a single man, once highly stimulated through improper exposure, finds himself in a desperate plight. There is only one answer to the single man's dilemma in our contemporary culture—that is, if he chooses to remain single. It is Paul's answer to young Timothy who was also single and who lived in a provocative society. You must "flee from youthful lusts, and pursue righteousness" (2 Tim. 2:22).

Think Right

✗Men should fortify themselves through regular study of the Word of God and prayer.

Nothing dulls a desire for communication with God and the study of His Word so much as indiscriminate exposure to illegitimate sexual stimuli. And nothing is so effective in combating temptation and lust as an effective prayer life and Bible study program. Thus, the apostle Paul wrote:

> Whatever is true, whatever is honorable, whatever is right, whatever is pure, whatever is lovely, whatever is of good repute, if there is any excellence and if anything worthy of praise, let your mind dwell on these things (Phil. 4:8).

Be Accountable

Every Christian man should have another Christian man as an accountability partner.

Having an accountability partner has become more and more necessary in the culture in which we live. In our church, we encourage this approach to maintain moral and spiritual integrity. An accountability partner is another man who helps each of us to keep from yielding to temptation, and when we do yield, to help us experience forgiveness and not to repeat the sinful action.

Some Accountability Questions

The following is a series of questions we distributed to the men in our church—questions one partner can ask the other, and vice versa:

1. How often did you meet with God this week?
2. What has God been saying to you through His Word this week?
3. What sins in your personal or business life did you experience this week that need confession?
4. Are you giving to the Lord's work regularly and proportionately as God has blessed you? What percentage did you give last month?
5. What movies did you see this past week? Do you feel good about viewing these movies? Would you be able to tell your fellow Christians in your church what you have seen without being embarrassed?
6. How did you influence your marriage and family this week? How positively? How negatively? What could you do to improve?
7. Did you pray for me/us this week?
8. What challenges or struggles are weighing on your mind?
9. What lives did you influence for Christ this week?
10. Did you just lie to me?

This final question always brings a chuckle. But it is important. Even a list of accountability questions are no guarantee we are being accountable. When all is said and done, an accountability system only works when we are men of integrity.

Seek Professional Counseling

Men should seek help from a competent Christian counselor if the moral problem seems beyond control.

This is particularly important, and absolutely essential, if you have a sexual addiction. If you lack understanding, sensitivity and communication in your married life, you may also need someone else to help you. On some occasions, I have seen the problem so severe that a husband is unable to verbalize his feelings directly to his wife. He needs a third person—an understanding counselor.

Perhaps, as a single man, you are fighting a losing battle with lust. Of all people, you need an understanding friend and helper—a prayer partner, a listener, an adviser. But never share your problems with a single girl, or a married woman. That can be lethal. You need a mature man of God who can help you work through your problems.

POINTS OF ACTION

The following personal projects are designed to help you maintain a life of moral purity:
- If married, ask your wife to read this chapter on her own. State that your purpose is to form a common basis for discussion.
- Next, discuss the chapter with your wife, using the following questions as guidelines:

  1. How do you as a woman differ from me as a man, especially in your sexual feelings, needs and attitudes?
  2. How do you as a man differ from me as a woman, especially in your sexual feelings, needs and attitudes?
  3. What can each of us do in our attitudes and behavior to better meet each other's needs sexually?

- If single, list three of the greatest problems you face that are related to your sexual nature.
- Study these problems carefully and then honestly answer the following questions:

  1. What am I doing to accentuate these problems?

2. What can I do on my own to solve these problems?
3. Can I solve all of these problems alone, or do I need help from a competent counselor?

- If either married or single, pray and ask the Lord to help you find another Christian man who will be your accountability partner. Jose' Garcia + Ronald Walke

THINKING AND GROWING TOGETHER

The following questions are designed for group discussion after reading and studying the content of this chapter:

1. What are some specific things we can do to maintain moral purity? What has worked in each of your lives? What hasn't worked?
2. What are some things we can do to begin communicating with our wives? How can we avoid threatening them and yet be honest?
3. Why do some men have more difficulty in maintaining moral purity?
4. How can we avoid sexual addictions? If this is a problem, how can we overcome it?

SET A GOAL

Write out one goal you'd like to achieve as a result of this study:

_____
_____
_____
_____

4

MAINTAINING
BALANCE

An overseer, then, must be above reproach,
*the husband of one wife, **temperate**.*
—1 TIMOTHY 3:2

Ask the average man what he thinks the word "temperate" means and he will probably refer to someone who is not self-indulgent, particularly in what he drinks. This is understandable because *Webster's* number one definition is as follows: "Not extreme or excessive: moderate in indulgence of appetite or desire: moderate in the use of intoxicating liquors."[1]

As we will see in a later chapter, being temperate is certainly a mark of spiritual maturity. But Paul seems to have had a much broader idea in mind when he used the word *hephalios*, which is translated in the *New American Standard Bible* as being "temperate." The *King James Version* uses the word "vigilant."

COOL, CALM, AND COLLECTED

Paul was describing a man who has a clear focus on life. Practically speaking, a temperate man doesn't lose his physical, psychological and spiritual orientation. He is stable and steadfast, and his thinking is clear.

A WELL-ORDERED PHILOSOPHY OF LIFE

I also like to describe a temperate man as one who has a correct perspective on life in this world. He knows where history is going. He knows God is in control of the universe as well as the affairs of mankind. But a temperate man also knows he is responsible to do all he can to carry out God's purposes for him in the world. If married, he tries to be a loving husband, a responsible father and a good provider for his family. He works hard at being a faithful employer or employee and a devoted member of his church. His consistent goal is to be a dynamic Christian witness wherever he is, by the way he lives and by what he says.

A temperate man doesn't go to extremes. On the one hand, he doesn't believe he is responsible to solve all of the problems in the world, allowing himself to get sidetracked from his priority as a Christian. On the other hand, he does what he can to solve humankind's social ills, but again without neglecting his biblical priorities.

I am Extreme [handwritten margin note]

A SENSE OF SECURITY

A temperate man doesn't go on emotional tangents. He has a sense of inner peace and security, no matter what is happening in life generally. This doesn't mean he never has periods of anxiety, but overall he has a sense of stability. In the words of James, he is not a "double-minded man" (Jas. 1:8).

Our Nation Is Crumbling

I was speaking at a special Bible conference one day, and during the coffee break, one of the participants began to talk nervously about the way our society is deteriorating—that things are going from bad to worse. I immediately sensed this person had an unusual amount of insecurity, an obsession with the idea that our nation is crumbling and falling apart morally, economically and politically. I didn't add to this person's sense of well-being when I responded, "If you think it's bad now, just wait awhile."

This Couldn't Be Happening to Us

I could almost hear a gasp. "Oh, God wouldn't allow that to happen in America, would He?"

I intensified the anxiety when I again responded with a comment that wasn't too reassuring. "Why not?" I asked. "Why wouldn't God allow bad things to happen in America? After all, we know from history that every nation that has departed from God's standard of righteousness has deteriorated and eventually collapsed."

Where Is Our Citizenship?

Frankly, I wasn't trying to be insensitive, though some may question my direct response. Rather, I wanted to make an important point that our hope should not be based on how well things are going in our society. According to the Scriptures, we are just "strangers" passing through (1 Pet. 2:11). "Our citizenship is in heaven" (Phil. 3:20). America, or any country, is not our real home.

When we respond as this person did, we are *not temperate.* We are afraid we might lose everything down here in our temporary home. We have lost sight of what the Christian life is all about.

Don't Misunderstand

I love America. And if you are an American, I am sure you do, too. I hope we'll be strong and secure for years to come. But God never intended for our country to be our source of security. No matter what happens down here on earth, we have hope in Jesus Christ. He is our true source for stability and security in life.

Again, don't misunderstand. When I stop and think about what is *really* happening in the American culture, I am also concerned, very concerned. I can also get particularly anxious when I think about my grandchildren and what they might face in years to come.

On the other hand, when I stop and consider that God is still God and that He is in control of the universe and our nation, I once again refocus my thoughts and feelings and get back in balance.

A PROPER FOCUS

Today, it is easy for Christians to get sidetracked onto peripheral issues. We can become obsessed with the problems in our society. We can devote all of our time and energy trying to clean up "the outside of the plate" and forget that it's what is on the inside that must be changed.

Let me say it carefully. God never called us as Christians to save America—as a nation, that is. Rather, we are to be "light" and "salt" in a world that desperately needs Christ. The greatest contribution we can make is to be everything God wants us to be, as individuals, as families and as local churches. We'll then see people come to know Jesus Christ and experience personal salvation. Hopefully, God will then bring renewal and revival to our nation.

POLITICAL INVOLVEMENT

This does not mean we should not be good citizens. We should be informed. We should take every opportunity to voice our opinions through the political process. We should speak out when we have a platform to do so.

In our own church, we have a committee of people called Current Issues Group (CIG). The group's task is to keep our church informed about what is happening in our society. As senior pastor, I look to them for guidance and help in leading our church to be active in being a positive voice in our society. For example, I preach a sermon at least once a year on the evils of abortion. Thankfully, our people have responded en masse to participate in the "Walk for Life" sponsored by Texans United for Life.

We also keep our people alerted to their responsibilities to vote in local and national elections, attempting to elect officials who are not only good leaders, but also men and women who are committed to the biblical values that made America great.

Our church also takes seriously Paul's admonition to pray for "all who are in authority, in order that we may lead a tranquil and quiet life in all godliness and dignity" (1 Tim. 2:1,2). But we try not to forget the ultimate purpose for this kind of praying: God "desires all men to be saved and to come to the knowledge of the truth" (2:4).

Yes, we are to be good citizens, but we must also realize that the world loves darkness more than light. Generally, those who have chosen to rely on their own wisdom will not listen to God's wisdom. And if they do not listen, God will judge our nation. But remember that our salvation is secure, no matter what happens around us. This is why New Testament Christians could be joyful in the midst of trials and tribulations.

THE OTHER END OF THE CONTINUUM

Paul used the word "temperate" in his first letter to the Thessalonians when he was talking about the coming day of judgment (see 5:2,3). They were not to "sleep as others do" but to be "alert and **sober** [temperate]" (v. 6).

These believers had an opposite problem, as do many of us. They were being lulled to sleep.

Everything's Great

Paul warned that some people will talk about "Peace and safety!" (v. 3), indicating that all is going well, and that we have nothing to fear.

In the same way, some Christians today believe that humans are in control of what is happening in our society. They believe that human genius will solve our problems and keep us safe and free from danger. Why worry about overpopulation, pollution and the threat of nuclear war? As intelligent human beings, we can handle these problems.

Don't Be Lulled to Sleep

At this point, Paul issued his warning: "While they are saying, 'Peace and safety!' then destruction will come upon them suddenly like birth pangs upon a woman with child; and they shall not escape" (v. 3). Because this is a prophetic statement, it is just as relevant today as it was the day Paul penned these words.

This is the other end of the continuum in terms of the illustration I used at the beginning of the chapter. It is possible to allow ourselves to get caught up in the false security of what appears to be human progress. This, too, is not being temperate. We are not walking in the "light" of the Word of God but rather in the "darkness" of the word of man (1 Thess. 4,5).

In conclusion, this leads us to a principle that brings balance to our lives and keeps us in the middle of the continuum. A mature Christian man has a correct view regarding the temporariness of this life and everything in it. He doesn't allow this temporary perspective, however, to derail him from God's main track.

ANOTHER BALANCING INSIGHT

We must remember that all of us go through momentary periods in our lives when we are temporarily confused and our thinking becomes distorted and blurred. This often happens when our minds

are overloaded with problems and crises, or when we are exhausted.
Elijah—one of God's greatest servants—faced this time of confusion
in his life. Being "a man with a nature like ours" (Jas. 5:17), he came to
a point where he could no longer cope with the problems in his life. He
wanted to die (see 1 Kings 19:4). He believed he was the only one left in
Israel who had not turned away from God, when in reality at least 7,000
people in Israel had not worshiped Baal (see v. 18). But this was a predictable period in Elijah's life. He had faced incredible pressures that
had built up for more than three years, culminating in his battle with the
prophets of Baal on Mount Carmel. Although he had been victorious, he
fell apart physically, emotionally and spiritually when Jezebel went for
his jugular. In his own words, he'd had "enough" (v. 4).

But Elijah's bout with depression was temporary. After eating
well, sleeping well and having some quality time with the Lord, he
once again became a clear-thinking, faithful prophet. Significantly,
one of the things that helped him the most was to find a loyal friend
in Elisha (see v. 21).

All of us go through these down periods in our lives. Under certain circumstances, they are predictable. But if we are maturing in
Christ, they are "moments" in our pilgrimage compared with the
"periods" when our minds are clear, our focus is accurate and we are
living "temperate" lives.

HOW TO BECOME TEMPERATE

Paul went on in this Thessalonian passage to tell all of us how to
develop this quality of life—how to become "temperate" in the midst
of subtle human progress. But this passage also applies to times in
our lives when we get panicky. "Let us be sober [temperate]," wrote
Paul, "having put on the breastplate of **faith** and **love**, and as a helmet, the **hope** of salvation" (5:8).

A MAN OF FAITH

A *temperate* man is a *man of faith*. Like men of old—Abel, Noah,
Abraham, Isaac and Moses—and others who are cataloged so dramatically in Hebrews 11, a mature man of God steps out and acts on
the promises of God.

"Let Us Run...the Race" (12:1)

Notice the "faith and action" of each of these men:

- By faith Abel *offered*...a better sacrifice than Cain (11:4)
- By faith Noah,...*prepared* an ark (v. 7)
- By faith Abraham,...*obeyed* by going out (v. 8)
- By faith Abraham,...*offered* up Isaac (v. 17)
- By faith Isaac *blessed* Jacob (v. 20)
- By faith Moses,...*left* Egypt (vv. 23,27)

All of these Old Testament men listed here "died in faith, without receiving the promises, but having seen them and having welcomed them from a distance, and having confessed that they were **strangers** and **exiles** on the earth" (v. 13).

"Fixing Our Eyes on Jesus" (12:2)

Today, a "temperate" man believes God and acts on His promises although he doesn't understand what lies ahead on this earth. And though the present world and the progress of humans seems to indicate that "all is well" and that peace is here—or if everything seems to be crumbling around us—a temperate man keeps on looking for the Second Coming of Jesus Christ to deliver him from the wrath to come (see 1 Thess. 5:9). Furthermore, he encourages other believers with this truth and helps build up all members of the Body of Christ, helping them to look forward to that day (see v. 11). By word and example, he practices the exhortation in Hebrews:

> Let us also lay aside every encumbrance, and the sin which so easily entangles us, and let us run with endurance the race that is set before us, fixing our eyes on Jesus, the author and perfecter of faith (Heb. 12:1,2).

A MAN OF HOPE

Closely aligned with the quality of "faith" is "hope," which refers to both the object of our faith as well as our present attitude and state of being (see 11:1).

Our Eternal Inheritance

Hope as the object of our faith refers to our eternal inheritance (see 1 Pet. 1:3,4). Our hope is laid up for us in heaven (see Col. 1:5). It is the "hope of salvation" (1 Thess. 5:8). It is "the hope of eternal life, which God, who cannot lie, promised long ages ago" (Titus 1:2). All of this will be culminated with our "blessed hope and the appearing of the glory of our great God and Savior, Christ Jesus" (2:13).

Steadfastness and Stability

But hope is also described as a present state of being. A man of hope is steadfast (see 1 Thess. 1:3). He has fixed his hope "on the living God" (1 Tim. 4:10), rather than on the "uncertainty of riches" and the things of this world (6:17). He holds fast the confession of his hope "without wavering" (Heb. 10:23), and has fixed his "hope completely on the grace to be brought...at the revelation of Jesus Christ" (1 Pet. 1:13).

In summary, a temperate man is a man of hope. And a man of hope is a mature, stable man because he is sure of his future state of being. Present circumstances do not give him false security, nor do they create insecurity. His past, present and future perspectives are clear, sharp and theologically correct.

A MAN OF LOVE

A temperate man is also a man of "love" (1 Thess. 5:8). This, Paul says, is the greatest thing, the most important of all these qualities. "But now abide faith, hope, love, these three; but **the greatest of these is love**" (1 Cor. 13:13).

Paul defined love in chapter 13:

> Love is patient, love is kind, and is not jealous; love does not brag and is not arrogant, does not act unbecomingly; it does not seek its own, is not provoked, does not take into account a wrong suffered, does not rejoice in unrighteousness, but rejoices with the truth (vv. 4-6).

The Spectrum of Love

Henry Drummond classifies these verses in 1 Corinthians 13 as the "spectrum of love"—nine ingredients that must be present for true love to exist:

Patience, kindness, generosity, humility, courtesy, unselfishness, good temper, guilelessness, sincerity.[2]

And why is love the greatest thing? Because, wrote Paul, it "bears all things, believes all things, hopes all things, endures all things" (v. 7).

Love Is Foundational

Love, then, is really the capstone for faith because love "believes all things." It is also the capstone for hope, because love "hopes all things." And furthermore, love is the greatest, because it "never fails" (v. 8).

Faith, hope and love, then, are foundational for having a clear perspective on life. Again, remember Paul's encouraging words:

> Since we are of the day, let us be sober [temperate], having put on the breastplate of **faith** and **love**, and as a helmet, the **hope** of salvation (1 Thess. 5:8).

POINTS OF ACTION

The following personal project is designed to help you develop the quality of "temperance."

Some Probing Questions

• Answer the following questions as honestly as you can:

1. How strong is my faith in God and His Word? Do I *really* believe He exists and that Jesus Christ is coming again? If I do, how is my faith revealed in my *actions*?

2. How aware am I of the "hope of [my] calling" (Eph. 1:18)? How fully do I understand "the riches of the glory of His inheritance in the saints, and what is the surpassing greatness of His power toward us who believe" (vv. 18,19)? Have I fixed my hope on the things of this world, or on eternal values (see Matt. 6:33)?

3. Am I a man of love? How well do I measure up to the criteria described in 1 Corinthians 13? Am I patient? Am I kind? Am I

generous? Am I humble? Am I courteous? Am I unselfish? Am I controlled? Am I pure in motives? Am I sincere?

Some Practical Suggestions

• Proceed to develop your *faith, hope* and *love*. Here are some suggestions:

1. Develop a plan for personal Bible study and prayer. Remember that "faith comes from hearing, and hearing by the word of Christ" (Rom. 10:17).
2. Learn to claim the promises of God's Word.
3. Interact with mature Christians. Seek advice and wisdom from other members of the Body of Christ.
4. Read biographies of great Christians.
5. In times of conflict, learn to submit and ask God what He is trying to teach you.
6. Set biblical priorities.
7. Discern what is temporal and what is eternal.
8. Verbalize praise and thanksgiving to God for loving and saving us.
9. Get plenty of rest and relaxation. Remember that it is easy to lose perspective when we are mentally and emotionally exhausted. (Read the story of Elijah in 1 Kings 18:1–19:8. Note particularly Elijah's loss of perspective in 19:1-4. Notice also God's solution in 19:5-8.)

THINKING AND GROWING TOGETHER

The following questions are designed for group discussion after reading and studying the content of this chapter:

1. How can we keep balance in our lives when we face so many pressures in our changing society?
2. How can we determine if we are getting too caught up in the issues in our society? How can we determine if we are not active enough in addressing these issues?
3. How can we help our pastor maintain balance in these areas?
4. How can we determine if we are growing in faith, hope and love?

SET A GOAL

Write out one goal you'd like to achieve as a result of this study:

_____

_____

_____

_____

Notes

1. *Merriam Webster's Collegiate Dictionary, Tenth Edition* (Springfield, MA: Merriam-Webster, Inc., 1993), p. 1213.
2. Henry Drummond, *Addresses* (Philadelphia: Henry Altemus, 1892), pp. 27-28.

5

A MAN OF
WISDOM

An overseer, then, must be above reproach,
*the husband of one wife, temperate, **prudent**.*
—1 TIMOTHY 3:2

The Greek word translated "prudent" in the *New American Standard Bible* is *sophron*. It literally means "sound in mind," and is translated "self-controlled" in the *New International Version*.

Sophron can also be translated "discreet," "sober," "temperate" or "sensible," depending upon the context. Frankly, I like the word "prudent" because *Webster's* reminds us that a prudent man is "shrewd in the management of practical affairs."[1] Subsequently, we can say that a prudent man is a "man of wisdom."

WE REMEMBER PRUDENT MEN

I had the special privilege of knowing the late Dr. William Culberson, who served for a number of years as president of Moody Bible Institute in Chicago, Illinois. I served on the Moody faculty for 13 years, and during that time I observed Dr. Culberson's actions and reactions in a variety of situations. I sat with him in hundreds of faculty meetings, listening to his sage advice and wise comments. I heard him open the Word of God in chapel sessions each week, making the Scriptures practical and applicable to our lives, both as faculty members and as students. I played hours of volleyball on our faculty team, sometimes with him and sometimes against him. (Incidentally, he was one of the best "set up" men with whom I have ever played. As a "spiker," he made me look real good!)

Personal Conversations
On two occasions, I had the opportunity to be involved in doing special research regarding the ministry of Moody Bible Institute. On one occasion, I was assigned to evaluate graduate and current-student responses to our ministry, which we called "The President's Questionnaire." On another occasion, I had the privilege of researching and writing the official history of Moody Bible Institute. During these lengthy periods of time, I spent hours interacting with Dr. Culberson and getting his perspectives.

Quick to Hear, Slow to Speak
Today, as I reflect on my associations with Dr. Culberson, I remember a "prudent" man. The late Dr. Wilbur Smith served with Dr. Culberson on a special Bible translation team. Dr. Smith once commented that Dr. Culberson's greatest strength was to be able to sit and listen to everyone share personal opinions, and then near the end of the discussion he would give the correct answer with clarity and great wisdom. Dr. Smith, too, considered Dr. Culberson a "prudent" man. Dr. Smith's comment reminds me of the following proverbs:

> A wise man will **hear** and increase in learning (Prov. 1:5).
> The wise in heart shall be called **prudent** (16:21, *KJV*).

SOUND JUDGMENT

One of my favorite passages of Scripture explaining what Paul had in mind when he used the word "prudent" to describe maturity is what he wrote to the Romans:

> For through the grace given to me I say to every man among you not to think more highly of himself than he ought to think; but to think so as to have **sound judgment** [that is, to think **soberly, sensibly** or **prudently**], as God has allotted to each a measure of faith (Rom. 12:3).

Paul was concerned that we have a proper view of ourselves in relationship to God and to other Christians (see Rom. 12:4-8). Evidently, some believers in Rome—as well as in Corinth (see 1 Cor. 12:14-27)— had an overly exalted view of their position in the Body of Christ. Some thought they were God's "special gift" to the church. Consequently, Paul exhorted them to be "devoted to one another in brotherly love" and to "give preference to one another in honor," rather than putting each other down while they were building themselves up (Rom. 12:10).

More than any other characteristic of maturity, Paul related this concept to all members of the Body of Christ. Within a span of five verses of Scripture, he instructed Titus to exhort older men, older women, younger women and younger men to be "sensible" or "prudent":

> Older men are to be temperate, dignified, **sensible** [prudent], sound in faith, in love, in perseverance. Older women likewise are to be reverent in their behavior, not malicious gossips, nor enslaved to much wine, teaching what is good, that they may encourage the young women to love their husbands, to love their children, to be **sensible** [prudent], pure, workers at home, kind, being subject to their own husbands, that the word of God may not be dishonored. Likewise urge the young men to be **sensible** [prudent] (Titus 2:2-6).[2]

RECOGNIZING PRUDENCE

Humility

1. • **A prudent man is a *humble* man.**

This kind of man has a proper view of himself, and he is keenly aware of one basic thing: all that he has (his gifts, abilities and possessions) are from God. Without Him, he could not speak, write, walk, make decisions or breathe. He understands and practices what Paul wrote to the Philippians:

> Do nothing from selfishness or empty conceit, but with **humility of mind** let each of you regard one another as

more important than himself; do not merely look out for your own personal interests, but also for the interests of others (2:3,4).

Gratitude

II. A prudent man has a proper view of the grace of God.

This kind of man realizes that he is lost without Christ and that all of his human abilities and achievements are useless in winning any favor with God. He understands that God in His boundless love sent His Son to die for lost humanity, "while we were yet sinners" (Rom. 5:8).

Paul set the example in demonstrating this kind of "prudence." Though he was "circumcised the eighth day," though he was "of the nation of Israel" and "of the tribe of Benjamin," and not only "a Hebrew of Hebrews," but also "a Pharisee"; yet all of these human accomplishments Paul "counted as loss for the sake of Christ" (Phil. 3:5-7).

Disciplined by Grace

Paul never forgot about God's reaching out to him in grace with the salvation message, including when he was on his way to Damascus to persecute Christians. How *could* he think more highly of himself than he ought to think? A prudent man is taught and disciplined by God's grace. Writing to Titus, Paul underscored this point:

> For the grace of God has appeared, bringing salvation to all men, instructing us to deny ungodliness and worldly desires, and to live **sensibly** [or **prudently**], righteously and godly in the present age (Titus 2:11,12).

Prayerful

III. A prudent man knows how to pray.

The apostle Peter associates this quality of maturity with prayer. He wrote, "Be of **sound judgment** [be **prudent**] and sober spirit for the purpose of prayer" (1 Pet. 4:7). An attitude of pride and an inaccurate view of God's grace leads to bad judgment and immature thinking in our prayer lives. A "prudent" man goes to his knees in humble and prayerful adoration, and then rises to a new level of righteous and holy living.

MEEKNESS IS NOT WEAKNESS

Having a correct perspective regarding our place in God's family does not mean we should be withdrawn and inhibited. It doesn't mean we should lack self-confidence and be burdened down with a sense of worthlessness.

Fear and Intimidation

Timothy apparently had a problem in this area of his life; he felt intimidated by those who opposed God's work. Paul charged Timothy to never "be ashamed," either of the Lord or of the Lord's servants (2 Tim. 1:8). Thus, Paul wrote to Timothy:

> For God has not given us a spirit of timidity, but of power and love and **discipline** [*sophronismos*—that is, of a **sound mind**, *KJV*] (v. 7).

Shoulders Back, Head Held High

What Paul wrote to Timothy applies to all of us. As Christians, we should never be ashamed or intimidated. If we are truly "prudent," we'll recognize that we are unworthy to be called children of God and members of the family of God. On the other hand, we can stand straight with our shoulders back and our heads held high. When we do, we have achieved that divine balance in our lives between being men whose gifts and abilities God can use and men who give all glory and honor to Jesus Christ.

PAUL'S EXAMPLE

The apostle Paul never hesitated to commend himself when he was falsely accused and belittled. At the same time, however, he made sure he had pure motives and that these motives were understood—that he was defending himself because of what God had done in his life.

This is clear in Paul's letter to the Corinthians. Some people questioned his apostleship as well as his motives. Thus, he wrote: "For if we are beside ourselves, it is for God; if we are of **sound mind** [that is, **prudent**] it is for you" (2 Cor. 5:13). We might paraphrase Paul's comments as follows:

> You may think we are bragging and are proud. If you feel that way, it is because of what God has accomplished in our lives. We are only glorifying the work of God in our own experience. In other words, we want you to see us as sober, prudent and sensible men—men who are humbly acknowledging that we are what we are because of God's marvelous grace (chaps. 11–12).

MODELING PRUDENCE TODAY

Earlier, we noted that the apostle Paul instructed Titus to "urge the young men to be sensible [*sophroneo*—that is, "prudent"]" (Titus 2:6). Paul then described in greater detail what he meant:

> In all things show yourself to be an example of good deeds, with purity in doctrine, dignified, sound in speech which is beyond reproach, in order that the opponent may be put to shame, having nothing bad to say about us (vv. 7,8).

The Only Way to Learn

Some biblical truths can be taught with words alone, such as who Jesus is, how to be saved and many other Bible doctrines. But some things must be taught by *both* instruction and example. In fact, without modeling, some words are meaningless. "Prudence" is one of those words. This is why Paul told Titus he must demonstrate "prudence" if young men are to learn to demonstrate the same quality in their lives.

A Conversation I'll Never Forget

I had a personal and meaningful experience one day while I was thinking about the concept in this chapter. I was having breakfast with my son, Kenton; at the time he was a sophomore at Baylor University. Our conversation that morning reached a deeper level than ever before. We were talking about a series of letters I had written to him—a series I began to write when he was in high school. These letters to Kenton were based on Paul's words to Timothy:

> Don't let anyone look down on you because you are young, but set an example for the believers in speech, in life, in love, in faith and in purity (1 Tim. 4:12, *NIV*).

I wrote seven letters in all, and each letter was based on one of the qualities outlined in this verse. At one point in our conversation, Kenton shared with me something he had never said before. "Dad," he said, "I want you to know you're my model, and I want to be like you."

I had two reactions to Kenton's statement. First, I was overwhelmed with gratitude to God. It was a humbling experience.

Second, Kenton's comment caused me to continue to evaluate my attitudes and actions. His words have stayed with me. When I am tempted to violate the will of God in my life—and I am sometimes tempted, as is every other Christian man—I think about my son's statement "Dad, I want to be like you."

Kenton's comment and his confidence in me as a role model have halted my actions on several occasions. For example, when I am tempted to pick up an inappropriate magazine from a newsstand in an airport and thumb through it, I think of my son's statement. When I am tempted to watch an inappropriate movie in my hotel room when I am traveling, which is just a flip of a switch away from reality, I think of my son's statement. When I am tempted to rent a video that features activities and language that violate the will of God, I think of my son's statement. It has been as if Kenton were sitting or standing beside me, listening, observing and taking mental, emotional and spiritual notes on my behavior.

In many respects, this is the kind of heavy responsibility Paul was laying on Titus's shoulders when he wrote, "Urge the young men to be sensible [prudent]" (Titus 2:6).

We Can't Be Perfect

I need to clarify something highly important. Paul is not teaching us that we have to be perfect. My son said something else to me that morning. "Dad," he explained, "I know you make mistakes. And so do I. But you're still my model."

This comment ministered to me as much, if not more, than his initial statement. We do make mistakes. Those who associate closely with me know that more than anything—especially my children. It encourages me to know that my son could see beyond my mistakes and my sins to my heart and see what I really want to be.

POINTS OF ACTION

The following personal project is designed to help you become a prudent man, a person who is wise and balanced in judgment. More specifically, it means you must develop a proper self-image.

The Peril of the Pendulum

As Christians, it is easy to go to extremes. Either we see ourselves as *nothing* or we are caught up in an *exalted* view of ourselves. The more immature we are, the more we vacillate between these two attitudes.

Both extremes are improper. On the one hand, we should recognize that all we are and have is because of God's grace. On the other hand, we should understand that God has given us special abilities and He wants us to use those abilities to accomplish great exploits for God.

- **Recognize that there are reasons for this imbalance to exist and persist. The following checklist will help you to begin to isolate the reasons for this imbalance.**
1. An unfortunate series of circumstances beyond human control
   - ___ Loss of a parent or parents
   - ___ Bad experiences in school or in the neighborhood
   - ___ Negative influences from others
   - ___ Hereditary factors or physical illness that have created feelings of inferiority
2. An incorrect theology
   - ___ You've been taught for so long that you are "nothing," you actually feel and believe you are "nothing."
   - ___ You've tried so hard to "crucify self," that you have downgraded your self-image and the image of God in you.
   - ___ You have an incorrect view of forgiveness and being right

with God. For example, you are trying to become "nothing" so that God will accept you.

Remember: You can do nothing to become right with God. You cannot even become "nothing." You must come to God just as you are and accept His free gift of salvation.

3. Parents who were unwise
   ___ They withheld praise and attention, creating in you an unnatural thirst and desire for recognition.
   ___ They were unwise in giving you too much of a prominent position, creating an emotional need to always be "first in line" and in the limelight.

Too Little or Too Much

As a pastor, I have discovered that Christian parents especially often withhold praise and attention from their children for fear they will create a prideful attitude. In actuality, when we withhold positive feedback, we will create the problem we are trying to avoid. This is also a surefire way to rear a child who will be starved for attention. Ironically, this child will also have a pride problem later because he or she has not learned how to emotionally handle success. Consequently, it is far better to give too much attention rather than too little. This problem is much easier to correct.

• **If you have isolated the source of your problem, interact with someone you trust, someone who is wise and *prudent*.**

Ask this person to help you develop perspective and to pray with you about your struggle. *WHAT IS MY SOURCE?*

• **Set up specific goals for your life to develop a proper self-image.**

Be careful not to rationalize immature behavior on the basis of past circumstances and experiences. Become a responsible person. Never blame your problems on someone else, though they may have contributed to the problem.

Ask God to help you overcome your problem. Remember that the Word of God says:

> But if any of you lacks wisdom, let him ask of God, who gives to all men generously and without reproach, and it will be given to him (Jas. 1:5).

THINKING AND GROWING TOGETHER

The following questions are designed for group discussion after reading and studying the content of this chapter:

1. What passage of Scripture referred to in this chapter meant the most to you? Why?
2. What specific struggles face us in being men of wisdom as described in this chapter?
3. How can we be "meek" in our relationships without being "weak"?
4. What personal experiences can we share with each other that will help us to encourage one another, pray for one another, love each other more and build up one another?
5. What is your special need for prayer?

SET A GOAL

Write out one goal you'd like to achieve as a result of this study:

To have God's image before my eyes throughout the day.

Notes

1. *Merriam Webster's Collegiate Dictionary, Tenth Edition* (Springfield, MA: Merriam-Webster, Inc., 1993), p. 941.
2. Note Paul's special application of the word "prudent" to women in 1 Timothy 2:9,15. Here this characteristic is related to the way she adorns herself. She is to adorn herself "with proper clothing, modestly and **discreetly** [prudently], not with braided hair and gold or pearls or costly garments" (1 Tim. 2:9). Paul, of course, is not saying women should not be attractive; rather, he is exhorting them to be truly humble and to keep their motives pure, not attracting attention to themselves merely through external means.

6

ADORNING
THE GOSPEL
OF CHRIST

*An overseer, then, must be above reproach, the husband
of one wife, temperate, prudent, **respectable**.*
—1 TIMOTHY 3:2

When my family and I moved to Dallas, Texas, in 1968, we built a new home in what was known as the "White Rock" section of Dallas. This description in itself indicates the problem we faced. We indeed built our house on the "solid rock," but we had a terrible time putting in a lawn. After hours of work hauling in dirt, spreading it and planting seed (and losing it all the first time in a Texas rainstorm), we finally made it.

I remember one day in August when it was about 105 degrees. I was perspiring profusely while I was raking and picking up rocks and trying to prepare the lot for topsoil. An eight-year-old neighbor girl had been watching me for several days. As she stood there sucking on her lollipop, she made a comment I will never forget: "My mommy says you work awfully hard for a preacher!"

I have laughed about this little girl's comment many times. But I was also grateful. You see, I knew I had impressed her parents, and at the same time changed their view of "preachers." This was an important step in becoming a witness for Christ in our whole neighborhood. As some enjoyed saying, people never did see me as a typical "man of the cloth."

THE GREEK WORD KOSMIOS

The New Testament word *kosmios*, which is variously translated in 1 Timothy 3:2 as being "of good behavior," "well behaved" or "respectable," actually means being orderly or well-arranged. In essence, it is speaking of a man who is living a well-ordered life.

To Adorn

Jesus Christ used the word kosmios to describe a "well-ordered" house (see Matt. 12:44), "decorated" tombstones (see Matt. 23:29), and "well-trimmed" lamps (see Matt. 25:7). Jesus also referred to the Temple that "was **adorned** with beautiful stones and votive gifts" (Luke 21:5).

The most powerful use of the word kosmios, however, appears in Paul's letter to Titus when he urged slaves to "be subject to their own masters in everything" (2:9). They were to be "well pleasing, not argumentative," and they were not to steal from their masters (v. 9). Rather, they were to "**adorn** the doctrine of God our Savior in every respect" (v. 10).

Cosmetics to the Gospel

Our English word "cosmetics" comes from the same basic word kosmios. We see this connection when the verb *kosmeo* is translated to "adorn." In essence, Paul is teaching that our lives are to be like "cosmetics to the gospel."

As all of us know, cosmetics make us attractive when properly used. They make us look good and smell good. In the same way, when non-Christians observe our lives and how we live them, they should be attracted to the gospel message and to the One who incarnates that message.

This illustration broadens the concept of respectability tremendously. No matter what our positions or professions, we are to live in such a way that our lives are "becoming" to the teachings of the Word of God.

A MODERN PARABLE

A certain man and his wife in a certain city bought a home and moved in. This man was a Christian, and the man from whom he purchased the house was also a Christian. And both were Christian ministers.

In a few short days, it became apparent that certain neighbors were disturbed that another minister had moved next door. For behold, the former minister had paid little attention to the outward appearance of his property. He allowed the grass to grow long, and when he did mow it certain sections were left uncut. And where he mowed, mounds of dry grass accumulated, creating a shabby appearance. Dandelions grew rampant, and other assorted weeds became a permanent part of the landscape. This man had planted no trees or shrubs, but allowed his large and spacious lawn to become a hay field.

It just so happened that certain neighbors in this particular community paid special attention to the outward appearances of their homes. True, many were not Christians and they were materialistic. Their houses and their lawns appeared to be their "gods."

But the neighbors were totally turned off by this minister's irresponsibility and lack of orderliness and unwillingness to do his part to add to the natural beauty of the neighborhood. Consequently, the minister moving in after the former one moved away found great communication barriers with his non-Christian neighbors. They were utterly convinced that Christians (ministers particularly) are a bad lot, that they are disorderly, unconcerned and irresponsible about keeping up their property and how this neglect affects their neighbors.

The Interpretation

This twentieth-century parable is true. It happened to me. I was the man who moved into the neighborhood and faced the communication barriers. I have shared it with you now because it illustrates how a man can be a Christian, even a Christian leader, and not be "respectable."

Because of this Christian man's reputation in the community, it took my wife and me many months to build trust with our neighbors. The way we accomplished it, however, was simple. But it was not easy because we had to prioritize our budget and do a lot of hard work.

What we needed to do first was apparent; we mowed regularly and sprayed the lawn to kill the weeds. And rather than fixing up the inside of the house, we postponed that ongoing project and allocated money to buy shrubs and trees. And because we couldn't afford to buy these yard items, as well as have them planted by someone else, we dug the holes ourselves and planted everything—a rather huge task. But we got the job done. And would you believe that when the neighbors—particularly those who resented us the most—saw our efforts, they warmed up and became relatively good friends.

I am thankful for this experience because it taught me a great lesson. If as Christians we choose to live in a particular neighborhood, we are responsible to keep up our property so we can also be a good testimony to those who live there.

WALKING WORTHY OF OUR CALLING

A respectable man is a man who lives in such a way that his total life adorns the teachings of the Bible. Whether it is his dress, his speech, the appearance of his home, his office or the way he does business— all are to be in harmony with biblical principles and doctrines. Because God is a God of order, a man of God should also be orderly and proper. He is to be a Christian gentleman in every area of his life.

When I think of being a man who lives a respectable life, I think of what Paul wrote to the Ephesian Christians about our Christian walk:

> I, therefore, the prisoner of the Lord, entreat you to **walk in a manner worthy of the calling** with which you have been called (Eph. 4:1).

Paul followed this *general exhortation* with the following *specific exhortations*:

- This I say therefore, and affirm together with the Lord, that you **walk no longer just as the Gentiles also walk**, in the futility of their mind (v. 17).
- Therefore be imitators of God, as beloved children; and **walk in love**, just as Christ also loved you, and gave Himself up for us, an offering and a sacrifice to God as a fragrant aroma (5:1,2).
- Therefore do not be partakers with them; for you were formerly darkness, but now you are light in the Lord; **walk as children of light** (vv. 7,8).
- Therefore **be careful how you walk**, not as unwise men, but as wise, making the most of your time, because the days are evil (vv. 15,16).

POINTS OF ACTION

The following personal project is designed to help you develop the quality of being "respectable."

Some Probing Questions
• Use the following questions to evaluate your lifestyle openly and honestly before God.

1. What about my external appearance? Does it measure up to what is considered proper both biblically and culturally?
   Remember: It is important to keep these two in balance. Usually, but not always, the culture itself makes certain demands on people. Non-Christians also have certain expectations regarding what is appropriate and what is inappropriate. It is important for a Christian to take into consideration cultural expectations and at the same time not violate biblical principles and teachings.

2. What are my motives in relationship to what I wear? Am I merely attracting attention to myself or to the Lord Jesus Christ who lives within me?
   Remember: You can dress elaborately to attract attention to yourself, or you can be shabby, unkempt or unclean to attract attention to yourself. Both lead to a lack of respectability.

3. What about the house I live in? Did I buy it to impress people, or did I buy it to glorify Jesus Christ?
   Remember: This question, as all of these questions, has to be handled individually. Don't judge others. Examine your own heart. Size, cost and location are not the most important issues; however, your motives are.

4. What about my speech? Do I use words to build up others or to build up myself? Do I glorify God with my words, or do I glorify myself? And furthermore, is my speech becoming to a Christian? Does it adorn the doctrine of God?

LISTEN TO YOURSELF

On one occasion, we were constructing a new building for one of the churches where I served as founding pastor. One of the men on our executive team was a general contractor and he volunteered to oversee the construction. We also hired another man from the church to do the on-site supervision.

One day the man who was to oversee the day-to-day operations came to me and was very concerned. The man who volunteered to serve as a general contractor (the man on our executive committee) was using expletives on the job site that were not becoming to a Christian man, let alone one who was in a leadership position in the church. As the senior pastor, it became my responsibility to discuss the issue with the contractor. It was a difficult and painful experience for me because the man chose to resign from his leadership role in the church. What made the experience so difficult is that this man was also my friend, and still is.

Two Different Personalities

Since the experience with my contractor friend, I have discovered other Christian businessmen who live this kind of dichotomous life. They never use this kind of language around their families or close friends, but once they walk into their offices, they seemingly become different personalities. Somehow they justify their language as being necessary to win respect. Sadly, the opposite happens. They lose respect.

A Disappointing Experience

I remember reading some of the manuscripts published after the late Richard Nixon resigned as president of the United States because of the Watergate fiasco. The American people became privy to what happened behind closed doors and the kind of language Mr. Nixon used to communicate with his staff. I will never forget my disappointment and my loss of respect for this high-profile man.

A Mark of Insecurity

Frankly, I have concluded that many men use bad language because they are threatened. This is their way of covering up their feelings of inferiority. This became particularly obvious to me one day when I was sitting in a graduate-school classroom in a course on statistics. The professor was going to great lengths to scribble extensive and complicated formulas on the chalkboard. The man sitting beside me happened to be rather proficient in statistics, although he was a student. He had told me earlier that some of the formulas the professor was using were not accurate.

This day, my fellow student couldn't contain himself any longer. He put up his hand and graciously questioned the professor's accuracy.

I will never forget the explosion that occurred. In the twinkling of an eye, the professor's language changed. He began to cuss and swear. His expletives were shocking, although this was a class filled with obvious unbelievers.

As I reflect on what unfolded in the classroom that day, it became apparent that my friend had threatened the professor in the worst way. Rather than admitting his error, the professor tried to cover up his insecurity with bad language. Unfortunately, some Christian men do the same.

Intense Anger

Closely related to feelings of insecurity is anger. Anger, too, can cause a man to use bad language. If you have difficulty believing this, talk to any professional football player and find out what happens on the field when tempers flair. Bad language and anger go hand in hand.

Frequently, however, insecurity and anger run on the same track, which leads to double trouble. Insecurity often *causes* anger and this can cause a verbal explosion that is anything but edifying.

CHECK YOURSELF

• **Use the following scriptural exhortations as a checklist to determine the degree of respectability you have with both Christians and non-Christians.**

Note: Check those areas where you believe you are particularly strong (✓) and mark those areas where you need to improve (X).

Your Business Life

✓ "But we urge you, brethren, to excel still more, and to make it your ambition to lead a quiet life and attend to your own business and work with your own hands, just as we commanded you; so that you may behave properly toward outsiders and not be in any need" (1 Thess. 4:10-12).

X "Whatever you do, do your work heartily, as for the Lord rather than for men; knowing that from the Lord you will receive the reward of the inheritance. It is the Lord Christ whom you serve" (Col. 3:23,24). *Sometimes I work for the eyes of men.*

✓ "And let those who have believers as their masters not be disrespectful to them because they are brethren, but let them serve them all the more, because those who partake of the benefit are believers and beloved" (1 Tim. 6:2).

Your Social Life

✓ ✓ "Whether, then, you eat or drink or whatever you do, do all to the glory of God. Give no offense either to Jews or to Greeks or to the church of God; just as I also please all men in all things, not seeking my own profit, but the profit of the many, that they may be saved" (1 Cor. 10:31-33).

X "Conduct yourselves with wisdom toward outsiders, making the most of the opportunity. Let your speech always be with grace, seasoned, as it were, with salt, so that you may know how you should respond to each person" (Col. 4:5,6). *Sometimes my language is filthy*

✓ "Keep your behavior excellent among the Gentiles, so that in the thing in which they slander you as evildoers, they may on account of your good deeds, as they observe them, glorify God in the day of visitation" (1 Pet. 2:12). *since I've been in MIAMI*

X "Submit yourselves for the Lord's sake to every human institution, whether to a king as the one in authority, or to governors as sent by him for the punishment of evildoers and the praise of those who do right. For such is the will of God that by doing right you may silence the ignorance of foolish men" (1 Pet. 2:13-15). *I hate submitting to PAGANS!*

Your Church Life *- ESTABLISH A PEACE RECORD!!*

X "Only conduct yourselves in a manner worthy of the gospel of Christ; so that whether I come and see you or remain absent, I may hear of you that you are standing firm in one spirit, with one mind striving together for the faith of the gospel" (Phil. 1:27). *I need to get surly*

X "So then let us pursue the things which make for peace and the building up of one another" (Rom. 14:19). *I shoot off mouth*

? "Do nothing from selfishness or empty conceit, but with humility of mind let each of you regard one another as more important than himself; do not merely look out for your own personal interests, but also for the interests of others" (Phil. 2:3,4). *Do I look out for myself?*

✓ "But as for you, speak the things which are fitting for sound doctrine" (Titus 2:1).

EVALUATE

• From this study, isolate areas in your own life where you need to improve. Translate these areas into goals and then take action to reach these goals.

For example, if you are a person who never gets to work on time, make it your goal to get an early start. Concentrate on this goal until you have developed a new habit.

• Pray and ask God to help you achieve these goals. Realize, however, that prayer alone will not enable you to achieve goals. You must act as a *responsible* human being. As someone has said, we must "put feet to our prayers."

Remember: Bad habits are hard to break, but we must break them if we are to become respectable and be a good reflection of the life of Jesus Christ.

THINKING AND GROWING TOGETHER

The following questions are designed for group discussion after reading and studying the content of this chapter:

1. What do you think about the author's conclusion that some men use bad language because they are insecure or angry?
2. What other reasons may cause men to resort to this kind of communication?
3. What other areas in our lives should we look at carefully to determine whether or not we are living "double" lives?
4. What can we do to become consistent Christians in all areas of our lives? If we have lost respect, how can we regain it?

SET A GOAL

Write out one goal you'd like to achieve as a result of this study:

_____

_____

_____

_____

7

A Cup of Cold Water

An overseer, then, must be above reproach,
the husband of one wife, temperate,
prudent, respectable, hospitable.
—1 TIMOTHY 3:2

A beautiful story illustrates the quality of being "hospitable." Sam Foss was an enthusiastic traveler as well as a writer. On one of his trips through rustic England, he came to a small unpainted house that stood on top of a fairly steep hill. He was weary and thirsty. At the side of the road he noticed a crudely made signpost finger pointing to a well-worn path and a sign that read: Come in and have a cool drink. Following the path a short distance, he found a spring of ice-cold water, above which hung an old-fashioned gourd dipper. On a bench nearby, he saw a basket of summer apples with another sign that read: Help yourself.

Foss was curious. He sought out the old couple who lived in the little house and questioned them about the signs and the fruit. He learned they were childless and they just eked out a living from their little farm. But because they had such an abundance of cold spring water and fruit, they felt rich and wanted to share it with everyone who passed by. "We're too poor to give money to charity," the old gentleman said. "But we thought maybe in this way we could add our mite and do something for folks who pass our way."

This experience was the basis for Foss's beautiful poem "The House by the Side of the Road."

As I read Foss's poem, I couldn't help but think of Jesus' words: "And whoever in the name of a disciple gives to one of these little ones even a *cup of cold water* to drink, truly I say to you he shall not lose his reward" (Matt. 10:42).

A CULTURAL EXPECTATION

Hospitality is not a new concept and is not distinctive to Christianity. It has been a part of Oriental culture for a long time and is considered a sacred responsibility. The Greeks also considered hospitality a religious duty.

Merrill Unger reminds us that even today among the Arabs, we can see a reflection of this ancient custom: "A traveler may sit at the door of a perfect stranger and smoke a pipe until the master welcomes him with an evening meal and then tarry a limited number of days without inquiry as to his purposes, and depart with a simple 'God be with you' as his only compensation."[1]

A BIBLICAL EXPECTATION

The God of the Bible first introduced "hospitality" as a quality reflecting His own grace and love when He outlined for the children of Israel their responsibility to help people other than themselves. His instructions are specific:

> "When a stranger resides with you in your land, you shall not do him wrong. The stranger who resides with you shall be to you as the native among you, and you shall love him as yourself" (Lev. 19:33,34).

What was instituted by God in the Old Testament is reconfirmed in the New Testament, and given a greater prominence. Christians, of all people, are to be hospitable. It is considered a mark of Christian maturity. As in other religions, it is not to be just a sacred responsibility or religious duty, but rather an act of *Christlike love*. This kind of love is to provide the basic motivation for reaching out to others (see Rom. 12:13).

Practicing Hospitality

Paul's letter was clear when he wrote to the Roman Christians. He told them to be hospitable in order to meet "the needs of the saints" (Rom. 12:13).

The word "hospitable" means being generous and caring for others. That is why we call our medical centers "hospitals"—they are places where we can help people who are physically and emotionally hurting.

The church is also to be a "hospital," not only a place for spiritual healing, but also a place where Christians share with one another what they have so they can meet each other's physical needs.

It Started in Jerusalem

The circumstances in Jerusalem when the Church was founded were, of course, unusual. Thousands of Jews had come from throughout the New Testament world to worship the Lord for a special 50-day celebration. At the conclusion of that time, on the 50th day, the Holy Spirit descended on the small group of believers who were praying in the Upper Room.

The Church was born, and thousands were converted to Jesus Christ. Because the new converts did not understand God's total plan, they stayed in Jerusalem to see what would happen next. At this point, we see the greatest demonstration of hospitality in the history of Christianity. Luke recorded, "For there was not a needy person among them, for all who were owners of land or houses would sell them and bring the proceeds of the sales, and lay them at the apostles' feet; and they would be distributed to each, as any had need" (Acts 4:34,35).

This New Testament example illustrates an ongoing practice throughout church history. Unusual circumstances will always create special needs among God's people. In New Testament days, it was sometimes a famine, such as the one faced by the Jerusalem Christians several years later. In this instance, the church in Antioch came to the rescue (see 11:25-30). Later, Paul faced special needs because of his imprisonment in Rome, and the Philippian church rose to the occasion and met his needs (see Phil. 4:10-20).

The Need Is Still with Us

Special needs emerge in the same way today, and when they do,

God's people should respond to those needs. In our own church, we have a "love fund" for this purpose—a special account we try to monitor carefully to make sure it is used to show hospitality. It may also involve using our homes and resources to minister to others, just to share love and friendship.

Paul emphasized the same point in his letter to the Ephesians when he wrote:

> Let him who steals steal no longer; but rather let him labor, performing with his own hands what is good, in order that he may have something to **share with him who has need** (Eph. 4:28).

PRACTICING HOSPITALITY IN A REMOTE JUNGLE CAMP

While thinking about this concept of hospitality, I received word regarding what nine men who attend one of our sister churches in San Antonio were planning. They were planning to fly to a remote jungle camp in Ecuador to share of themselves and their resources to construct a facility for a special missionary.

A Shock Wave

In 1956, a shock wave circled the globe as five missionaries lay dead on the banks of the Curaray River in Ecuador, murdered by savage Auca Indians. Two years later, Rachael Saint, a sister of one of the martyred men, along with Dayuma, a runaway Auca Indian girl, courageously walked back into the tribe under God's guidance and protection. The result has been no less than earth shattering.

Jesus Changes Headhunters' Hearts

The first rough draft of the Auca New Testament was scheduled to be completed by 1988. Rachael had spent years living among the tribe. In conjunction with Wycliffe Bible Translators, she had learned the language, reduced it to writing, taught the people how to read and at that time was working to place the completed New Testament in their hands. This Saint among savages had seen all of her brother's killers converted to Jesus Christ and three of those men pastor Auca churches.

Rachael's Primitive Conditions

During the time Rachael lived among the Auca tribe, she had no running water, no bathroom facilities, no stove or conveniences we call necessities. At the age of 72, two hours of her day was spent boiling water, plus untold precious time used just making do. This valuable time could have been spent completing her translation work.

Lightening Rachael's Load

The crew of nine men from Fellowship Bible Church of San Antonio, Texas, flew to this remote jungle camp to spend 10 days constructing facilities to lighten Rachael's load so that the job of translation could be finished on time. The materials for the project were flown into the jungle by Missionary Aviation Fellowship and constructed on the site by these nine men who personally raised the money to complete the project.

What I have just illustrated is a contemporary demonstration of applying Paul's exhortations in Romans 12:13 *(NIV)*: "Share with God's people who are in need. Practice hospitality."

"WITHOUT COMPLAINT"

As stated earlier, the basis of hospitality is true Christian love. Peter made this point clear when he wrote: "Above all, keep fervent in **your love for one another,** because love covers a multitude of sins" (1 Pet. 4:8). He then followed this powerful admonition by saying: **"Be hospitable to one another *without complaint"* (v. 9).

Unselfish motives are the true test of Christian love. We are not to respond to others' needs because it is our responsibility or simply a duty. Rather, it is to come from our hearts. We are not to love others for reward, but because God first loved us.

Rewards *will be* granted. You cannot truly reach out to others without eventually receiving. But receiving is not to be a part of our basic motivation in demonstrating hospitality.

A Classic Prayer

Saint Francis of Assisi captured this concept of unselfish motives better than anyone I know:

Lord, make me an instrument of Your peace;
Where there is hatred let me sow love;
where there is injury, pardon;
where there is doubt, faith;
where there is despair, hope;
where there is darkness, light;
where there is sadness, joy.

O Divine Master, grant that I may not so much seek
to be consoled as to console;
to be understood as to understand;
to be loved as to love.
For it is in giving that we receive;
it is in pardoning that we are pardoned;
and it is in dying that we are born to
eternal life.

ENTERTAINING STRANGERS

Once again, the context for showing hospitality is Christian love. Note the total context in the letter to the Hebrews:

> Let love of the brethren continue. Do not neglect to show hospitality to strangers, for by this some have entertained angels without knowing it. Remember the prisoners, as though in prison with them, and those who are ill-treated, since you yourselves also are in the body (Heb. 13:1-3).

A Word of Caution

As Christians, we must be cautious in attempting to practice the kind of hospitality described in Hebrews. Some people make it a consistent practice to deceive believers and take advantage of them. This is understandable because they know Christians are told to be caring and generous.

Through the years, I have experienced this kind of deceit on several occasions and I must admit, I have made some bad decisions. In short, I have been taken. I have had to learn to ferret out what is a real, honest need.

You Never Know When It Will Happen

One day, I was sitting in my favorite donut shop. Next to me was a woman my wife and I had tried to befriend and had gotten to know well. Her life had been a disaster. She was a divorcee and had several children. Since her divorce, it was obvious she had been "living around" with guys she had met. She wasn't secretive about her private life. To add to her plight, she was uneducated, though definitely intelligent, but she had never learned to read.

As I came into the donut shop that morning, I sat down beside her and began to plan my day. At first, we exchanged hellos as we normally did, and then I went about my personal business.

Caught Off Guard

Several minutes later, she leaned over and quietly asked me if I could lend her 20 dollars to fill her car with gas. "I'll pay it back," she said, "as soon as I get my next paycheck."

My heart was immediately moved. I started to get my billfold, but then realized I had only enough money with me to pay for my donut and a cup of coffee. "I'm sorry," I said. "I don't have any money except enough to pay my bill, but if I did, I'd help you out."

I probably would have lent her the money, and I probably would never have gotten the money back. That, of course, would not have been a disaster, but had I given her the money, it probably wouldn't have been the wisest thing to do. It would have only reinforced her irresponsibility.

"This Girl Ain't No Angel"

Later, when I was a little more objective, I thought about several things. First, she had enough money, and always had, for cigarettes. She was a chain-smoker and had plenty of cigarettes that morning. Second, she commented later in our conversation that she should have been at work, but was running late, and she didn't seem to care much. She continued to sit at the counter, smoke up a storm, eat donuts and drink coffee. And third, I thought, *I know I'm supposed to show hospitality because I might be entertaining an angel unaware, but this girl ain't no angel.*

DETERMINING TRUE NEED

Ways can be found, of course, to determine true needs and to discover if people are trustworthy. The writer of Hebrews is not teaching us that we should be indiscreet and respond to everybody who asks for a handout. Some people are irresponsible and downright manipulative. It would not be the loving thing to do to allow them to continue this kind of behavior. This is why we should be cautious.

But, the cumulative teaching of the Bible is that we should care about those in need, including people we don't know. Let us not exclude those who have real needs. By sharing only a cup of cold water, we are sharing in effect with Jesus Christ Himself (see Mark 9:41). As Christians, we are to be generous and hospitable. This is one of the outstanding marks of Christian maturity. I believe that is why Paul lists hospitality as one of the positive qualities in his letter to Titus (see Titus 1:8). It reflects Christian maturity and helps us to develop good reputations.

HOSPITALITY BEGINS AT HOME

The overall teaching from Scripture regarding the quality of hospitality as a sign of maturity definitely focuses on the way we use our homes. This was particularly true in the New Testament because the churches had no permanent place to meet except *in* homes. If a man were going to be a spiritual leader, chances are the church would meet in his home. How could he be qualified without being generous in the area of hospitality in his life?

But the quality of hospitality is a mark of maturity in any Christian man. We are all to be hospitable, using our homes to serve others. True, our economic circumstances influence how much we are able to entertain. The size of our homes makes a difference in the number of people we can entertain. But on the other hand, in our own church, I have seen people who have small homes demonstrate hospitality just as often as people who have large homes. True Christian love transcends economic status. And when it does not, it should. That is why James wrote:

> But let the brother of humble circumstances glory in his high position; and let the rich man glory in his humiliation, because like flowering grass he will pass away (Jas. 1:9,10).

Cultural Dynamics

We must realize that culture also influences the way people are able to use their homes to be hospitable.

Behind the Iron Curtain

When I ministered in Romania before the "walls" between East and West came crashing down, it was against the law to have more than a few people in a home at the same time regularly. This was not just a restriction against Christians but for all people, regardless of their religious or political philosophy. Ceauseseu was fearful of any kind of conspiracy. In view of the revolution that took place in the city square in Timisoara, we can understand this Communist leader's paranoia.

But Ceauseseu's law *did* influence the church in a special way; it limited the members' activity. They were forced to meet in public church buildings where their every move could be monitored. This, however, did not keep these believers from practicing hospitality. They found a way, although they were unable to use their homes as they should under normal circumstances.

High-Rise Apartments in Hong Kong

I saw a similar problem in Hong Kong, but not because of government restrictions. It related to the dense concentration of people in this area of the world, plus the limited space in terms of land. Understanding the problem is easy because several million people live within the size of the Dallas-Fort Worth airport.

In terms of living quarters, those living in Hong Kong had little choice but to live in small skyscraper apartments. This makes it difficult for them to use their "homes" to entertain. But I noticed these Christians spend a lot of time meeting together in the thousands of Chinese restaurants that permeate Hong Kong. They, too, had found a way to "practice hospitality." Again, we see this biblical principle transcending culture.

Points of Action

The following personal projects are designed to help you develop the quality of hospitality.

Love Is the Key

• **You'll never develop hospitality as you should without becoming a "man of love."**

As we have seen, love is foundational in developing this quality in our lives. Almost every passage in the New Testament that refers to "being hospitable" is encased in a context that emphasizes Christian love.

Remember: Biblical love *is not a feeling.* It is an attitude and involves action. Christian love is patience, kindness, generosity, humility, courtesy, unselfishness, good temper, guilelessness and sincerity. Review the "spectrum of love" from 1 Corinthians 13:4-7 (see chapter 4, pages 62-63).

Love Is Doing What Is Right

• **Begin to show hospitality no matter how you feel about it.**

Some people wait for a *desire* to show hospitality. This may never come. You may need to start showing hospitality before you begin to sense any reward whatsoever at the feeling level.

Let's face it. Thinking about showing hospitality may threaten you. But remember, "perfect love casts out fear" (1 John 4:18). As you begin to practice biblical love, fear and threat begin to subside.

Develop a Plan

• **Decide on some specific ways to show hospitality.**
  1. Look for opportunities to share your home with spiritual leaders—pastors, missionaries and other Christian workers. Invite them for dinner or to stay in your home.

Angels Unaware

Some Bible interpreters believe that the reference to entertaining "angels without knowing it" refers to "messengers" who are serving Jesus Christ as apostles, prophets, evangelists, pastors and teachers. In other words, these were "angels/messengers" who had been assigned to missionary responsibilities by Jesus Christ to equip and build up the universal Body of Jesus Christ (see Eph. 4:11-13). In other words, if this is a correct interpretation, among the strangers who knocked on the doors of the homes of New Testament Christians might have been true servants of God who were called in a special way to carry out the Great Commission.

2. Look for opportunities to share your home with other members of the Body of Christ who comprise your own local church.

Remember: A special physical need is not necessary for you to show hospitality. The need might be social, emotional and spiritual. Many Christians are lonely and in need of fellowship, and may be too bashful to reach out to others. They are waiting for an invitation to share their lives with someone else.

A Word to the Timid

If you are bashful and reserved and tend to wait for an invitation, and then are tempted to criticize others for being unfriendly, you need to reach out to others even though you are afraid. You will be surprised at how quickly others will respond to you, and you will begin to receive "in giving."

3. Begin to show hospitality to non-Christians by beginning with the people around you—your neighbor across the street or the person who works beside you at your job.

Remember: You are the Christian. You are the one who should be reaching out. Invite these people to dinner or ask them to join you in an evening of relaxation and social activity.

A word of caution: Don't get overly ambitious. Begin by building friendships with one or two non-Christians. Frequently this will set the stage for an invitation to a Bible class in your home or for you to personally witness for Jesus Christ.

4. Open your home for an informal Bible study, either for Christians or non-Christians.

Remember: To invite non-Christians to your home for a Bible study means building friendships first. You must learn to love people because they are people and not just because you want to win them to Christ.

Set Some Simple Goals

• Set up some specific but simple hospitality goals.

For example, you might plan to invite a Christian couple to your home for dinner. Or you might plan to invite your neighbors to join you for a picnic dinner in your backyard.

These goals are simple. But when you have achieved them, you can then proceed to set up additional goals that are more extensive and long range. But, by all means, begin now!

THINKING AND GROWING TOGETHER

The following questions are designed for group discussion after reading and studying the content of this chapter:

1. What are some of the ways you are practicing hospitality?
2. Why do we hesitate to practice hospitality as we should?
3. What can we do to overcome the barriers that keep us from practicing hospitality?
4. Can you think of something you'd like to do immediately to begin to develop this spiritual quality in your life? Would you mind sharing it with us?

SET A GOAL

Write out one goal you'd like to achieve as a result of this study:

_____

_____

_____

_____

Note

1. Merrill F. Unger, *Unger's Bible Dictionary* (Chicago: Moody Press, 1967), p. 502.

8

ABLE TO TEACH

*An overseer, then, must be above reproach,
the husband of one wife, temperate, prudent,
respectable, hospitable, **able to teach**.*
—1 TIMOTHY 3:2

I have a close friend and fellow elder at Fellowship Bible Church North where I pastor. His name is Mike Cornwall. Mike has been involved in the banking industry for years. At one point in time when he was CEO of one of the largest savings and loans in the state of Texas, he and his wife, Sharon, had an unusual experience.

A SATURDAY MORNING SHOCK

Mike and Sharon were sitting at home having breakfast one Saturday morning when they heard some commotion in front of their home. They looked out the window and saw a group of people walking back and forth in front of their house. It didn't take but a moment to conclude that they were being picketed.

A Definite Setup
In a few minutes, someone knocked on the front door. Standing there was a man with a document. Standing beside him was another man with a camera. Mike had never seen these people before and for a

moment, was puzzled. But very quickly he got the picture loud and clear. This man wanted him to sign the document confessing that his savings and loan organization was "redlining" minorities.

The facts are, the government had passed legislation that could give the impression of redlining. And because Mike's organization was one of the most prominent in the state of Texas, they targeted his savings and loan—and Mike particularly as the CEO—to let the government know they were not happy.

It was clear that they never expected to get Mike's signature but, rather, an argument or a slammed door. It would look great on the front page of the *Dallas Morning News* the next day—hence, the man with the camera.

An Unexpected Invitation

Nonplussed, these men got neither an argument nor a slammed door. Rather, Mike invited them and all the picketers to come into his family room for a cup of coffee and an open discussion. At first, these people couldn't believe what was happening, but they soon discovered Mike was sincere.

As they sat in comfort and while Sharon served them coffee, Mike began to share his own journey as a long-term resident in Dallas. He told them of his concern for minorities through the years, and his own involvement in helping build the Martin Luther King Center.

Mike's Ministry Moment

Mike then shifted his comments to an important event in his own life that forever changed his perspective on others. He told his visitors of his conversion to Christ in a Bible study in the home of one of his neighbors. At that point, mouths began to drop open, and Mike began to get some positive affirmations. Apparently, some in the group at least understood the gospel.

To make a long story short, these people eventually left, each one thanking Mike and Sharon for their hospitality. Not another word was ever mentioned about their grievances. The picketers got on the bus, drove away and Mike never heard from them again.

A Marvelous Example

I heard Mike share this story at one of our elder/pastor retreats. As he shared, I thought of Paul's use of the word *didaktikos* in his second letter to Timothy, which is translated "able to teach." Once Mike sat down, I stood up and shared the following passage to demonstrate how Mike had fleshed out in his life that Saturday morning what Paul told Timothy:

> But refuse foolish and ignorant speculations, knowing that they produce quarrels. And the Lord's bond-servant must not be quarrelsome, but be kind to all, **able to teach**, patient when wronged, with gentleness correcting those who are in opposition, if perhaps God may grant them repentance leading to the knowledge of the truth (2 Tim. 2:23-25).

WHAT WOULD YOU HAVE DONE?

I often ask myself this question: What would I have done if I had been in Mike's shoes? Frankly, I may have triggered an argument very quickly, falling into the trap that had been set. After all, they would have been invading my space. This was *my* home. They were on private property. And to make matters worse, they would have been accusing me falsely. This was clearly a setup.

But that's not the way a mature man responds. Mike quickly understood the picketers' grievances. He didn't go on the defensive. He was "kind to all." He was "patient when wronged." He corrected his opponents with "gentleness." In short, Mike was "able to teach," and because he was, his opponents changed their attitudes. And most importantly, they heard Mike's testimony regarding his relationship with Jesus Christ and how it changed his life. Hopefully, some of them came to a "knowledge of the truth."

DIDAKTIKOS

The little phrase "able to teach" that Paul used to describe a mature man of God is a fascinating concept. As already mentioned, it comes from one Greek word, and though hundreds of references in the New Testament refer to some form of the word for "teaching," this particular word is used only twice—in the list of qualities in 1 Timothy 3:2 and in Paul's second letter to Timothy, the passage just quoted.

Our tendency is to see the phrase "able to teach" through our own mental grid. We tend to think of "good teachers" we have known through the years—people who are effective communicators, those who are able to use skillful methods and who can motivate people to learn. More than likely, we might think of high-powered lecturers, people who can hold us spellbound for an hour. In actuality, we are thinking about their abilities and their skills and their expertise.

A QUALITY OF LIFE

Didaktikos has a far broader meaning than just pedagogical skill. Dr. Phil Williams, one of my best friends through the years—a Greek professor who is now with the Lord—believed that this word could be translated "teachable" because of its root meaning and its use in classical Greek. I certainly respect Phil's opinion because he studied both classical Greek and Koine—the language of the New Testament. I believe, however, that didaktikos has a far more profound meaning—the ability to communicate in a humble, sensitive, nondefensive and, yes, "teachable" way. You see, the meaning of didaktikos in classical Greek does mean "teachable." By the time it came into the Greek language known as Koine, however, it had developed a broader meaning. It incorporated both the concept of "teachability" as well as a person's spiritual and psychological maturity in using pedagogical skills.

A Powerful Cluster of Words

You can see this concept clearly when you look at the passage quoted earlier from 2 Timothy 2. Note that the English phrase "able to teach" is surrounded by significant words that describe not skills, but qualities of life. In his communication, Timothy was to avoid *arguments*. He was to be *kind* to all people, Christians and non-Christians. He was to be *patient* even when he was falsely accused and personally attacked. He was to correct those who were opposing him in a *gentle* manner. And note: Sandwiched right in the middle of these qualities of life is the phrase "able to teach."

What Does This Mean?

To demonstrate the quality of being "able to teach" means that a man must possess certain personal qualities that enable him to communicate with others in a nonthreatening, nondefensive manner. He is not the kind of person who goes around looking for arguments or stirring them up. He is sensitive to people, including those who are confused and obstinate and bitter. When verbally abused, he doesn't reciprocate with cutting words and put-downs. In short, a man who is "able to teach" is a person who is not in bondage to himself. He is secure as a person and in control of his mind and emotions.

A Personal Confession

I remember one time as a young Bible institute teacher, I did not demonstrate this quality of being "able to teach" well. A man who was several years older than I kept disagreeing with me in one of the classes I was teaching. He was also obnoxious. One day I became so infuriated with his behavior that I gathered up my lecture notes, dismissed the class and walked out the door, leaving the students to fend for themselves.

Later, I found out why this man tried so hard to intimidate me. He took the initiative to come to my office and ask for forgiveness. You see, I began dating a girl on campus, who is now my wife. He confessed that he had his eye on the same girl and I had "beat him to the draw." I, of course, was completely unaware of his intentions and feelings. Once he unraveled his story, it all made sense.

But had I been more experienced, I could have handled the situation more maturely. If I had it to do over again, I would have asked this student to see me personally after class to discuss his concerns. I would have probably found out the real reason for his attitudes and actions. Furthermore, I would have demonstrated more Christlikeness to the students, that I was really "able to teach" in the full sense of what the phrase means.

I have never forgotten that experience. It taught me a great lesson. In similar circumstances, I have handled these situations in a much more godly fashion, which also means we become more mature in our Christian lives through actual hands-on experience. Some of our greatest spiritual lessons can come from our failures.

OUR ATTITUDE TOWARD SCRIPTURE

Consider another significant dimension to the meaning of being "able to teach." Although Paul does not use the word didaktikos in his letter to Titus, he makes several statements that clearly refer to the same concept—being "able to teach." He states that a mature man is "self-controlled, holding fast the faithful word which is in accordance with the teaching that he may be able both to exhort in sound doctrine and to refute those who contradict" (Titus 1:8,9).

Demonstrating Self-Control

Here in this paragraph, Paul makes it clear that a man who is able to "exhort in sound doctrine and to refute those who contradict" must also be a man who is "self-controlled." The Greek word Paul uses here is *enkratees*, which literally means to be able to control oneself. In other words, when confronting people who are contradicting what you are teaching, Paul states that we should be self-controlled, in the same fashion as described with the words "nonargumentative," "kind," "patient" and "gentle" in 2 Timothy 2:23-25 where Paul uses the word didaktikos, or being "able to teach."

This Doesn't Mean Compromise

This does not mean a man who is nonargumentative, kind, patient and gentle does not have certain convictions regarding the Word of God. Furthermore, it does not mean he ever compromises these convictions. A mature man of God is to "hold fast" to the "faithful word." But at the same time, he does not allow himself to get involved in "foolish and ignorant speculations," a phrase Paul uses in his second letter to Timothy (2:23). Again, we see a significant correlation between Paul's comments to Timothy and his comments to Titus.

Some "Must Be Silenced"

Paul was not teaching that this gentle, sensitive approach will always work in confronting people who disagree with God's Word. We also see this in his letter to Titus. Following his exhortation to continue "holding fast the faithful word" (1:9), Paul went on to explain that there were "many rebellious men, empty talkers and deceivers" in Crete (v. 10). In no uncertain terms, Paul told Titus these men "must be silenced because they are upsetting whole families, teaching things they should not teach, for the sake of sordid gain" (v. 11).

Is This a Contradiction?

In some respects, this does not sound like the same man who explained "gentleness," "kindness" and "patience" when he wrote to Timothy. Is this a change in Paul's philosophy of communication? Not at all. The reason for Paul's stern approach to the problems in Crete becomes clear when we study more carefully the nature of the problems and the characteristics of the men who were creating these problems. The difficulties in Crete were beyond the stage of "gentle" dialogue. Titus was facing those who were totally corrupt—men who had consciously rejected the "faithful word." They had deliberately chosen the path of corruption and unbelief. To them, nothing was pure. Paul wrote that "both their mind and their conscience are defiled" (v. 15). When this combination of traits is true in a man, he has reached the lowest point in degeneration. He is no longer self-deceived, but deliberately setting out to thwart God's purposes.

Mixing Truth with Error

What made this problem worse, these men in Crete had purposely mixed truth with error in order to deceive more people. This is why Paul wrote:

> They profess to know God, but by their deeds they deny Him, being detestable and disobedient, and worthless for any good deed (v. 16).

These are strong words. A "gentle" approach would only serve to further their own selfish endeavors. Paul is saying there is only one way to reach men who deliberately lie, men who destroy people's families without a twinge of conscience and who rip people off "in the name of God." They must be directly confronted with the Word of God by godly people whose motives are pure and whose lives exemplify the characteristics of Jesus Christ.

Paul's ultimate hope, of course, was that these men would respond to this kind of a direct confrontation. And even more, Paul wanted the Body of Christ in Crete delivered from these deceitful men's destructive influence.

OUR UNDERSTANDING OF SCRIPTURE

A man who is "able to teach" not only is self-controlled and convinced that the Word of God is true, but he also understands the Scriptures sufficiently to be "able both to exhort in sound doctrine and to refute those who contradict" (v. 9). We cannot communicate God's truth without a knowledge of the Word of God. This is why Paul also wrote to Timothy:

> And the things which you have heard from me in the presence of many witnesses, these entrust to faithful men, who will be able to teach others also (2 Tim. 2:2).

As maturing Christian men, we must constantly be learning more and more of God's Word, and understanding it. Only then can we teach it. This is why Paul also wrote the following words to Timothy:

> Be diligent to present yourself approved to God as a workman who does not need to be ashamed, **handling accurately the word of truth** (v. 15).

TO SUM UP

A man who is "able to teach" must demonstrate three significant qualities. First, he must be characterized by spiritual and emotional maturity—being able to handle himself in threatening situations. Second, he must have a firm conviction that the Word of God is true. Third, he must understand the Word of God's teachings sufficiently to be "able to teach" all men. Put another way, a maturing Christian man must:

- *Learn* more and more of the Word of God (see 2 Tim. 2:2).
- *Believe* more and more of the Word of God (see Titus 1:9).
- *Live* more and more of the Word of God (see 2 Tim. 2:24,25).

POINTS OF ACTION

The following project is designed to help you develop the quality of being "able to teach."

A Quality for Every Christian Man

• **Realize that every Christian man should strive to develop the quality of being "able to teach" in his life.**

Being "able to teach" is essential to being a good father. Paul underscored this when he wrote to the Ephesians:

> And, fathers, do not provoke your children to anger; but bring them up in the discipline and instruction of the Lord (Eph. 6:4).

This quality is also essential for being a participating member of your local church. Paul also underscored this point in his letter to the Colossians:

> Let the word of Christ richly dwell within you, with all wisdom **teaching and admonishing one another** with psalms and hymns and spiritual songs, singing with thankfulness in your hearts to God (Col. 3:16).

Study Scripture

• **Develop a regular program of Bible study, either personally and/or in a group.**

This should be more than a devotional study. It should be serious Bible study designed to learn the basic content and doctrines of the Bible.

Following are some suggestions:

1. Take a Bible correspondence course.[1]
2. Enroll in a Bible class, such as one that is offered at a local evening Bible college or seminary.
3. Become involved in a Bible study group in your church, prefer-

ably a discussion kind of study where you are able to participate by asking questions and interacting with others.

Mature Psychologically

• **Begin now to develop your psychological and spiritual maturity so you will not be threatened when discussing the Word of God with all kinds of people.**

A mere knowledge of Scripture and doctrine will not automatically solve this kind of personality problem. Many people who know the Bible from cover to cover are defensive and highly threatened people and frequently use the Scriptures as a "personal" sword rather than as the "sword of the Spirit."

The following are some practical suggestions for developing this quality of life:

1. If someone attacks you personally, never retaliate out of threat or embarrassment. Respond warmly and with openness. Draw them out even more.

Remember: "A gentle answer turns away wrath, but a harsh word stirs up anger" (Prov. 15:1).

If you are too emotional at the moment to respond objectively, it is better to refrain from commenting until you have developed a degree of objectivity and are in control of yourself. To help you achieve this goal, memorize the words of James:

> This you know, my beloved brethren. But let everyone be quick to hear, slow to speak and slow to anger; for the anger of man does not achieve the righteousness of God (Jas. 1:19,20).

2. Try not to embarrass people publicly, although they may attack you publicly.

Seek to speak to them in a private setting. This is also true when disciplining your children.

3. If you continue to have problems with insecurity and feelings of threat, seek out a mature Christian friend or counselor.

Attempt to understand the reasons for your defensiveness. Be open and honest about your feelings and why you believe this happens.

4. Gently force yourself to function in threatening situations. This

is difficult, but it is necessary. You will develop confidence as you begin to act and succeed in areas that are threatening.

Warning: Don't run away when you fail. Learn from the failure, and the next time you will succeed.

Remember: The more you succeed, the more confidence you will develop.

Learn Effective Methods

• **Learn how to teach creatively.**

Once you have begun to study the Scriptures more carefully and have developed a greater sense of security, don't forget to also begin thinking creatively regarding the teaching-learning process. In other words, learn how to use effective methods to help people learn.

To learn this, you might enroll in a class designed to help you learn *how* to teach. Better yet, begin to teach. Learn by experience. This will be more beneficial than a how-to course in all aspects of teaching. You will learn Bible content as you prepare to teach others, and you will also develop a sense of security the more you teach. And when you teach, ask someone to sit in and give you an evaluation after the session.

Remember: Teaching involves more than working with a group; it is also a one-on-one process (see 1 Thess. 2:11). You may find one-on-one teaching the most productive, particularly when it comes to working with your children. Paul used this family model in discipling new Christians. This is clear from his first letter to the Thessalonians:

> Just as you know how we were exhorting and encouraging and imploring **each one of you** as a father would his own children, so that you may walk in a manner worthy of the God who calls you into His own kingdom and glory (vv. 11,12).

THINKING AND GROWING TOGETHER

The following questions are designed for group discussion after reading and studying the content of this chapter:

1. What communication experiences have you had that were threatening? How did you handle them?

2. Who are some of your favorite teachers who model the true meaning of being "able to teach"? Why?
3. Can you describe some communication experiences you wish you could do over again?
4. Describe the communication experience, positive or negative, where you have learned the greatest lesson.

SET A GOAL

Write out one goal you'd like to achieve as a result of this study:

_____

_____

_____

_____

Note
1. Write to Moody Correspondence School, 820 N. LaSalle St., Chicago, IL 60610.

9

AVOIDING OVER-INDULGENCE

*An overseer, then, must be above reproach, the husband of one wife, temperate, prudent, respectable, hospitable, able to teach, **not addicted to wine**.*
—1 TIMOTHY 3:2,3

Several years ago, I received a letter from an irate mother. She was having some serious problems with her teenage son. He was drinking. How seriously, I am not sure. Someone recommended that she give her son a copy of my book *The Measure of a Man* (the original edition). She thought it was a good idea but decided to read the book herself before giving it to her son, which is certainly commendable. When she got to this chapter on avoiding overindulgence, however, she became extremely angry, tore up the book and threw it in the trash can. In her letter, she accused me of false teaching and condemned me for perverting the Word of God and leading people astray.

Evidently, she had read only the first paragraph and decided I was a heretic. Let me share that first paragraph and you will understand *why* she was so upset.

If Paul were living today in our twentieth-century Western culture, would he condone drinking alcoholic beverages?

Not necessarily, as will be shown later. But the issue before us in 1 Timothy and Titus is *not* total abstinence from any form of alcoholic beverage. The basic word *paroinos* used in these verses literally means a man "who sits too long at his wine." In other words, he *overdrinks*, and consequently, is brought into bondage and loses control of his senses.

When I responded to this woman's letter, I graciously attempted to point out to her that her son may have known the true biblical perspective on alcoholic beverages. Consequently, when she tried to convince him that the Bible taught total abstinence in all situations, he may have lost respect for her, and perhaps overindulged just to prove his point. I also pointed out the possibility that if she communicated with him in the same manner as she had communicated with me, it may have driven him in the opposite direction. Not surprisingly, I never heard from this woman again.

WINNING BATTLES AND LOSING WARS

In all seriousness, this woman's letter saddened me. There is an important principle here. We should never try to convince people to live in a certain way based on a false interpretation of the Bible. If we do, and people accept it as gospel truth and then discover they have been given an incorrect perspective on Scripture, they may also overreact and become rebellious, perhaps rejecting any scriptural teachings. When this happens, they have not only lost respect for us, but also respect for the Scriptures. This is a tragedy. We may have won a battle, but we have lost the war.

FACTS OR FICTION?

The fact is that the Bible does *not* teach total abstinence. As Merrill Unger reminds us, in most of the passages of the Old Testament where the common word for wine is used, the reference "certainly means fermented grape juice."[1] The same is true in the New Testament. There is no way to prove that references to wine were to only nonalcoholic grape juice. Rather, all cultural and exegetical evidence points in the opposite direction.

To be true to Scripture, we must also interpret Paul's references to "wine" in his letters to Timothy and Titus in the same way. Paul was stating that a mature man of God is *not* to be "addicted to wine." Paul was emphatic in both of his letters (1 Tim. 3:3; Titus 1:7). He did not say a mature man should not *partake* of wine. Rather, he stated he was *not* to be *addicted* to it. Common sense tells us it is impossible to be "addicted" to grape juice or any other unfermented drink.

WHAT THE BIBLE TRULY TEACHES

The Bible does not teach against drinking alcoholic beverages per se. Don't misunderstand. Total abstinence, particularly in our culture, is certainly commendatory. Before you complete this chapter, you may decide to make this your goal. If not, I would hope you develop a cautious approach to drinking alcoholic beverages.

Drunkenness Is Condemned

The Bible clearly teaches against drunkenness. This is true in both the Old and New Testaments. In Proverbs we read:

> Do not be with heavy drinkers of wine, or with gluttonous eaters of meat; for the heavy drinker and the glutton will come to poverty, and drowsiness will clothe a man with rags (23:20,21).

The Price People Pay

Later in the same chapter of Proverbs, we discover a series of questions: "Who has woe? Who has sorrow? Who has contentions? Who has complaining? Who has wounds without cause? Who has redness of eyes?" (v. 29). Following this series of specific questions, we find the answer to all of them: "Those who linger long over wine, those who go to taste mixed wine" (v. 30).

A Serious Warning

Following this explicit paragraph on the price people pay when they indulge, we discover a serious warning:

> Do not look on the wine when it is red, when it sparkles in

the cup, when it goes down smoothly; at the last it bites like a serpent, and stings like a viper. Your eyes will see strange things, and your mind will utter perverse things (vv. 31-33).

"Be Filled with the Spirit"

The New Testament writers are just as clear in their teaching against overdrinking that leads to drunkenness. Paul wrote to the Ephesians:

> And do not get drunk with wine, for that is dissipation, but be filled with the Spirit (5:18).

WATERED-DOWN WINE

The wine of New Testament days was not like most of our wines today. This is not totally clear from the biblical texts, but it is clear from other reliable sources. Dr. Norman Geisler, in his excellent book entitled *To Drink or Not to Drink*, summarizes Robert H. Stine's excellent article in the June 20, 1975, issue of *Christianity Today*, "Wine Drinking in New Testament Times." Geisler states:

> Stine researched wine drinking in the ancient world, in Jewish sources and in the Bible. He pointed out that wine in Homer's day was 20 parts water and one part wine (Odyssey 9.208.9). Pliny referred to wine as eight parts water and one part wine (Natural History, 14.6.54). According to Aristophanes, it was stronger, three parts water and two parts wine. Other classical Greek writers spoke of other mixtures....The average was about three or four parts of water to one part of wine.[2]

Geisler goes on in the magazine article to point out that "wine today has a much higher level of alcohol than wine in the New Testament. In fact, in New Testament times, one would need to drink 22 glasses of wine in order to consume the same amount of alcohol in two martinis today!" Again quoting Stine, Geisler concludes, "In other words, it is possible to become intoxicated with wine mixed with three parts of water, but one's drinking would probably affect the bladder long before the mind."[3]

In view of this historical evidence, we must be careful not to equate wine drinking in today's world with wine drinking in the New Testament culture. The difference is notable. What we drink today would be classified in the Bible as strong drink, wine that is "red" and that "sparkles in the cup" (Prov. 23:31). A Christian must never "linger long" over this kind of wine.

BIBLICAL GUIDELINES

Avoid Overindulgence

• **Overdrinking and overindulgence is in conflict with God's will.**
Overindulgent drinking is sinful. Paul underscored this point in his first letter to the Corinthians when he identified "drunkenness" along with many other sinful actions:

> Or do you not know that the unrighteous shall not inherit the kingdom of God? Do not be deceived; neither fornicators, nor idolaters, nor adulterers, nor effeminate, nor homosexuals, nor thieves, nor the covetous, **nor drunkards,** nor revilers, nor swindlers, shall inherit the kingdom of God. And such were some of you; but you were washed, but you were sanctified, but you were justified in the name of the Lord Jesus Christ, and in the Spirit of our God (6:9-11).

Avoid Addictions

• **Drinking alcoholic beverages is also out of God's will when we become addicted.**
Paul wrote, "All things are lawful for me, but not all things are profitable. All things are lawful for me, but I will not be **mastered by anything**" (v. 12).
Some people indulge in drinking and violate the will of God. But some people indulge and also become addicted. They are empowered by alcohol. They *consistently* overindulge. Today, we classify these people as alcoholics.
Addiction to alcohol was Paul's primary concern in his letters to

Timothy and Titus. Any man who was selected to minister in a special way to others in the Body of Christ must "not be addicted to wine." This would apply, of course, to any other kind of alcoholic beverage.

Startling Statistics
America has become a society permeated with alcoholics. As far back as 1985, the National Council on Alcoholism reported that 18.3 million adults in the United States were considered "heavy drinkers." Imagine what it is today. A heavy drinker consumes more than 14 drinks a week. Of this 18.3 million, 12.1 million showed one or more symptoms of alcoholism. A year later (in 1986), the Richardson Independent School District (in the Dallas area) reported that 80,000 Texan adolescents were alcoholics.

These statistics are continuing to rise in American society. Many people are greatly concerned about the large number of college students who are considered heavy drinkers. It is not a good omen for our future.

Disease or Sin?
Christians differ in their opinions regarding alcoholism. Some classify it as a sin; others as a disease. My personal opinion is that it is both.

We cannot ignore the evidence that the alcoholism affliction is a sickness. But many other sinful actions, including homosexuality, rape, addiction to pornography, prostitution, various forms of crime (including stealing, lying and murder), may have their roots in psychological problems or sicknesses. This does not disqualify these actions from being regarded as sinful. They are terribly wrong. Unless they are recognized as "acts of the sinful nature" as well as acts caused by other factors in the personality, these problems will not be dealt with properly. People too easily rationalize sinful behavior.

This is not to say that alcoholics do not need understanding. Most alcoholics do not need more condemnation because they already feel condemned by themselves as well as others. Often their self-image is at zero and below. They need to experience God's forgiveness in Jesus Christ. They also need to feel accepted by others. But they must also recognize that they are accountable for their actions, both to God and to man.

Avoid Being a Stumbling Block

• Drinking alcoholic beverages is out of the will of God when it causes others to sin.

The Bible teaches that we should not cause others to stumble and fall into sin. Paul wrote to the Romans:

> It is good not to eat meat or to drink wine, or to do anything by which your brother stumbles (14:21).

Do As I Say, Not as I Do

The National Council on Alcoholism has discovered that children of alcoholics run a risk of becoming alcoholics themselves four times greater than that of children of nonalcoholics. True, we can engage in the age-old argument regarding what causes these kinds of problems—heredity or the environment. Both are involved. Some people (some say one in five) are born with a propensity toward alcoholism, but it is still true that *modeling* plays a great part in causing them to start drinking. When children have a propensity to become addicted, they are simply moved in that direction by bad parental examples. Furthermore, what we do speaks so loudly that they cannot hear what we say. More than likely, children will do what we do, not necessarily what we say they should *not* do under these circumstances.

Peer Pressure

The issue is far greater than having children who exhibit a natural inclination toward alcoholism, either psychologically or physically or both. Although we, as their parents, may be moderate drinkers, our children live in an alcoholic society. They experience incredible peer pressures. An adolescent has to be well adjusted to withstand the pressures to indulge with his or her friends. Social acceptance is a tremendous force, and even children who have good parental models can be led astray.

Beware of Judging One Another

Within a period of two weeks, two men in the church I pastor approached me regarding drinking alcoholic beverages. Both men were growing Christians who desired to do the will of God. But the factor that triggered their concern about their actions was their young children.

Both of these men were well aware of the problems in our society. They knew the dangers of alcoholism, and they were concerned about the example they might set for their children.

Was it worth the risk to drink, although drinking may not be sin for them? Would their freedom in Christ eventually cause one of their children to fall?

As we discussed the matter, they both came to the conclusion that drinking alcohol was not worth the risk. One decided on total abstinence. The other decided on abstinence in front of the children. Both made decisions based on principles of Scripture (see Rom. 14:1-23).

Honor God with Your Body

• **Drinking alcoholic beverages is out of the will of God when we hurt ourselves or others.**

If we are Christians, our bodies are temples of the Holy Spirit. He dwells within us. Therefore, we are not to harm ourselves. We are not our own. We were bought at a price. "Therefore," Paul concluded, "glorify God in your body" (1 Cor. 6:20).

It's Relaxing, But...

Research demonstrates that overindulging does harm our bodies and does affect our minds. One of the men who consulted me mentioned a second reason he wanted to quit drinking. After a hard day at the office, it did quiet his spirit and soothe his nerves to have several drinks. But he went on to point out that it put him in a state of lethargy. He had no desire to do anything but sit and watch TV or sleep. When his children and wife needed his attention, he lacked motivation to respond, which he noticed was directly related to his alcohol consumption.

More Startling Statistics

Listen to these sobering facts:

1. Alcohol is the number three public health problem in the United States.

2. Alcohol is the number one cause of death among young people (ages 15-24).
3. Alcohol causes problems in more than one-third of all American families.
4. About 200,000 Americans are killed each year in alcohol-related incidents. This is nearly four times as many Americans as were killed in the entire Vietnam War.
5. One-half of all traffic accidents involve alcohol.
6. Drinking drivers are three to four times more likely to cause an accident than are nondrinkers.
7. Alcohol is the third greatest cause of birth defects.
8. A high percentage of wife and child abuse cases are a result of alcohol consumption.
9. A high correlation exists between alcohol consumption and crimes such as suicide, homicide, rape, assault and robbery.

These facts speak for themselves. Every Christian should consider not only what the Bible teaches, but also what research has revealed regarding drinking in our culture. Is it worth the risk to become part of the statistics that state that 7 out of 10 Americans use alcohol as a beverage? You must decide in the light of biblical principles.

DON'T OVERINDULGE IN ANYTHING

Overeating

Notice how often *eating* and *drinking* are mentioned together in the Bible. I know of Christians who overeat regularly but would never touch a drop of alcohol. And some of these Christians are the most vociferous in judging others who drink socially. Yet, they are consistently overweight, not because of glandular problems but because of a lack of self-discipline.

Jesus Christ had some strong words to say to these kinds of Christians:

> "And why do you look at the speck that is in your brother's eye, but do not notice the log that is in your own eye? Or how can you say to your brother, 'Let me take the speck out of your eye,' and behold, the log is in your own eye? You

hypocrite, first take the log out of your own eye, and then you will see clearly to take the speck out of your brother's eye" (Matt. 7:3-5).

Tobacco, Too

I have never preached a sermon against smoking, although I have not smoked during my adolescent and adult life. Ironically, I smoked more as a child when two of my cousins taught me at age four and five to pick up cigarette butts along the highway. In retrospect, I thank God that my parents moved when I was six and I got away from this negative influence. Otherwise, I probably would have become addicted to cigarettes, along with millions of other Americans.

We cannot deny the harmful effects that smoking has on our bodies. The statistics are piling up. Listen to these observations from the American Lung Association:

1. Cigarette smoking is the major cause of emphysema, chronic bronchitis, lung cancer and heart disease.
2. Pregnant women who smoke have more spontaneous abortions, premature births and low-weight births than women who do not smoke.
3. Nearly one million teenagers start smoking every year (more girls than boys are now smoking).
4. More than 350,000 people die yearly from diseases associated with smoking.
5. One-third of the deaths from heart disease are caused by smoking.
6. If people never smoked, 85 percent of lung-cancer deaths would be avoided.

Again, these observations speak for themselves. As Christians, we should do nothing that will interfere with our health. Again, we must remember that Jesus Christ dwells within us and He wants to use our bodies to glorify Him and to carry out His purposes on this earth.

Drugs

While flying back home from Denver one evening, I was seated beside a man who was reading *Newsweek* magazine. The feature article was entitled "Kids and Cocaine." I was particularly interested in the article and told the man why. When he finished reading, he shared the magazine with me. After I had read the article, we launched into an unusual discussion. He was a Jew and I was a Christian.

Together, we agreed that no one is free from the dangers of drugs. No family is automatically protected from the problem, regardless of what we do. Teenagers are always open to experimentation, and drugs are so available and addictive that sometimes one exposure can send the teenager in the wrong direction.

MAINTAINING OUR CHRISTIAN WITNESS

Be Proactive

One day I had a conversation with a woman who was trying to witness to the people in her office by letting them know she didn't drink. I shared with her that she need not concentrate on letting them know she didn't drink, they knew that simply by her actions. Neither did she have to drink to win them. In our culture, people respect people who refuse alcoholic beverages, if the refusal is handled properly. The woman could tactfully refrain from using alcohol and concentrate on building friendships with her non-Christian coworkers, looking for opportunities to share with them her personal relationship with Christ, not her nonalcoholic habits.

Non-Christians Are Perceptive, Too

While doing biblical research on the subject of this chapter, I was staying in a motel in Denver, Colorado. At about 5:00 that evening, I went to the restaurant to get a cup of coffee and to continue my research. Because it was dinnertime, however, they hesitated to seat me in the main dining room and suggested that I go into the bar. "It's dark in there," I said. "I need to be in a place where I can read and study."

They pointed out that I could be seated next to a window in the bar. Sure enough, this was a spot where I could see. The sun was still coming through a large-pane window. So I sat in this little bar with my open Bible, drinking a cup of decaffeinated coffee and researching what the Bible had to say about not being "addicted to wine."

Surprise! Surprise!

Seated behind me were two couples who noticed I was reading my Bible. I overheard a bit of their conversation, and it was obvious they were somewhat ill at ease with my presence and a Bible in the bar. Finally, one of them asked me what I was doing. To their amazement, they found out I was a pastor preparing a message for the weekend. This opened the door for personal witnessing.

I was rather amazed that they thought my Bible and the bar did not mix. The very presence of the Word of God made them feel uncomfortable. Their uncomfortableness eventually caused me some uncomfortableness, and I got up and left.

The point is that those who have worldly views—especially in our culture—know that certain things in the Word of God and Christianity are not compatible with their lifestyles. We don't have to concentrate on telling them—most of them already know. Our task is to share Jesus Christ and not be threatened by their behavior.

POINTS OF ACTION

The following personal project is designed to help you develop a Christian lifestyle that conforms to biblical principles.

Don't Judge Others

• **Evaluate your own attitudes and prejudices.**

You may consider yourself a mature Christian, having developed certain boundaries for your own life. However, have you made absolute for other Christians what God has created to be a freedom?

For example, God has allowed you the freedom to totally abstain from drinking any alcoholic beverage. But God has also given other Christians freedom to partake, although as has been shown, He has set definite boundaries.

Christian Liberties

Are you judging your fellow Christian who is taking a liberty you do not take? If you are, you are violating a commandment of God. Listen to the apostle Paul:

Let not him who eats [or drinks] regard with contempt him who does not eat, and let not him who does not eat judge him who eats, for God has accepted him. One man regards one day above another, another regards every day alike. Let each man be fully convinced in his own mind (Rom. 14:3,5).

Basis for Admonishment

We have looked at three reasons a Christian should lovingly admonish another Christian when it comes to drinking alcoholic beverages. *First,* the person is overdrinking and overindulging, which is resulting in unclear thinking and irresponsible behavior. *Second,* a Christian has become addicted to alcohol. *Third,* a Christian's freedom in this area is causing a weaker Christian to stumble and sin, to overindulge or to become addicted.

A Higher Principle

• **Never violate the principle of love and concern for others.**

Although Paul did not teach total abstinence and although he instructed Timothy to "use a little wine" for health reasons, he also told the Romans, "It is good not to eat meat or to drink wine, or to do anything by which your brother stumbles" (Rom. 14:21). The issue Paul was concerned about in Romans 14 was not the *meat* or the *wine* per se. Rather, it was the idolatrous associations and the problems partaking may have created for weak Christians. Paul was saying that at times total abstinence is the better way to live. *Love and concern for others is the higher principle,* and a mature, sensitive Christian is willing to avoid certain activities, although they may be legitimate in themselves. Does anything in your life violate this broader and higher principle?

Personal Discipline

• **Never partake of anything that harms your body, clouds your thinking or brings you into bondage.**

If you believe you lack discipline in your life in any area, the following specific suggestions may help you:

1. Isolate the problem.
2. Discuss the problem with several other mature Christians to see if they concur that it is really a problem or just an oversensitive conscience.
3. If others concur that the problem is real, ask them to pray regularly for you.
4. Write out the problem on a piece of paper, and then write out a specific goal you wish to accomplish in overcoming the problem. Read your goal several times a day if necessary.
5. Develop a regular time to study the Scriptures, and to meditate and pray about the problem.
6. If necessary, join a Christian accountability group to help you overcome the problem.

Remember: Many Christians fail consistently because they are programmed for failure. If you want to overcome a problem, program yourself for victory in Jesus Christ.

A FINAL SUGGESTION

If you cannot overcome your problem by following these six suggestions, seek help from a competent Christian counselor. It may be that that you need to understand and come to grips with some deeper roots of your problem. For example, overdrinking and overeating are frequently a reflection of emotional problems such as fear, anxiety, insecurity and anger. If this is true, you need professional help to support you and guide you in overcoming your problem.

THINKING AND GROWING TOGETHER

The following questions are designed for group discussion after reading and studying the content of this chapter:

1. What is your thinking regarding the guidelines in this chapter? In other words, do you agree or disagree?
2. What personal experiences can you share that verify the importance of following these biblical guidelines?
3. How can a Christian avoid judging others in the area of drinking

alcoholic beverages? How can this be done in other areas, including Christian liberty?

4. How can Christians avoid using their Christian liberty in ways that cause others to stumble and fall into sin?

SET A GOAL

Write out one goal you'd like to achieve as a result of this study:

_____

_____

_____

_____

Notes

1. Merrill F. Unger, *Unger's Bible Dictionary* (Chicago: Moody Press, 1967), p. 1168.
2. Dr. Norman Geisler, *To Drink or Not to Drink* (P.O. Box 471974, Charlotte, NC 28247: Quest Publications, 1984), p. 16. This self-published book is no longer in print.
3. Ibid., p. 17.

10

OVERCOMING SELF-CENTEREDNESS

For the overseer must be above reproach
as God's steward, not self-willed.
—TITUS 1:7

During my college years, I had a self-centered roommate. This was not only my opinion. Everyone who had a close relationship with this young man came to the same conclusion. In fact, almost everyone who knew I shared a room with this person felt a bit sorry for me.

Because I am by nature basically a tolerant and forgiving person, I did my best to make this relationship work. But the more I gave in to my roommate's whims and wishes, and the more I tolerated his irritating behavior, the more he seemed to take advantage of me.

As we sat together talking one evening, his actions pushed me over the edge, and all the resentment and frustration I had allowed to build up within me for many months came pouring out. I told him not only how I felt, but also how everyone else felt.

Fortunately, God used this confrontation to get my roommate's attention. As I shared my frustration and deep feelings of hurt and anxiety, I literally wept. Although I certainly could have improved my method of communication that day, God used it nevertheless.

Somehow my roommate saw beyond my frustration and anger to my personal concern for his welfare and his reputation as a Christian. Furthermore, he knew in his heart that I had patiently put up with a lot of self-oriented behavior on his part.

I was rather amazed at the results. Although he didn't acknowledge at the time that what I shared was true, he made some dramatic changes. He immediately began to be more sensitive and others-oriented. I could tell that he was attempting to make some midcourse corrections in his life.

My great reward, however, came several years later, after we had parted ways. He acknowledged that everything I had said was true. He wanted me to know that while I was pointing out these things to him, he knew *then* that it was true. However, he couldn't bring himself to admit it. He now wanted me to know he had changed.

RUBBING OTHERS THE WRONG WAY

I share this story not to put down my friend or to make myself look good, for I had my own share of immaturity and still do. My purpose is to illustrate that a mature Christian man is "not self-willed." Self-centered, self-pleasing and self-oriented personalities do not have a good reputation. They are overbearing and frequently rub others the wrong way.

AUTHADEES
The Greek word *authadees* is translated "self-willed" in Titus 1:7, and is used in only one other place in the New Testament—in Peter's second epistle, where the apostle Peter warned Christians against false teachers and how to recognize them. They "will follow their sensuality...and in their greed, they will exploit you with false words" (2:2,3). They "despise authority" and they are "daring" and "self-willed" (v. 10). Their hearts are "trained in greed" (v. 14), and they speak with "arrogant words of vanity" (v. 18).

The Profile Is Clear
The self-willed man is a self-centered man. He is his own authority. He is often greedy and vain. Joseph H. Thayer defines this characteristic as self-pleasing and arrogant.[1] In essence, a self-willed man

builds the world around himself. He wants to "do as he pleases" (Beck translation). Williams translates that a man who is *not* self-willed is "not stubborn."

THAT'S NOT ME

Because Peter used the word "self-willed" to describe a person whose arrogance and self-centeredness were blasphemous and horribly sinful, it is easy for a Christian man to rationalize and conclude that he doesn't display this kind of characteristic in his life. The fact is that we may be appalled at what Peter describes, but still be *self-willed, self-oriented* and *self-pleasing* Christians. We have simply sugarcoated our sinful behavior with regular church and Bible study attendance and religious language. We may have strong biblical beliefs and yet be guilty of failure in this area of our lives. Although our basic doctrines—what we believe about God, Jesus Christ, the Holy Spirit and how to be saved—may be correct, we may still be arrogant and self-willed. We are still reflecting the "deeds of the flesh," or as the *NIV* reads, "The acts of the sinful nature" rather than "the fruit of the Spirit" (Gal. 5:19,22).

The "Self-Willed" Continuum

Self-centeredness comes in various degrees. Even mature Christians have a tendency toward self-centeredness and can fall into this trap. We will find it easy to be self-pleasing and overbearing until Jesus Christ takes us home to heaven. But at some point this kind of behavior breeds resentment, lack of respect and lack of trust. If we persistently demonstrate the trait to be self-willed, people will not feel comfortable around us nor respect us.

Why We Avoid Confronting the "Self-Willed" Person

It is difficult to confront a self-willed Christian because teachability is not a self-willed person's long suit. Most people will resist telling such a person their true feelings because they are afraid, intimidated and often fear rejection. Rather, they work hard to please and to be accepted by the overbearing person, in the meanwhile secretively talking about the person.

MARITAL RELATIONSHIPS

Nothing is more devastating to a marriage relationship than a self-oriented spouse. Selfishness probably destroys more marriages than any other negative characteristic.

In some respects, I found it easier to live for Christ when I was single than when I got married. Having to relate to my wife was far more demanding than having to relate to my friends, my fellow Christians and the larger Christian community. To love my Christian neighbors as Christ loved me is one thing. But to love my wife as Christ loved the Church is yet another thing. That is why I believe Paul emphasized this point in his letters to the Ephesians and Colossians (see Eph. 5:25; Col. 3:19) after he had clearly stated that all Christians are to love one another as Christ loved them (see Eph. 5:2; Col. 3:14).

Paul knew that marriage puts far greater demands on our commitment to Christ. Not only am I made more aware of my own selfish tendencies, but I am also faced with the challenge of living with my mate's weaknesses. The truth is that no husband is perfect and no wife is perfect. Unless we are truly committed to practicing God's principles of love, our imperfections are likely to create alienation rather than mutual Christian growth and edification as God intended.

AS MEN, WE ARE PARTICULARLY VULNERABLE

Although both husbands and wives can be guilty of being self-centered (it lies just below the surface for most of us), a man can perhaps stumble and fall more easily. This happens for several reasons.

Our Sin Nature
By God's design, a Christian man is to be a godly leader in his home. Because of our sinful nature, however, including Christians, our *natural tendency* is to abuse our position of leadership.

Our Pride and Ego
A man's ego is easily threatened—this is one of our greatest weaknesses. This can quickly lead to selfish reactions. And if we were honest with ourselves and others, we would admit this is often a smoke

screen to cover up our feelings of insecurity and a weak self-image.

Our Rational Tendencies

A man tends to operate at the rational level more than at the feeling level. Consequently, we often don't understand how our overbearing approach to leadership is affecting our wives. When our wives try to tell us how they feel, rather than listening, we give them 10 reasons why they shouldn't feel that way.

Again, if we were really honest with ourselves, we would know we often respond to our wives with logic because we are threatened by their negative feelings. We are not only trying to prove to them that they shouldn't feel the way they feel, but we are also trying to prove to ourselves that we are not to blame for their feelings.

PARENT-CHILD RELATIONSHIPS

Our ability to be humble and kind to others is tested even further in our relationships with our children. A self-willed father can devastate and discourage his children. Though this is true for both parents, it is particularly applicable to fathers. That is why Paul wrote:

> And, **fathers**, do not provoke your children to anger; but bring them up in the discipline and instruction of the Lord (Eph. 6:4).

In his letter to the Colossians, Paul stated this truth more specifically:

> **Fathers** do not exasperate your children, that they may not lose heart (Col. 3:21).

Paul is telling us that a self-centered, self-willed father can easily create intense anger and resentment in his children. This should not surprise us because this kind of behavior creates anger and resentment in all of us, including adults. I am amazed at how often we expect children to tolerate our adult weaknesses and our own immature behavior to a greater degree than we tolerate the same kind of behavior in ourselves or in other adults.

WHAT CAUSES SELF-CENTERED BEHAVIOR?

Overindulgence

Some people have simply learned to be self-centered and self-willed. They are spoiled and conceited. They were overindulged as children. They have always had their own way, and they still want their own way as adults.

A non-Christian who develops self-centered traits is a candidate for sensual and selfish living that defies description. On the other hand, a Christian who is self-willed often lives a life of pious behavior in certain realms, but turns into a selfish and self-centered person in other circumstances. Tragically, I have seen men rationalize this kind of behavior by using biblical statements ripped out of context. For example, some pastors become authoritarian and lord it over others (see 1 Pet. 5:2,3). They use their God-ordained position inappropriately.

I have also seen husbands rationalize self-centered behavior because God says they are to function as "the head" of their wives. Again, they use their positions of authority to become authoritarian, domineering and controlling. Somehow they do not see that this is a total contradiction to loving their wives just as Christ loved them (see Eph. 5:25).

Ignorance

For several years, I conducted an open-line talk show in Dallas. People were allowed to call in and talk about any concerns they had. I will never forget receiving a call one day from a young man whose wife had just left him.

"What happened?" I asked.

"Well," he said, "she believes that I'm too controlling—that I'm too much in charge."

"Are you?" I asked.

"I'm just trying to do what God says I should do," he responded. "Didn't God say that I was to 'rule over' her?"

I couldn't believe what I was hearing. I hurriedly went on to explain that what he was doing was the *result* of sin. God was not telling us to dominate and control our wives as a result of Eve's failure, and Adam's failure as well. Rather, the Lord spelled out the results of that original sin for both husbands and wives. From that point forward, every wife's tendency would be to usurp the authority of her husband. And every husband's tendency would be to dominate and control his wife.[2]

CHILDHOOD REPRESSION

Some people become extremely self-willed for another basic reason. It is much more difficult to understand and sometimes hard to detect by the person himself. When you are talking about the problem, a person may blurt out, "I really don't know *why* I am so negative." Or, "I really don't understand my selfishness."

The "Self-Willed" Phase

"Self-willed" behavior often relates to early childhood. Between ages two and three a child goes through a natural self-will phase. It is a normal phase in every child's life, a time when he moves from extreme dependency to independence. It is biological as well as psychological. The child begins to learn to control the world around him, including people.

A Child's Greatest Gift

Some parents desperately and unintentionally misunderstand this self-willed phase in a child's behavior. They immediately become fearful that their children are suddenly becoming overly "strong-willed." They envision children who will grow up trying to control others the rest of their lives. Rather than seeing this natural bent as one of God's greatest gifts to the child that needs to be channeled and directed, they attack it and try to break the child's will. Unfortunately, parents only end up crushing the child's will, causing the child to repress strong, aggressive feelings. Often these emotions are buried deep within the child, and periodically try to emerge but again are repressed.

When Our Efforts Backfire

Tragically, this crushing approach to child-rearing often produces the opposite effect of what parents had in mind. Rather than overcoming the self-willed syndrome, which automatically happens at about age three or four when the will is naturally channeled, the child instead grows into a strongly self-willed person, even as an adult. This kind of person honestly has difficulty understanding why he is so self-cen-

tered and hard to get along with. But it is relatively easy to understand when you understand the psychological roots. Unfortunately,
it is not as easy to overcome the problem.[3]

A CHILD'S NATURAL BENT

The truth of a child's natural bent is beautifully illustrated in one of
the proverbs:

> Train up a child in the way he should go, even when he is
> old he will not depart from it (Prov. 22:6).

Often we interpret this verse from Proverbs as a parent's responsibility to educate a child in the way that the parent thinks the child
should go. More specifically, as Christians, we interpret this as training the child to go the way God wants him to go. But this is not what
the proverb means. Rather, we are to "train up a child" according to
the way God has created that child. We are to consider the natural
bent. We are to consider the natural phases that are part of his childhood development. When we do this, we will not be working against
God but with God in helping the child to develop and accept God's
truth in the natural context of life. This is indeed a profound truth,
and it correlates beautifully with what we have learned about childhood development from the social sciences.

TO SUM UP

A strong self-will, generally speaking, can come from two sources.
First, we may be overindulged, pampered and spoiled. We have been
given too much freedom and too many bad examples. As a Christian,
or as a non-Christian, this kind of experience can produce selfishness
and self-centered behavior.

Second, rather than having too much freedom, we may have been
overly restricted and repressed, particularly as young children. Our
natural self-will phase was never culminated, which leads naturally
to more cooperative traits. To this day, we are still trying to get
through this phase of learning to control the world, but never achiev-
ing our goal. We have deep-rooted feelings of resentment and bitter-

ness that are still controlling us. These feelings are also regularly getting us into trouble with those around us.

Whatever the source—whether spiritual or psychological—a mature Christian is not to be "self-willed." We must face ourselves realistically, and by God's grace, overcome this negative trait.

POINTS OF ACTION

This personal project is designed to help you overcome self-centered and self-willed behavior.

Self-Will Versus a Strong Will

• **Develop a proper perspective on self-will.**

A "strong will" is not necessarily the same as "self-will," as Paul used the term. "Willpower" is one of the greatest possessions we have. A spiritually and psychologically mature Christian, however, does not use his willpower to dominate and crush others. He is also able to maintain a balance between being strong willed and humble. The apostle Paul was certainly this kind of man.

Determine the Root Cause

• **If you struggle with being a self-willed person—even to a certain extent—attempt to isolate the cause.**

A man who is self-willed because of overindulgence and the development of bad habits can usually isolate the problem quickly. On the other hand, a man who is self-willed because of being overly restricted or repressed frequently has difficulty understanding why he does what he does. The reason is that this kind of behavior often stems from unconscious motivations.

Take Action

• **When you isolate the root cause of your problem, take steps to cease being "self-willed."**

If you are self-willed because you have always been allowed to get your own way, be thankful. It is relatively easy to stop acting that way. Allow Jesus Christ to control you. Study the Word of God. Find out what the Bible says about being a gracious, loving and unselfish Christian and then start loving people. Stop using people for your own means. Allow the Holy Spirit through the Word of God to produce His fruit in your life. Remember the words of Paul:

> But the fruit of the Spirit is love, joy, peace, patience, kindness, goodness, faithfulness, gentleness, self-control; against such things there is no law. Now those who belong to Christ Jesus have crucified the flesh with its passions and desires. If we live by the Spirit, let us also walk by the Spirit. Let us not become boastful, challenging one another, envying one another (Gal. 5:22-26).

On the other hand, if your problem has psychological roots that are difficult to understand, you may need some professional help from a competent Christian counselor. You may need someone who can help you understand *why* the problem exists, and then help you set up goals to overcome the problem.

Be Careful

It is easy for self-willed people to rationalize their behaviors once they understand the reasons for their behaviors, and then continue to live irresponsible lives. They choose to go on in their sin, while at the same time blaming someone else for creating their problems.

Remember: God holds all men responsible for their actions, no matter what the cause of the problem. The Lord understands and sympathizes, but we must begin to act responsibly by using the resources He has given us.

THINKING AND GROWING TOGETHER

The following questions are designed for group discussion after reading and studying the content of this chapter:

1. Without being specific, can you describe men you work with who are self-willed, as described in this chapter? How do these men affect you and others they associate with closely?

2. Have you ever had a problem with being self-willed? How has it affected your relationship with your wife? Your children? Other fellow Christians?
3. If you have ever struggled with this problem, can you describe the main cause? Would you be willing to share it with us?
4. How are you overcoming this problem? What progress have you made?

SET A GOAL

Write out one goal you'd like to achieve as a result of this study:

_____

_____

_____

_____

Notes

1. Joseph H. Thayer, *Greek-English Lexicon of the New Testament* (Grand Rapids: Zondervan Publishing House, 1962), p. 83.
2. For a careful exegetical analysis of the Hebrew text in Genesis 3:14-16, see Ronald C. Allen's *Majesty of Man* (Portland, OR: Multnomah Press, 1984), p. 147.
3. An overly restricted child can also develop a "weak will." The child just gives up, and the rest of his life he is afraid to project and exert himself.

11

DON'T LET THE SUN GO DOWN

For the overseer must be above reproach as God's
*steward, not self-willed, **not quick-tempered.***
—TITUS 1:7

I grew up in an environment where I came to believe that angry feelings are sinful. My father, although a wonderful, loving and caring man, tended to be passive. I never saw him lose his temper, although he faced situations that would cause the average man to explode. I came to admire that quality.

I later discovered, however, that Dad often repressed his negative feelings. Like so many people, he was angry underneath. It just didn't show.

Fortunately, he was a sunup to sundown farmer and I am convinced he remained relatively healthy physically and emotionally because he literally worked off his inner tensions through sheer hard work.

As a young boy who loved his father, I naturally personalized his approach in handling my own angry feelings. In reality, I was repressing those feelings, just like my dad did. I really didn't allow myself to feel anger.

As I began to understand this dynamic in my life, I had to relearn how to handle angry feelings. Though it was a process, I began to stop denying that I felt certain things, although I discovered that repression had become an almost automatic response. Today, I have made good progress in understanding this God-designed emotion and have learned how to handle it biblically.

BE ANGRY, AND YET DO NOT SIN

Not all anger is sinful. It is impossible to live without getting angry. It is a normal emotion. Paul acknowledged this when he admonished the Ephesians, "Be angry, and yet do not sin" (Eph. 4:26). To deny this reality in ourselves and others can lead to some serious psychological, spiritual and, especially, physical problems.

Jesus Christ, the perfect Son of God, demonstrated that it is possible to express anger without sinning when He drove the "money-changers" from the Temple. Seeing them exploiting others in the house of God, He overturned their tables and scattered their money all over the courtyard. He also made a whip out of cords and drove the sheep and cattle out of the Temple area (see John 2:13-17).

WHEN DOES ANGER BECOME SINFUL?

As with many issues, we need a rather broad biblical perspective to answer the question: When does anger become sinful? But it *can* be answered, and clearly.

Flying Off the Handle

• Anger becomes sinful when it results in "quick-tempered" behavior.

This is why Paul told Titus to never appoint men to spiritual leadership who were "quick-tempered." It is a definite sign of spiritual and emotional immaturity. It is allowing angry feelings to get out of control and become sinful.

All of us understand what Paul was talking about, either through observing this kind of behavior in others or experiencing it ourselves. The word Paul uses in Titus 1:7 literally means "passionate." A quick-tempered person "flies off the handle," "loses his cool" and usually says and does things that hurt and offend others.

The Greek word *orgilos*, which Paul used here, literally means "prone to anger." The English word that probably comes closest to describing this kind of quick-tempered person is "irascible," meaning "hot-tempered" or "easily provoked" to anger.

This kind of anger is also persistent. Paul was not talking about isolated and periodic circumstances that push us over the edge. A quick-tempered person consistently and persistently loses his temper.

Physical Abuse

• **Anger becomes sinful when it hurts people physically.**

This kind of behavior correlates with another negative characteristic listed by Paul in the same text, and which will be the subject of our next chapter. A Christian who is violent is certainly immature. The concept here means to be a "striker"—to hurt people through physical force.

Bitterness

• **Anger becomes sinful when it persists and results in bitterness.**

Paul spoke directly to this kind of anger. He wrote, "Be angry and yet do not sin." Elaborating, he stated, "Do not let the sun go down on your anger, and do not give the devil an opportunity" (Eph. 4:26,27).

Time Becomes Our Friend

All of us need a cooling-off period when we get angry. It is virtually impossible to suddenly flip a switch and dissipate angry feelings. But time becomes our friend. It gives us an opportunity to understand what has caused our anger and to become more objective.

Personally, I have found it helpful to avoid writing letters or making telephone calls when I am angry. If I do write a letter when I am feeling angry, I always try to hold the letter for at least 24 hours and then reread it. Normally, I then make a lot of changes because I have become a lot more objective.

In most instances, I also have someone else who is close to the situation and knows the circumstances read the letter and give me feedback. On occasions, I have been advised not to send the letter. In some instances, it is much better to pick up the telephone and talk to the person directly, especially after I have developed more objectivity.

Quick to Hear, Slow to Speak

This leads to another practical suggestion from James, "Be quick to hear, slow to speak" (1:19). I also try to avoid responding verbally to a person, or situation, when my feelings are unusually intense. If I do respond, I will usually say things I regret.

There is a fine line here, for at times we should respond immediately. It may be the right time to deal with the problem. But in doing so, we should be able to respond maturely and in a nonvindictive and nondefensive way.

Don't Misunderstand

It is not wrong to share our feelings of anger. But when we do, we should not attack the other person. For example, I might say, "I'm feeling very angry right now. I feel threatened and hurt and misunderstood, though I'm sure I don't understand all the factors involved," which is always true although we may feel we have an accurate perspective. There are *always* circumstances we don't understand.

This approach is quite different from the person who shouts, "I'm angry. Why do *you* always pick on me? What's the beef? What's *your* problem? Why are *you* so insensitive? Can't *you* see what you're doing to me and everyone else?"

Avoidance

- **Anger can easily become sinful when we prolong communications.**

One day I sensed a strain in my relationship with my wife. Frankly, I couldn't understand what was happening. At first, I thought it was just one of those moments in the stream of life that we all experience and that it would pass. But it didn't.

I Was Amazed

Finally, I awakened one morning and broached the subject, trying to be teachable myself. I was amazed at what I heard. She was interpreting certain things in my attitudes and actions that had precipitated her responses. I had in turn responded that way because of some things she had said, which I had totally misunderstood.

What had happened is what happens in many marriages. We had a breakdown in communication that led to our mutual misinterpretation. Fifteen minutes of honestly and openly sharing thoughts and feelings in a nonjudgmental and nondefensive way changed our perceptions on the whole problem and resolved it. I was amazed at how two people can live together for nearly 40 years and so totally misunderstand each other's thoughts and feelings.

We've Let the Sun Go Down

To allow these situations of misunderstanding to persist can lead to bitterness and increasingly aggressive actions. We are allowing the sun to go down while we are still angry. We are giving the devil a foothold in our lives.

I don't believe Paul was speaking literally in terms of a 24-hour day. It is certainly a good idea to settle issues before the day ends, providing that is possible. But some problems erupt as the sun is going down.

The point Paul was making is that we need some time to think, reflect and cool off, but we should not allow anger to persist. If we do, it will inevitably become sinful. We will do things and say things that are out of the will of God.

Psychological Abuse

• **Anger becomes sinful when we hurt people emotionally and spiritually.**

On one occasion, I was enjoying a hamburger at McDonald's. A young mother sitting at another table suddenly began to verbally and mercilessly attack her young son. He must have been about five or six years old. I don't know what he did to irritate her (maybe he spilled something), but I will never forget his response to her angry outburst. I could see him withdraw physically, reflecting horrible humiliation on his face. He never said a word, nor did he cry. He simply withered like a green plant sprayed with powerful poison.

This mother's verbal abuse didn't stop inside the restaurant.

Minutes later they left, crossed the parking lot to her car, and before getting into the car, she cut loose again. This time she came at him with a pointed finger and strong language. She must have verbally abused him for a full two minutes, as the little guy turned his head away trying to escape this psychological beating.

You might guess what she said when he looked away. "Turn and look at me," she screamed. I clearly remember his efforts as he tried to raise his eyes and look into her ugly countenance.

My Own Anger Was Aroused

By this time, I was becoming angry. I can still feel the same emotions as I recount the story. I wanted to grab this woman and shake her and shout a few choice words. Obviously, I didn't know all the factors involved, but I was sure of one thing. Here was an angry, frustrated woman, and this little fellow was apparently a scapegoat. No matter what he did (and it couldn't have been much), the mother's behavior reflected a quick-tempered and verbally violent woman.

Don't Misunderstand

I am not saying children do not need discipline. But we should avoid publicly embarrassing our children. And we should never displace our anger on them, no matter what they have done.

Verbal abuse can be more devastating than physical abuse. It inevitably creates anger in the child, anger that cannot be expressed. To do so only intensifies the verbal beating. The only thing the child can do is to repress his angry feelings, which will eventually manifest themselves in other ways—either passively or actively. Passive anger leads to depression, self-condemnation and withdrawal. Active anger often causes a child to displace his angry feelings on other children—people he can verbally or physically attack without fear of losing the battle.

Retaliation

• **Anger becomes sinful when we become vengeful.**

It is natural to want to hurt those who hurt us—to get even. But that, God says, is not our right nor our responsibility. Paul wrote, "Never pay back evil for evil to anyone. Never take your own revenge, beloved, but leave room for the wrath of God, for it is written, 'Vengeance is mine, I will repay,' says the Lord" (Rom. 12:17,19). It is God's will for all of us to "not be overcome by evil" but to "overcome evil with good" (v. 21).

WHAT CAUSES SINFUL ANGER?

We allow angry feelings to lead to sinful actions for several reasons.

The Fall

• **We are made in God's image, which was terribly tarnished when sin entered the world.**

God is both a God of love and a God of anger. And because we are made in His image, we have a unique capacity to experience both of these emotions.

When Adam and Eve plunged the whole world into sin, our tendency to experience angry feelings became tremendously complicated.

We must understand, however, that anger is a God-created capacity that reflects His image. It should not surprise us that we experience this emotion so easily and so consistently. And in view of our sinful nature, neither should it surprise us that we have so much trouble with this emotion.

Poor Examples

• **We may have been exposed to bad models.**

Angry people nurture anger in others. This is why Solomon wrote:

> Do not associate with a man given to anger; or go with a hot-tempered man, lest you learn his ways, and find a snare for yourself (Prov. 22:24,25).

This is an especially serious problem when the bad model is a child's parent. Children cannot suddenly remove themselves from a negative home environment.

Good, Not Perfect Models

Don't misunderstand. Our children need good models, not perfect models. They need to be able to watch adults demonstrate how to handle anger in mature and appropriate ways.

Remember, too, that children can understand anger. If we totally hide our own anger from them, they may grow up thinking it is wrong to have angry feelings. This can lead to intense guilt feelings on their part when they feel anger.

My Iced-Tea Episode

I remember one incident when my son was about eight or nine years old. He was stirring his iced tea and kept clinking the spoon against the side of the glass.

Frankly, it upset me. I had had a pretty rough day and just the sound of the consistent clinking glass irritated me. So I asked him to stop. And he did, for a few seconds. Then he began to clink again.

Once again I asked him to stop, this time with a little more intensity in my voice. Once again he cooperated, for a few seconds.

The third time it happened, I turned to him, asked him to look me straight in the eye and said with more intensity than ever, "Kenton, I've asked you to stop two times already. Now please obey me. That noise makes me angry!"

My son looked at me somewhat startled. Then with a calm spirit, he said, "Oh, OK, Dad! I understand." This time he really understood and stopped. He needed to hear me share my anger in a direct, but nonabusive way. *That* he understood.

Habituation

• We can easily develop bad habits.

Angry outbursts can become a habit. We learn that we can sometimes manipulate others with this approach to problems. We have simply developed a bad habit, a way of responding.

Or we may have concluded from past experiences that becoming angry is the normal way to behave. It has become so much a part of our behavior that it is as natural as breathing. Unfortunately, we are responding in an inappropriate way simply because that is the way we have learned to respond.

Remember, too, that we can also learn to control other people with passive anger by giving them the silent treatment. Sensitive people are particularly vulnerable to being manipulated with this kind of behavior. Because they don't want people to feel hurt, they work hard at creating a peaceful environment—for example, apologizing or taking the blame for things they haven't done.

Unfortunately, when this happens, we are only reinforcing the passive-aggressive person's behavior and we have set the stage for the next episode. Unfortunately, the passive-aggressive person has only become more entrenched in a bad habit. Sadly, some people don't realize they are using this kind of manipulative behavior.

Abuse

• We may have been mistreated.

Abuse is the most difficult problem to correct and overcome. Unfortunately, children are most often the victims, although more and more the "battered spouse syndrome" is emerging. Most women who become victims are battered physically. Most men who are victims are battered psychologically.

Perhaps the most applicable point is to make sure we are not guilty of abuse ourselves. Certainly, if we know it is happening to others, we should do all we can to help, realizing that it is not always the easiest problem to resolve.

On one occasion, a close friend who lived in Chicago looked out of his window one evening. He saw a man in the middle of the street beating his wife. Because my friend was a good, concerned citizen, he went out and tried to break up the fight. Unexpectedly, when he pulled the man off the woman, she immediately turned on my friend and began to attack him. The response went something like this: "This is none of your affair. If my husband wants to beat me up, that's his business, not yours!"

A strange response indeed! Unfortunately, our efforts are not always appreciated by those who are victims.

POINTS OF ACTION

The following project is designed to help you overcome sinful anger.

• Develop a proper biblical perspective on anger.

Ask yourself the following questions and answer yes or no. Be as honest as possible.

1. Do I tend to get angry quickly and rather frequently?
2. Do I find that angry feelings persist and linger?
3. Do I want to take matters into my own hands and get even with others who make me angry?

If you answer yes to any of these questions, you are no doubt facing a serious anger problem in your life. It is also a sin problem. Begin by confessing this sin to God and claiming forgiveness through the blood of Christ (see 1 John 1:9).

Remember: You must be honest with God. If you have an anger problem, don't try to fake it with the Lord. Tell Him exactly how you feel, confess that your anger is sin and ask Him to help you overcome this problem.

• **Proceed to isolate the cause or causes of your anger problem.**
The following questions will help you:

1. Is it because of a bad parental example?
2. Is it simply because you have been spoiled and have developed into a self-centered person?
3. Is it because of insecurity?
4. Is it because of an overly restrictive childhood?
5. Is it because you have simply developed bad habits?
6. Is it because you have been abused and mistreated?

Remember: Most anger problems have multiple causes. To understand these causes and to overcome the problem, you will probably need to talk with someone you can trust, someone who will listen objectively to your problem and help you isolate and understand the causes.

• **Take action to overcome your problem.**
The following suggestions will help you:

1. Regardless of the cause, don't blame your problem on someone else. Don't feel you have to seek revenge. Allow God to make things right.

2. Learning to control anger calls for understanding and insight. Meditate on the following proverbs:

• He who is slow to anger has **great understanding** (Prov. 14:29).
• He who restrains his words has **knowledge**, and he who has a

cool spirit is a man of **understanding** (17:27).

✳• A man's **discretion** makes him slow to anger (19:11).

The more we understand the circumstances that cause anger in ourselves and others, the more we will be able to control that anger and handle it in ourselves and others. We need an accurate perspective.

3. Learn to overcome your anger problem through an intelligent and rational approach.

Some counselors believe that people can overcome anger simply by expressing that anger in nonhurtful ways. To a certain extent, this is helpful, and may be necessary. More recent research reveals, however, that if this kind of behavior is encouraged on a persistent basis, it will simply reinforce bad habits. In other words, a childhood problem cannot be ultimately solved by having an adult consistently react in childish ways. At some point, we must approach the problem rationally and responsibly.

4. Set specific goals for your life in the specific areas where you are troubled.

Write out your goals, read them regularly and ask God to help you achieve them. If you have learned to get angry through a bad example, learn to manifest Christlike characteristics. For example, set up "patience" as a goal for the situations that really bother you.

If you are a spoiled, self-centered person, get your eyes off yourself and onto others. See what you can do for others, rather than always thinking of what others can do for you.

If you are insecure and easily threatened, program yourself to avoid a negative and defensive response when someone challenges your ideas. Rather, learn to listen and ask more questions.

If you are an angry person because of an overly restrictive childhood, learn to respond to people positively. Don't allow yourself to continue to react in childish ways. Keep unconscious motivations from controlling you and causing you to strike out at others. Reprogram your reactions, and you will discover that you will be instantly rewarded with positive responses from others.

PREVENTATIVE MAINTENANCE

All human beings, including Christians, have a natural tendency to become angry. Furthermore, all of us need a program to keep our emotions under control. The following are some suggestions:

1. Stay in tune spiritually. Avoid getting out of fellowship with God. Keep your prayer life in order and listen to the voice of God as He speaks through the Scriptures.
2. Avoid having to face difficult and tense situations when you are physically and emotionally tired.
3. Engage in a regular program of physical exercise, especially if you work under pressure and consistent tension.
4. If you become angry and upset about a particular set of circumstances and you are unable to shake the problem, learn to express your feelings in an objective and straightforward manner. Don't brood. Communicate, but avoid sending "you" messages that will be threatening to the other person.
5. Learn to back off every aggravating situation and try to look at it objectively. Why did it happen? What problems may the other person involved be facing? Ask yourself what you can do to help become a part of the solution rather than the problem.
6. Memorize James 1:19,20. If anger is a problem in your life, meditate on these verses every morning before you begin your day's activities, and then ask God to help you put this truth into practice.

This you know, my beloved brethren. But let everyone be quick to hear, slow to speak and slow to anger; for the anger of man does not achieve the righteousness of God (Jas. 1:19,20).

THINKING AND GROWING TOGETHER

The following questions are designed for group discussion after reading and studying the content of this chapter:

1. What have you discovered is the best way to handle your anger?
2. What do you do when you feel you have no place to go to share your angry feelings?

3. What experiences can you share where you have seen anger out of control? What happened?
4. Do you know someone who has an anger problem and needs help? Can you share this need for prayer without violating a confidence?

SET A GOAL

Write out one goal you'd like to achieve as a result of this study:

_____

_____

_____

_____

12

NEVER RESORT TO VIOLENCE

For the overseer must be above reproach as
God's steward, not self-willed, not quick-tempered,
*not addicted to wine, **not pugnacious.***
—TITUS 1:7

The translators of the *New American Standard Bible* chose the word "pugnacious" to describe the Greek word *pleektees*. It is an appropriate word, but it may be vague to the average English-speaking person. Joseph H. Thayer defines this kind of man as a "bruiser," one who is "ready with a blow"; "a pugnacious, contentious, quarrelsome person."[1]

The *King James Version* leaves no question about what it means to be pugnacious. A mature man of God is not to be a "striker"—one who physically hurts others. Pugnaciousness, then, is really anger out of control—not just verbally, but physically.

A HORROR STORY

A young man who grew up in our church in Dallas was living in Austin, Texas. Unfortunately, at one point in his life he had become involved in drugs and alcohol. Fortunately, he admitted his problem and overcame the habit.

One evening this young man was attending a meeting of

Alcoholics Anonymous (AA). He and another friend arrived early. His friend went and sat on a couch beside a young woman who also attended AA regularly. Behind them was an open window. Hearing some commotion outside, the young woman stood up to see what was happening. At that moment, three shots rang out. A man standing outside the window fired two shots into the back of her head and then turned the gun on himself. Another man in the room jumped through the window to pursue the attacker. He found the man lying on the ground, mortally and violently wounded by his own hand, a victim of his own jealousy and rage.

The young man from our church rushed over to the young woman lying in a pool of blood on the floor and tried to administer first aid. His efforts were fruitless. She died 30 minutes later on the way to the hospital.

Needless to say, this young man was terribly traumatized by the violent act he had witnessed. He couldn't sleep all night. The next evening he turned on the TV to try to forget what had happened, and he began to watch a relatively mild detective show. But suddenly, the sound of gunshots and the sight of people falling wounded became so real and repulsive that he couldn't continue watching. Violence had become a reality.

This kind of a story is shocking, and it should be, but such events should not surprise us. When sin entered the world, humanity inherited an incredible capacity toward violence.

CAIN AND ABEL

Violence in its worst form began with our first parents' eldest son, Cain. He resented his younger brother because God accepted Abel's offering and rejected his own, probably because of Cain's sin and wrongdoing in the first place. God told Cain, "If you do well, will not your countenance be lifted up?" (Gen. 4:7).

The Lord then added a significant warning we should all heed:

> And if you do not do well, sin is crouching at the door; and its desire is for you, but you must master it (v. 7).

Cain, however, did not heed God's warning. He did not come to grips with his jealousy and anger. He "let the sun go down" on his wrath. Whether he planned his brother's death or struck out at him in a moment of rage we are not told, but while they were out in the field alone, "Cain rose up against Abel his brother and killed him" (v. 8).

MOSES' SERIOUS SIN

Some of God's choicest servants have allowed their anger to get out of control, leading to violent acts. Moses, for example, killed an Egyptian who was beating one of Moses' Hebrew brothers. Although Moses no doubt felt justified in what he had done—probably because of his high political position in Egypt as well as his heritage as an Israelite—it is clear from the story that he was taking both the law of the land and God's law into his own hands. Consequently, he brought down on his head the wrath of the king of Egypt and at the same time lost the trust of the very people he was attempting to defend. As a result, he had to flee into the wilderness to escape death (see Exod. 2:11-15).

DAVID'S HORRIBLE CRIME

David's violent crime probably represents the most frightening illustration in Scripture. It demonstrates that even a man after God's heart—a man who could write the beautiful twenty-third psalm—could commit violence against an innocent human being. In a moment of selfish desire, although he had access to hundreds of other women who in his culture were recognized as his legitimate wives, he used his kingly position and power to take another man's wife into his own bedchamber. When Bathsheba became pregnant, he tried to cover his sin with an insidious plot. He designed a scheme to have Uriah, Bathsheba's husband, killed on the frontlines in battle so that it appeared to be an accidental death.

Tragedy Strikes

David paid some horrible consequences for these sins—consequences that plagued him until the day he died. His son Amnon raped his own sister Tamar (see 2 Sam. 13:1-14)—another violent crime that has been around since the Fall. In turn, David's son

Absalom became angry with Amnon, and after two years of bitterness, schemed Amnon's death (see vv. 22-29).

But There's More

This sad story continues to unfold. Eventually, Absalom turned against his own father and devised another scheme to turn the children of Israel against David (see 15:1-12). Because David himself at times was such a violent man, God allowed his son Absalom to turn the hearts of the children of Israel away from David (see 16:5-12).

Although David was intensely repentant for his sin (and God certainly forgave him), he never escaped the consequences of his sin. His family's story is one of the most sordid and sad sagas in all of Scripture; it is filled with horrible violence.

THE NEW TESTAMENT CULTURE

Paul used the word *pleektees* in both his letter to Timothy and the one he wrote to Titus (1 Tim. 3:3; Titus 1:7). In both instances, the word follows the phrase "not addicted to wine." The connection in Paul's mind is clear. A person who loses control of his senses because of alcohol also tends to lose control of his anger. How many brawls have come out of barroom scenes where people have had too much to drink?

Christianity and Violence Don't Mix

You might ask why Paul had to refer to such an obvious quality—or lack of it—when screening people who might be in spiritual leadership roles in the church. Wouldn't any thinking person realize that physical violence is out of character with Christian behavior?

We could ask the same question about being a "husband of one wife." Isn't it obvious that living with more than one woman is a violation of God's plan for marriage?

Reflect for a Moment

These questions are not difficult to answer when we stop and think about the pagan culture out of which these New Testament

Christians were converted. Let's remind ourselves again of Paul's words to the Corinthians:

> Do not be deceived; neither fornicators, nor idolaters, nor adulterers, nor effeminate, nor homosexuals, nor thieves, nor the covetous, nor drunkards, nor revilers, nor swindlers, shall inherit the kingdom of God. **And such were some of you** (1 Cor. 6:9-11).

New Testament leaders had to constantly warn Christians not to allow characteristics from their previous pagan lifestyles to continue in their Christian lives. Paul admonished the Ephesians and the Colossians to "put away" these things and to walk worthy of their calling in Christ (Eph. 4:17-32; Col. 3:1-14).

A mature Christian man, then, is in control of his human spirit. Not only is he a person who is not "quick-tempered," but he also doesn't commit acts of physical violence.

TOO CLOSE FOR COMFORT

As I reflect on the subject of this chapter, I can't help but think about Nazi Germany and the violent acts committed against millions of Jews and many, many others. You see, I am German—mostly. I grew up in a German community. Many of my closest friends are German. Some were born in Germany and moved to the United States following World War II.

Ethnically, I represent some of the same people who so casually gunned down millions of Jews and herded them into gas chambers. I represent people who threw babies against brick walls and battered their brains out, and then went home to their own children, held them in their arms, rocked them and then tucked them into bed.

How Could This Happen?

Are all Germans psychopathic? Mentally sick? Insensitive and cruel? The answer, of course, is a decided no. But we, like all people, are sinners. And all of us—along with every human being alive—have the same capacity to engage in violence toward our fellow human beings and to follow the leadership of violent men—Hitlers,

Mussolinis and Stalins. Maybe these men were psychologically ill, as well as being spiritually degenerate, but why do men and women who are mentally and emotionally sound follow them and carry out their orders?

Believe It or Not

Whether you can accept it or not, the Bible teaches that all human beings have the same potential. We have a sin nature that can lead us to do horrible things and overshadow whatever semblance of good that remains in our hearts and personalities. The prophet Jeremiah said it well, "The heart is more deceitful than all else and is desperately sick; who can understand it?" (17:9).

Eichmann Is in All of Us

Relative to what happened in Nazi Germany, Chuck Colson recounted what he had seen on network television's "60 Minutes." Commenting on what he had seen, Colson stated the following:

> Introducing a recent story about Nazi Adolf Eichmann, a principal architect of the Holocaust, Wallace posed a central question at the program's outset: "How is it possible...for a man to act as Eichmann acted?...Was he a monster? A madman? Or was he perhaps something even more terrifying: was he normal?"
>
> Normal? The executioner of millions of Jews normal? Most self-respecting viewers would be outraged at the very thought.
>
> The most startling answer to Wallace's shocking question came in an interview with Yehiel Dinur, a concentration camp survivor who testified against Eichmann at Nuremburg trials. A film clip from Eichmann's 1961 trial showed Dinur walking into the courtroom, stopping short, seeing Eichmann for the first time since the Nazis had sent him to Auschwitz 18 years earlier. Dinur began to sob uncontrollably, then fainted, collapsing in a heap on the floor as the presiding judicial officer pounded his order in the crowded courtroom.

Was Dinur overcome by hatred? Fear? Horrid memories? No; it was none of these. Rather, as Dinur explained to Wallace, all at once he realized Eichmann was not the godlike officer who had sent so many to their deaths. This Eichmann was an ordinary man. "I was afraid about myself," said Dinur, "...I saw that I am capable to do this. I am...exactly like he."

Wallace's subsequent summation of Dinur's terrible discovery—"Eichmann is in all of us"—is a horrifying statement; but it indeed captures the central truth about man's nature. For as a result of the Fall, sin is in each of us—not just the susceptibility to sin, but sin itself.[2]

WHEN IT HITS HOME

The reality of what Chuck Colson pointed out in his editorial hit me one day in a personal way. My oldest daughter had a scary experience when she was driving to work. While pulling up to a stop light, she inadvertently and unintentionally irritated a driver in another car.

The driver jumped out of his car and ran up to hers and tried to pull open her door. Fortunately, it was locked. He next proceeded to beat his fists against her windows, trying to smash them in. He also pounded the hood and kicked the side of the car, and finally with his bare hands demolished her sideview mirror.

As my daughter looked on in horror, she noticed particularly the man's eyes. They were ablaze with fire and hatred, reflecting violent anger. My heart almost skips a beat when I think what might have happened to my daughter had this man been able to get inside her car.

Where Have All the Values Gone?

Where Have All the Values Gone? is the subtitle for a book written by Tim and Beverly LaHaye entitled *A Nation Without a Conscience.* They relate the following story:

A young black couple, married only five months, was driving

on Interstate 395 in Washington, D.C., one Saturday afternoon when a carload of total strangers drew up beside them.
One man in the car opened fire. The nineteen-year-old wife
died instantly, and the injured husband was barely able to
ease the car to a stop. When the police apprehended the
killer (who would have been in prison on another charge
had not a parole board cut his sentence by 60 percent in the
belief that the criminal had been "rehabilitated"), the mur-
derer gave this reason for the outrageous random shooting:
"I just felt like killing someone."[3]

ROOT CAUSES IN OUR CULTURE

Bob Vernon, who served in the Los Angeles Police Department for
37 years, and is a strong Christian, points out in his book entitled
L. A. Justice that the problems in our society have many root causes. But in terms of violence, Vernon made the following penetrating
analysis:

> Valuing material things and money above people is one of
> the true root causes of our culture's destruction. When the
> material is apprized more than people, people lose self-
> esteem and regard for others.
>
> Many people today lack a healthy sense of self-worth.
> The intensity of the problem varies from person to person,
> but at the extreme end of the continuum are those who hate
> themselves. They see no value in themselves. Their lives are
> miserable. And if they're just a bunch of garbage waiting to
> decay, so is everyone else.
>
> Those who have reached this extreme are very danger-
> ous. They're angry and bitter. Life for them is a grievous,
> sour joke, something to dull with drugs and sex until it mer-
> cifully ends. Since that's their view, it's easy to end the
> "worthless" life of another. When self-respect is nonexistent,
> so is respect for others.
>
> In the inner city, the overemphasis on possessions is obvi-
> ous. Many young lives have been snuffed out for a leather
> jacket, a ghetto blaster, or a pair of Air Jordans.[4]

SOME STARTLING STATISTICS

But, you say, Bob Vernon is talking about the ghetto. Consider the following statistics and observations:

- In Texas, one out of four women experiences domestic violence in her lifetime. Fifteen percent of Texas women are severely and repeatedly abused.
- Nationally, an incident of wife abuse occurs once every 18 seconds.

The Department of Human Resources in Dallas reports the following:

- They receive 250 to 300 calls monthly concerning child abuse.
- Of the above figures, 35 percent represent physical abuse, and 25 percent to 30 percent reflect sexual abuse.
- Eighty to 85 percent of abused children are under the age of three.

OUR MOST VIOLENT CRIME

Similar statistics could be reported in nearly every major city and in most states in America. But one of the most violent tragedies that occurs every day is that an average of 180 babies are "legally" killed every hour in the United States. Legalized abortion is probably one of the greatest crimes against humanity that exists in our society today. In essence, how far have we come from the crimes of Nazi Germany? How far are we from what was really happening in the Roman Empire? Perhaps in the mind of God, there is very little difference.

POINTS OF ACTION

The project designed for overcoming a "quick temper" in the previous chapter is also applicable to overcoming violent behavior. Here are some additional suggestions for dealing with the problem:

- Be sure you are not "striking out" at people verbally.
  Ask yourself the following questions:

1. How frequently do I talk about other people's problems?
2. With whom do I share this information?
3. How often do I repeat information about a particular person?
4. What kind of emotional reaction do I have when I talk about somebody else's problems?

If you talk frequently about others to a variety of people and enjoy repeating stories about a particular person, chances are you are "getting even" with someone. You are using a more culturally acceptable form of pugnacious behavior, but it is "striking out" just the same.

• Make sure you are following a biblical approach to handling personal offenses, forgiveness and sin. Study carefully the following Scriptures:

> "And if your brother sins, go and reprove him in private; if he listens to you, you have won your brother. But if he does not listen to you, take one or two more with you, so that by the mouth of two or three witnesses every fact may be confirmed. And if he refuses to listen to them, tell it to the church; and if he refuses to listen even to the church, let him be to you as a Gentile and a tax-gatherer" (Matt. 18:15-17).

> Brethren, even if a man is caught in any trespass, you who are spiritual, restore such a one in a spirit of gentleness; each one looking to yourself, lest you too be tempted. Bear one another's burdens, and thus fulfill the law of Christ. For if anyone thinks he is something when he is nothing, he deceives himself (Gal. 6:1-3).

• Once you have isolated areas of resentment in your own personality, proceed to deal with them.

You might follow this sequence:

1. Confess your sin to God.
2. Pray for God's help in overcoming the problem.
3. Write out some specific goals to help you overcome your problem. For example, you might write: "I will not talk about (Jim and Jane) in a derogatory way."

Or, "I will talk personally to (Jim and Jane) about their problem. If they have hurt me, I will communicate with them face-to-face rather than get even through gossiping about them."

4. If you have hurt someone's reputation, ask the person to forgive you.

• Seek professional help if you have a problem with physically abusing other people.

If you have a serious and persistent problem with anger and loss of emotional and physical control, and if you have not been able to overcome the problem through the previous suggestions, by all means seek professional help from a Christian psychiatrist or psychologist. You probably need someone to help you analyze the problem and its root cause and then support you in overcoming it.

Remember: You cannot expect someone else to solve your problem. Another person can only assist you. You must take the initiative and become a mature person in Jesus Christ, regardless of how difficult it is.

Warning: Abusive people are similar to alcoholics. They often live in a state of denial. Until they admit their problem, they cannot be helped.

THINKING AND GROWING TOGETHER

The following questions are designed for group discussion after reading and studying the content of this chapter:

1. Have you been physically abused? Would you be willing to share with us why it happened, how it affected you and what you are doing to overcome it?
2. Have you experienced verbal abuse? Would you be willing to share with us why it happened, how it affected you and what you are doing to overcome it?
3. Why do abused people frequently grow up and abuse others by repeating the same patterns? How can these patterns of behavior be broken?
4. Why has sexual abuse become so rampant in our society?
5. What can we do as Christian men to help solve this problem in our culture?

SET A GOAL

Write out one goal you'd like to achieve as a result of this study:

_____

_____

_____

_____

Notes
1. Joseph H. Thayer, *Greek-English Lexicon of the New Testament* (Grand Rapids: Zondervan Publishing House, 1962), p. 516.
2. Chuck Colson, *Jubilee* (July 1983).
3. Tim and Beverly LaHaye, *A Nation Without a Conscience* (Wheaton, IL: Tyndale House Publishers, 1994), pp. 3-4.
4. Robert L. Vernon, *L. A. Justice* (Colorado Springs: Focus on the Family Publishing, 1993), pp. 190-191.

13

BECOMING A FAIR-MINDED MAN

An overseer, then, must be above reproach,
the husband of one wife, temperate,
prudent, respectable, hospitable, able
to teach, not addicted to wine or
*pugnacious, but **gentle.***
—1 TIMOTHY 3:2,3

I must make a confession. The first time I studied the word "gentle," as used by Paul in this list of qualities that reflect Christian maturity, I missed something. You see, several Greek words are translated "gentle," which I mentioned in my first edition of *The Measure of a Man.* But as I once again studied this quality, I saw something I hadn't seen before. Paul chose this particular word (*epiikees*) to describe a particular kind of gentleness—"a spirit of forbearance." Joseph H. Thayer defines the word as being "equitable" and "fair"—and we might add, "reasonable."[1]

MEET TOM LANDRY

In looking for a man to illustrate the quality of being gentle, I thought of Tom Landry, former coach of the Dallas Cowboys. I first met

Mr. Landry in his office when a friend of mine and I introduced Tom to a young man named Tony Evans. Tony was an up-and-coming young black pastor—our first full-time missionary from the first Fellowship Bible Church—a man we believed could have a good influence on the Cowboys team as a spiritual counselor. We wanted Tom to meet Tony, and he welcomed us graciously.

Since then, I have met Coach Landry here and there—in airports, on airplanes, at banquets and in other special meetings. I have also read most everything that has been written about his life and career.

An EPIIKEES Man

Tom Landry has a lot of special qualities that reflect Christian maturity. But one quality stands out that I believe illustrates what Paul had in mind when he used the word *epiikees* in his letter to Timothy.

Coach Landry is a fair-minded man. Tony Dorsett, premier running back who at times frustrated Landry, made the following comment as he reflected back on his years with the Cowboys: "Maybe you didn't always like his decisions but he was fair. He would listen to all sides of an issue and then decide what was best for the team."[2]

Dorsett wasn't the only Cowboy who at times caused a lot of difficulties for Landry. Dwayne Thomas, another powerful running back, helped lead the Cowboys to a Super Bowl victory. But Thomas later got hooked on drugs, and his behavior became so bizarre, it became ridiculous.

And then Thomas (Hollywood) Henderson blew a potentially brilliant career for the same reason and later became a public embarrassment to the whole Cowboys organization.

Faith Made a Difference

As tough-minded as Landry could be, he demonstrated incredible patience and forbearance with these men on his team. In his book, *A Landry Legend*, Bob St. John summarizes Tom's approach: "His faith certainly was a factor in helping him to try to understand and cope with the much-troubled Dwayne Thomas and be more fair and understanding of a person such as Thomas (Hollywood)

Henderson and the somewhat different behavior patterns of Tony Dorsett."[3]

Randy White, an all-pro defensive lineman, put it this way, "Hey, I was there when he had a lot of those misfits, and Coach Landry would bend over backwards in giving them a second and even a third chance. That's two or three more than they'd have gotten from anybody else—or from anybody in any other kind of business. He did it because he has faith in people."[4]

Mike Ditka, who both played for the Cowboys and later coached, added, "Tom Landry is probably the fairest guy I've ever been around. He let a lot of players push him to the limit. But when they did, that was it!"[5]

Life Before Christ

The facts are that Tom Landry was not always this kind of "gentle" man. His life as an NFL coach began to change dramatically when he became a Christian. On one occasion, an older fan (a man who appeared to be in his 60s) stopped Landry and made this comment, "Tom, I saw you play when you were with the Giants. You seem so calm now. But you used to get pretty mad in those days. Yes, you had a temper alright. You were awfully fiery." Landry responded, "I guess we all grow a little, mature a little."[6]

Landry's Greatest Moment

As most people who follow professional football know, Landry's brilliant career as an NFL coach came to a disappointing end when he was fired by the Cowboys' new owner, Jerry Jones. Because of the way it was horribly mishandled—which Jones has admitted—all of Dallas and many fans and coaches around the league were appalled and angry. But in many respects, this was Landry's greatest moment to be a witness for Jesus Christ, and he rose to the occasion. When other lesser men would have allowed "the sun to go down on their anger," Landry faced the situation as a mature Christian should.

"I'm Not Bitter at All"

Though desperately hurt, Landry responded, "I'm not bitter at all. I knew what I was doing when I tried to bring this club back. This is the worst scenario, I guess, that could have happened. But I took that

chance....Things could have been handled better but you have somebody coming in who is awful new to this environment we live in. I'm
sure he was very excited about the possibility of owning the
Cowboys, and I doubt his thoughts went much further than that."[7]

Gentle and Considerate

I have chosen this Tom Landry illustration because it isn't often we
find a Christian man who is so well-known and who also demonstrates so dramatically what Paul had in mind with the word epiikees.
Strange as it seems, it is a form of "gentleness" and "patience" that is
unique. The translators of the *Amplified New Testament* captured this
meaning with these words, "Not combative but gentle and considerate, not quarrelsome but forbearing and peaceable" (1 Tim. 3:3).

Do as I Do

When the apostle Paul wrote to Timothy, outlining characteristics of
Christian maturity, he modeled these qualities in his own life, including epiikees.

Confronting the Corinthians

When Paul wrote to the Corinthians, many of whom were falsely
accusing him, he said, "Now I, Paul, myself urge you by the meekness and gentleness of Christ" (2 Cor. 10:1). Here the word "gentleness" is the same basic word Paul used in the list of qualities in his
letter to Timothy.

If you go on and read Paul's additional comments, however, he
didn't mince words with the Corinthian Christians. He pointed out
their sins, defended his apostleship and exhorted them to become
mature Christians.

Paul was a gracious, sensitive and fair-minded man. But he would
not compromise Christian truth and false accusations. He "defended
himself" without being "defensive." People could push him only
so far. In this sense, Paul demonstrated the "meekness and gentleness" of Jesus Christ. Our Lord, who often "turned the other
cheek," did not hesitate to overturn the moneychangers' tables and
to make a whip of cords to drive the animals from the Temple court
(see John 2:15,16).

Meekness Is Not Weakness

When Paul wrote his second letter to Timothy, he told this young pastor to be "patient when wronged, with gentleness correcting those who are in opposition" (2:24,25). But when Paul wrote to Titus, he told him to "silence" certain men who were "upsetting whole families, teaching things they should not teach, for the sake of sordid gain" (1:11).

Later, Paul told Titus, "Reject a factious man after a first and second warning, knowing that such a man is perverted and is sinning, being self-condemned" (3:10,11).

Paul's New Life in Christ

Although he was one of the most tough-minded men in all of Judaism—a man who approved of Stephen's martyrdom—Paul's life was changed when he became a Christian. As with all of us, it took time to change behaviors that were not in harmony with Christian virtues. But he made those changes and became not a perfect man, but a man who *could* write to the Corinthians without fear of contradiction and exhort them to be "imitators" of him, just as he was an imitator "of Christ" (1 Cor. 11:1).

CHRISTIANS SHOULD UNDERSTAND MERCY

Paul was particularly concerned that we demonstrate this kind of "gentleness" toward non-Christians. He also made this clear in his letter to Titus:

> Remind them to be subject to rulers, to authorities, to be obedient, to be ready for every good deed, to malign no one, to be uncontentious, **gentle, showing every consideration for all men** (3:1,2).

Overcome Evil with Good

Here again Paul used the word epiikees. Paul anticipated that some of the believers who lived in Crete might ask Titus *why* he insisted on treating unbelievers so graciously. Consequently, Paul explained why. First, he commented on these believers' lives before they were converted to Jesus Christ. "For we also once were foolish ourselves," Paul wrote. We too were "disobedient, deceived, enslaved to various lusts and pleasures, spending our life in malice and envy, hateful, hating one another" (v. 3).

Don't Forget God's Grace

Paul went on to remind them that although they as Christians were doing the same things, God had mercy on them:

> But when the kindness of God our Savior and His love for mankind appeared, He saved us, not on the basis of deeds which we have done in righteousness, but according to His mercy (vv. 4,5).

Paul was instructing Titus—and teaching us—that as Christians we, of all people, should show mercy toward people who are lost in sin. Although we may not be able to identify with the depths of sin into which some people fall, we must remember that it is only by God's grace that we may have been reared in a Christian home. It is only by God's grace that we have not been trapped in the mire of sin, that we have not grown up in a drug-infested ghetto.

A Stone Face or a Gentle Heart?

This is the kind of consideration Tom Landry extended to Dwayne Thomas and Hollywood Henderson, although they were flaunting a lifestyle that was contradicting everything he believed and lived. Landry wanted to see them have a chance.

Landry revealed his heart toward these men when he once said, "The most disappointing thing is I just couldn't help them enough. I feel guilty that I couldn't get them back on the right track. Once you get on coke or crack, you're destined for trouble."[8]

On another occasion, Landry added, "If I have a weakness, it may be that I'm too compassionate. I give people a chance to see whether they can turn it around. It didn't work out for me too often."[9] This is the gentle (epiikees) side of Landry many people never knew. They only saw him as the stone-faced coach calling plays from the sidelines.

A WORD FROM JAMES

James, the half-brother of Jesus Christ, described this unique quality of gentleness in his letter to Christian Jews who were scattered throughout the New Testament world. He contrasted the behavior that reflects *worldly wisdom* with the behavior that reflects *God's wisdom.*

> But if you have bitter jealousy and selfish ambition in your heart, do not be arrogant and so lie against the truth. This wisdom is not that which comes down from above, but is earthly, natural, demonic. For where jealousy and selfish ambition exist, there is disorder and every evil thing. But the wisdom from above is first pure, then **peaceable, gentle** [that is, epiikees], **reasonable, full of mercy** and good fruits, unwavering, without hypocrisy (Jas. 3:14-17).

The Gentleness of Wisdom

The cluster of words James used surrounding the word "gentle" helps us to understand what the word really means. This kind of attitude correlates with behavior that is "peaceable" and "reasonable." It is "full of mercy." In fact, James earlier encouraged his readers to demonstrate good behavior with the "**gentleness** of wisdom" (v. 13). Here the word "gentleness" comes not from epiikees, the word we have been studying; it comes from *prautees*, a word meaning "meekness," a concept that is closely associated with the kind of "gentle" qualities Paul was referring to in 1 Timothy 3 when he wrote: "An overseer, then, must be...gentle" (vv. 2,3).

BLESSED ARE THE GENTLE [MEEK]

Now that we have looked specifically at the way the Scriptures describe this special kind of "gentleness," let's look more broadly at other forms of "gentle" behavior. The following are scriptural texts that speak for themselves.

PRAUTEES (Gentle, Mild, Meek, Humble)

- But the **fruit of the spirit** is love, joy, peace, patience, kindness, goodness, faithfulness, **gentleness**, self-control; against such things there is no law (Gal. 5:22,23).

- Brethren, even **if a man is caught** in any trespass, you who are spiritual, restore such a one in a spirit of **gentleness;** each one looking to yourself, lest you too be tempted (6:1).
- **Walk in a manner worthy** of the calling with which you have been called, with all humility and **gentleness,** with patience, showing forbearance to one another in love (Eph. 4:1,2).
- And so, as those who have been chosen of God, holy and beloved, **put on** a heart of compassion, kindness, humility, **gentleness** and patience; bearing with one another, and forgiving each other (Col. 3:12,13).
- But **flee from these things,** you man of God; and **pursue** righteousness, godliness, faith, love, perseverance and **gentleness** (1 Tim. 6:11).
- But sanctify Christ as Lord in your hearts, always being ready to **make a defense to everyone** who asks you to give an account for the hope that is in you, yet with **gentleness** and reverence (1 Pet. 3:15).

EEPIOS (Mild, Gentle)

- But we proved to be **gentle** among you, as **a nursing mother** tenderly cares for her own children (1 Thess. 2:7).
- And **the Lord's bond-servant** must not be quarrelsome, but be kind to all, able to teach, patient when wronged, with **gentleness** correcting those who are in opposition, if perhaps God may grant them repentance leading to the knowledge of the truth (2 Tim. 2:24,25).

POINTS OF ACTION

The following project is designed to help you develop the quality of "gentleness" in all of your relationships.

Come to Know Christ Personally

• **Put your faith in Jesus Christ for salvation and be born again.**
Whatever form of "gentleness" we are attempting to display, we must realize that God will help us when we put our faith in Christ for

salvation, experience the new birth and then allow the Holy Spirit to take control of our lives.

In this chapter, I have used Tom Landry to illustrate the quality of "gentleness" mentioned by Paul in his maturity profile. Coach Landry would be the first to acknowledge that the changes that came into his life happened because of his conversion experience.

Do You Feel Empty Inside?

Tom Landry confesses to an emptiness that came into his life, in spite of his great football accomplishments. He puzzled about what was lacking. During this search, he turned his thoughts toward Jesus Christ. He had certainly read about Jesus Christ throughout his life, but who was this man, really? Did Christ actually accept him? Landry concluded that if he accepted Jesus Christ, then he must accept what Christ said. And if he accepted what Christ said, he needed to change the way he was living his life.

Join a Bible-Study Group

Landry's search began in a Bible study after the 1958 football season. A friend had invited him to join a group of men who often met at the Melrose Hotel for breakfast, followed by a Bible study. At first, Landry was skeptical. But he kept attending, and ultimately his life was changed. He met Jesus Christ personally.

Jesus Christ Will Change Your Life

Regarding his conversion to Christ, Landry made these comments:

> At some period during the spring of 1959, all my so-called intellectual questions no longer seemed important, and I had a joyous feeling inside. Internally, the decision had been made. Now, while the process had been slow and gradual, once made, the decision has been the most important one in my life. It was a commitment of my life to Jesus Christ and a willingness to do what He wanted me to do as best I could by seeking His will through prayer and by reading His Word.[10]

It is true that many of the qualities outlined by Paul might be seen—at least to a certain extent—in people who do not know Jesus Christ personally. But the facts are, we cannot consistently reflect Jesus Christ and His life as we should unless we come to know Him personally. Do you know Jesus Christ in this way?

Pursue Gentleness

✘• Set this kind of "gentleness" as a goal for your life.

The Christian life involves personal discipline. Once we come to know Jesus Christ personally, we not only have a new source of strength, but we also have the capacity to pursue Christian qualities. This is why the apostle Paul wrote to Timothy:

> But **flee from these things,** you man of God; and **pursue...gentleness** (1 Tim. 6:11).

Seek Wisdom from Above

✘• Discover God's wisdom through the Word of God and prayer.

Listen to God

Remind yourself again of the words of James:

> But the **wisdom from above** is first pure, then...**gentle** (3:17).

Here James uses the same word for "gentle" that Paul used in his maturity profile in his letter to Timothy. By learning God's Word, which is filled with wisdom from above, we can begin to develop and display this quality in our lives.

Converse with God

James also reminded us that we have access to this kind of wisdom through prayer. Thus he introduced his letter with these words:

> But if any of you lacks wisdom, let him ask of God, who gives to all men generously and without reproach, and it will be given to him (1:5).

Evaluate Your Life

✸• Isolate those relationships in your life where you have difficulty demonstrating this kind of "gentleness."(*ac a*)

Following are some suggestions to help you isolate areas in your life where you need to improve:

1. If you are married, ask your wife and children to help make you aware of times when you are not fair-minded, equitable and considerate.

✸2. Ask a close friend to evaluate your relationships with other people, to give you feedback in any area where you do not demonstrate this quality of life.

3. If you are a teacher, an employer or anyone who supervises other people, ask them to fill out an evaluation form. Include a question regarding how they view your relationships with others in terms of being fair and objective, and if you are able to listen to all sides of an issue before making a decision.

4. Develop a regular Bible-study program. There is no substitute for the Scriptures in serving as a mirror to reflect those areas in our lives that are not reflective of Jesus Christ.

THINKING AND GROWING TOGETHER

The following questions are designed for group discussion after reading and studying the content of this chapter:

1. What are some relationships in your life where you have difficulty being fair-minded and gentle in handling people?

2. How have you developed an approach in working with people that has helped you improve in this area of your life?

3. How can we maintain a better balance between being accepting, tolerant and fair, and yet make tough decisions "gently"?

4. How have people taken advantage of your efforts at being tolerant, fair and considerate? Do you feel you were too compassionate? Or would you take the same approach again?

5. Can you cite the times people took advantage of Jesus Christ

when He demonstrated this kind of "gentleness"? What about the apostle Paul? What about your pastor?

SET A GOAL

Write out one goal you'd like to achieve as a result of this study:

_____

_____

_____

_____

Notes

1. Joseph H. Thayer, *Greek-English Lexicon of the New Testament* (Grand Rapids: Zondervan Publishing House, 1962), p. 238.
2. Bob St. John, *The Landry Legend* (Dallas: WORD Inc., 1989), p. 283.
3. Ibid., p. 156.
4. Ibid., p. 291.
5. Ibid., p. 157.
6. Ibid., p. 23.
7. Ibid., p. 286.
8. Ibid., p. 157.
9. Ibid.
10. Ibid., p. 154.

14

BLESSED ARE THE PEACEMAKERS

An overseer, then, must be above reproach,
the husband of one wife, temperate, prudent,
respectable, hospitable, able to teach,
not addicted to wine or pugnacious,
*but gentle, **uncontentious**.*
—1 TIMOTHY 3:2,3

The translators of the *Amplified New Testament* give us a good functional definition for what Paul had in mind when he stated that a mature man of God is "uncontentious." He is "gentle and considerate, **not quarrelsome**, but forbearing and peaceable" (1 Tim. 3:3). Conversely, a contentious man generates debate and arguments.

This kind of behavior—like most of the characteristics outlined by Paul—can be viewed on a continuum. If we are honest, most of us are mildly contentious. We periodically stir up arguments, and then evaluate our motives, recognize what has happened, back off and change our approach. When necessary, we ask forgiveness.

Some people are on the other end of the continuum. In the extreme, they always say no when others say yes. They say "black" when others say "white." When the majority favor a decision, they form a minority of "one" and oppose the majority.

"Mr. Charge Ahead"

I have a close friend who now serves with me as an elder in the church where I am senior pastor. Those who knew him best called him "Mr. Charge Ahead"! In his younger days, he was known as "Fast Eddie"! He knew this trait at times got him into trouble, especially since he was a good debater—which at times was interpreted as being argumentative, insensitive and even contentious.

Is This Man Qualified?

Before this man was selected to be an elder, we followed a standard procedure we regularly use in evaluating whether a man and his wife are qualified for this level of leadership. We asked all of our other elders (and their wives) and our senior staff pastors (and their wives) to fill out an evaluation form on each prospective candidate and his wife (if married). This form is based on the 20 characteristics outlined by Paul in his letters to Timothy and Titus and explained in each chapter in this book. We asked each person to use a seven-point scale (from 1-7) to express his or her degree of satisfaction or dissatisfaction with this person's behavior on all 20 of these characteristics. For example, the first question reads: "How do you evaluate this person's reputation as a Christian?" (see chapter 20, pp. 277-280).

When my friend was being considered for eldership, we followed this procedure. When the forms were returned, he was consistently marked down in several related areas, one area being "contentious." His wife, however, had almost perfect scores.

Where the Rubber Meets the Road

I—as senior pastor—and one other elder, were asked to sit down with this man and his wife and report on these responses. Frankly, I was nervous about it, as I always am under these circumstances. This kind of communication is always difficult for me, especially when it is someone to whom I feel close.

A wonderful thing happened. My friend sat and listened, obviously surprised. He was totally open and nondefensive. He thanked us for our time and openness with him and his wife and assured us he would think and pray about what we had shared.

The True Test

My friend then did what mature men do. He later asked his wife for her opinion. Did she agree with our evaluation? She did. What she said surprised him. The following is Eddie's account of what happened!

> When Maureen said that she agreed with the evaluation that I could be contentious, argumentative and too bold in defending the views I held strongly, I knew that God wanted to get my attention—big time. I also knew down deep that the evaluation was correct. As I asked God for help, He made it clear to me that I needed to develop the fruit of the Spirit known as gentleness. He also gave me a plan. I was to get my family to hold me accountable. One evening I called my family together and asked each one to forgive me for not being gentle and to ask for their help. I explained to them that every time they saw me using my verbal skills to steamroll over them, raise my voice, show anger or be contentious in any way, they were to put an *X* on the family calendar in the kitchen. To my dismay, the next day I got five *X*s. I considered changing the rules! But I was committed and my family helped me learn to be gentle. What started out as a crushing blow to my Mr. Charge Ahead ego has turned into a wonderful blessing in my life. I now know that viewpoints spoken in gentleness with energy is much more acceptable and effective with the listener. I certainly have not arrived at my goal but I am on my way.

Our Communication Style

The changes this man made were immediately obvious to all who knew him well. He eventually became an elder and today I consider him one of our most faithful board members. He has a heart for God, a heart for the ministry and a heart for people. The facts are, he really always did. He simply needed to change his style of communication. He didn't mean to appear contentious, authoritarian, or argumentative and controlling. But when he learned that other mature leaders thought he was, he made some permanent and lasting changes.

True Humility and Teachability

You see, how this man handled our communication about these issues also demonstrated his level of maturity and desire to reflect Jesus Christ in all of his relationships. Had he responded defensively, had he walked away angry, had he left the church—as some men do—he would have verified that he had a serious problem. But he didn't do these things, demonstrating true humility and teachability and a deep desire to become more mature in Jesus Christ.

THE CONTENTIOUSNESS CONTINUUM

All of us at times fall somewhere on this continuum, and for various reasons. At times, we are simply vulnerable. We may feel insecure. At other times, we are just plain obstinate. Or perhaps we have been hurt and are simply in a negative mood. We may also be getting even with someone for something he or she has done to irritate or insult us.

As with most of the characteristics we have looked at, Paul was concerned about the man who *habitually* demonstrates inappropriate attitudes and actions. He was also concerned about the person who is *unpredictable*, the man who at times is congenial and at times, without seeming provocation, stirs up arguments and throws a "wrench in the spiritual machinery" that God designed to create peaceful relationships.

THE PAUL AND BARNABAS ARGUMENT

Don't misunderstand. It is not wrong to disagree or to challenge incorrect thinking or inappropriate behavior. Some of the most godly people don't see eye to eye on all issues.

Paul and Barnabas certainly illustrate this reality. They were the best of friends and close missionary companions. They disagreed, however, regarding whether to take John Mark on a second mission trip. Mark had bailed out on the first trip. Paul lost confidence in him and wanted to leave him behind. But Barnabas wanted to give him another chance. Luke recorded, "There arose such a **sharp disagreement** that they separated from one another, and Barnabas took Mark with him and sailed away to Cyprus. But Paul chose Silas and departed, being committed by the brethren to the grace of the Lord" (Acts 15:39,40).

Who Was at Fault?

This passage from Acts has puzzled Bible students. Who was right and who was wrong? Paul was such a strategic leader in God's scheme of things that some find it difficult to fault him in this situation. We forget, however, that he was human and it may be he was being impatient and intolerant.

Personally, I believe Paul was being driven by a strong commitment to the task God had given him, and became insensitive to Mark. Barnabas, who was known for his strong "people orientation," didn't want to see this young man devastated and perhaps lost to the ministry.

I also believe Paul learned a significant lesson because of this disagreement with Barnabas, which is later reflected in his relationship with Timothy and other coworkers (cf. Col. 4:10). Paul became a more sensitive and gentle man without losing his strong commitment to carrying out the Great Commission in the midst of tremendous opposition and difficulties.

PAUL'S CONFRONTATION WITH PETER

On another occasion, Paul confronted Peter—yes, the great apostle Peter—and accused him of being a hypocrite. Paul minced no words in his letter to the Galatians:

> But when Cephas came to Antioch, I opposed him to his face, because he stood condemned. For prior to the coming of certain men from James, he used to eat with the Gentiles; but when they came, he began to withdraw and hold himself aloof, fearing the party of the circumcision. And the rest of the Jews joined him in hypocrisy, with the result that even Barnabas was carried away by their hypocrisy (2:11-13).

It is difficult to place blame in these situations but it appears Paul was clearly right in what he did. Peter was compromising, which became a stumbling block to Paul's close friend Barnabas.

One thing, however, is clear. Although God greatly used the apostles to carry out His work in the world, they were human and made mistakes. They too, were in the process of becoming mature in Jesus Christ, along with those they were nurturing.

THE "SONS OF THUNDER"

One thing about the divine author of Scripture—the Holy Spirit is open and honest. He exposes weaknesses as well as strengths, even in God's greatest servants. James and John are classic examples. They were so contentious at times that Jesus called them the "Sons of Thunder" (Mark 3:17). There is no question that their motives were often selfish, even as the time grew near for Jesus to be crucified. On one occasion, James and John and their mother made a "power move" and asked Jesus if they could sit on His right and on His left in the Kingdom (Matt. 20:20-28; Mark 10:35-45). When the other 10 men found out about it, they were indignant. James and John had stirred up a hornet's nest.

At this moment, Jesus taught all of them, and us, a powerful lesson:

> And calling them to Himself, Jesus said to them, "You know that those who are recognized as rulers of the Gentiles lord it over them; and their great men exercise authority over them. But it is not so among you, but whoever wishes to become great among you shall be your servant; and whoever wishes to be first among you shall be slave of all. For even the Son of Man did not come to be served, but to serve, and to give His life a ransom for many" (Mark 10:42-45).

WE ARE ALL ON A SPIRITUAL JOURNEY

It is encouraging to know that the 12 men Jesus chose to change the world were human. All of them had serious flaws in their characters, including the apostle Paul. But God changed all that, not overnight, but over a process of time. The apostle John, who was initially motivated by greed and selfishness, years later reflected that change when he defined love:

> We know love by this, that He laid down His life for us; and we ought to lay down our lives for the brethren (1 John 3:16).

JESUS' PRAYER FOR UNITY

No concept is more important in the Scriptures than *unity*. This was one of Jesus' greatest concerns. Knowing that the time was quickly coming for Him to complete the work He had come to do on earth, He prayed in earnest to the Father for His disciples, and for us:

> "I do not ask in behalf of these [the apostles] alone, but for those also who believe in Me through their word [all of us who are Christians]; that they may all be one. I in them, and Thou in Me, that they may be perfected in unity, that the world may know that Thou didst send Me, and didst love them, even as Thou didst love Me" (John 17:20,21,23).

Unity among Christians demonstrates to the world the deity of Jesus Christ and the unity He has with God the Father. It communicates the very essence of Christianity—"that God was in Christ reconciling the world to Himself" (2 Cor. 5:19).

God is particularly pleased when we strive to create unity within the Body of Jesus Christ. This is why Jesus said:

> "Blessed are the **peacemakers** for they shall be called sons of God" (Matt. 5:9).

PAUL'S CONCERN FOR UNITY

Although Paul at times failed the Lord—just as we all do at some points in our Christian lives—he had a major concern when he wrote to various churches. Consider the following exhortations that focus on being "peacemakers" rather than on being "contentious."

- Be of the same mind toward one another; do not be haughty in mind, but associate with the lowly. Do not be wise in your own estimation (Rom. 12:16).
- If possible, so far as it depends on you, be at peace with all men (v. 18).
- So then let us pursue the things which make for peace and the building up of one another (14:19).

- Now may the God who gives perseverance and encouragement grant you to be of the same mind with one another according to Christ Jesus; that with one accord you may with one voice glorify the God and Father of our Lord Jesus Christ (15:5,6).
- I, therefore, the prisoner of the Lord, entreat you to walk in a manner worthy of the calling with which you have been called,...being diligent to preserve the unity of the Spirit in the bond of peace (Eph. 4:1-3).

ROOT CAUSES

We become "contentious" for various reasons.

Our Sin Nature

- "All have sinned and fall short of the glory of God" (Rom. 3:23).

When we consider the fact that we all have sinned, it shouldn't surprise us that we tend to be selfish and self-centered, which always stirs up contention. We must always be on guard that we don't allow ourselves to reflect the "deeds of the flesh," which include "enmities, strife, jealousy, outbursts of anger, disputes, dissensions, factions" (Gal. 5:19,20). But when we "walk by the Spirit" (v. 25), we will reflect the "fruit of the Spirit," which reflects "love, joy, peace, patience, kindness, goodness, faithfulness, gentleness, self-control" (vv. 22,23).

Bad Models

- Some children are constantly exposed to bad parental examples.

Some people grow up in this world seeing nothing but contentiousness in their family setting. They don't know there is a different way to live. Consequently, they live life reflecting what they have learned from their parents.

Bad Habits

- Some people learn to survive by controlling others.

Bad habits are closely related to bad models. It is possible, however, for people to have good parental examples but to simply grow up in a competitive society where they learn to succeed by having the last word. This is their way of winning. They seldom stop to think how many other people become losers because they take this approach, including their children and their marital partners. Unfortunately, this always causes resentment that will ultimately reveal itself in one way or another.

Insecurity
• **Some people are contentious because they have deep feelings of insecurity.**

Insecurity can drive people in one of two directions. Some become reclusive and withdrawn. They seldom open their mouths and they retreat from any kind of competition.

Insecure people who move in the opposite direction often become domineering and authoritarian. They cover up their insecurities by trying to control everyone else. They can't accept or admit defeat. It threatens them terribly. They are often the people who become winners. They tend to overachieve and then work hard to stay on top. When their positions are threatened in any way as king of the mountain, even as Christians they resort to sinful tactics to defend themselves against their fears of failure.

An insecure man will often put other people down in order to build himself up. He becomes a victim of a subtle, unconscious selfishness that can reflect itself in all kinds of ways—authoritarian, argumentive, quarrelsome, gossiper, backbiter, critical—he also curses and may use physical violence.

Christian leaders who have this problem are particularly dangerous. They tend to rationalize their behaviors and may use the Word of God as a weapon to reach their self-centered goals. They interpret Scripture through their own psychological grid. They take advantage of their "spiritual" positions and begin to lord them over others (see 1 Pet. 5:3). If anyone resists their authoritarian tactics, they quickly "beat them down" and control their opposition's conscience with such verses as, "Obey your leaders, and submit to them" (Heb. 13:17).

Bitterness
• **Persistent resentment can cause people to be contentious.**

The bitter man has "let the sun go down on [his] anger" (Eph. 4:26). He has given "the devil an opportunity" in his life (v. 27).

Most often, this bitter spirit begins with feelings of anger toward one or two people. It can generalize to include almost everyone, however, including the person himself. This is anger turned inward. When this happens, it is reflected in a general "contentiousness," a chip-on-the-shoulder attitude that affects many, many people.

As we have seen, Paul warned New Testament Christians against this sin. The author of the Hebrews expressed the same concern:

> Pursue peace with all men, and the sanctification without which no one will see the Lord. See to it that no...**root of bitterness** springing up causes trouble, and by it many be defiled (12:14,15).

POINTS OF ACTION

The following personal project is designed to help you overcome contentiousness in your personality.

Evaluate

• **Attempt to isolate the root problem that causes you to be contentious.**

The following questions will help you discover what causes you to be contentious. The stories are designed to help you identify your own problem.

1. Am I contentious because of selfishness and jealous attitudes that simply reflect my sinful nature?

> John is an only child. He got his way in most everything he wanted. His parents seldom disciplined him for inappropriate behavior. Now that he is older, he can't stand having anyone else be the center of attention. Consequently, he has become an insensitive person. As long as people can remember, he has manipulated and used other people to achieve his own ends.

2. Am I contentious because of bad parental models?

> Sam grew up in a home where his parents always seemed to argue. Furthermore, they never got along well with their

neighbors. They seemed to be out of harmony with everyone, including themselves. Sam simply grew up thinking this is the way "normal people" live. Today, he lives his life the way his parents lived.

3. Am I contentious because of bad habits?

Tim grew up in a good family, but was quickly exposed to a competitive world. Because he was athletic, he became involved in sports early in life. Because of his natural talents, he became a winner. Now that he is grown, he can't stand to lose. He quickly loses his temper when he is on the losing side. Tim has simply developed some bad habits.

4. Am I contentious because of insecurity?

Jim is one of several children. He has an older brother and two younger sisters. He was a normal child with average intelligence. He was likeable and mildly athletic. But his brother was a genius in almost every way. Jim's dad always favored his older brother, and at the same time, tended to put Jim down. Jim was forced to compete. If he withdrew, he was teased.

As he grew older, Jim learned that by working real hard, he could win at most everything. His older brother's natural ability to achieve soon took on a lazy tone and soon Jim was outdistancing him in almost everything he did. At last, he had the applause of his father and others.

Unfortunately, this approach to life became a security habit for Jim. He feels uncomfortable unless he always wins and is the center of everything. He must win every argument, must have the final word and must have his ideas accepted to feel secure.

5. Am I contentious because of a root of bitterness?

Tom's father is an alcoholic. As long as he can remember, his dad mistreated his mother and abused the other children. He can't remember a time that he did not have angry, bitter feelings toward his father. In fact, John feels anger toward almost everyone now. Consequently, he is always hurting someone's feelings with nasty remarks and put-down attitudes and statements.

Confess Your Sins

• **No matter what the cause of your contention, confess it as sin and seek God's forgiveness (see 1 John 1:9).**

A place to start with any sin problem is to confess it to God. The wonderful truth is that He will forgive us (see 1 John 1:9). You must believe this to be true and accept it as a reality. There is no more wonderful feeling than to be at peace with God.

Ask Forgiveness

• **Confess your sin to those you have hurt and ask forgiveness.**

It may be that you have hurt the local body of believers where you fellowship. If so, confess your sin to the body as a whole and ask for their forgiveness and prayers so that you might change your attitudes and behavior. Public confession, however, is not necessary unless it involves the total group. You may only need to ask forgiveness from a small group—your wife, your children and others who may know you well. If you are confused about confession, seek advice from your spiritual leaders. They can advise you regarding to whom you should confess and from whom you should seek forgiveness.

Set Goals

• **Write out *specific* goals that relate to your *specific* problems with *specific* people.**

Read these goals every day. Use them as personal prayer requests.

If you are a contentious element in your family, you may want to write out something such as the following:

> I will not start any quarrels when we are eating together. I will listen to what others are saying without automatically disagreeing with someone.

If you cannot solve your problem with these suggestions, seek professional help. You may find it difficult to isolate and discover the root cause of your problem. If so, seek out a Christian counselor and take some tests to help you understand your personality conflicts.

THINKING AND GROWING TOGETHER

The following questions are designed for group discussion after reading and studying the content of this chapter:

1. Can you describe a relationship that is difficult because of "contentiousness"?
2. Can you identify where you are on the "contentiousness continuum"? Would you be willing to share this with us?
3. If you become "contentious," what tends to trigger this reaction?
4. How does "contentiousness" reflect itself in other negative characteristics listed by the apostle Paul in his letters to Timothy and Titus?
5. Do you have a specific prayer request regarding "contentiousness" in your life or in another person to whom you are having difficulty relating?

SET A GOAL

Write out one goal you'd like to achieve as a result of this study:

_____

_____

_____

_____

15

BECOMING A GENEROUS MAN

An overseer, then, must be above reproach,
the husband of one wife, temperate, prudent,
respectable, hospitable, able to teach, not addicted
to wine or pugnacious, but gentle, uncontentious,
free from the love of money.
—1 TIMOTHY 3:2,3

Being a "Christian" and being "generous" *should* be inseparable concepts. How can we who have been *given* the greatest gift ever *given* be anything but generous? Unfortunately, being generous is not true of many who claim to have received what Paul calls an "indescribable gift!" (2 Cor. 9:15).

AN EXPERIENCE THAT CHANGED MY LIFE

I once heard a non-Christian businessman speak about how to become successful. Among other things, he said, "You must be generous."

Frankly, I was jolted. You see, being generous implies more than simply giving. It involves our attitude. Here was a non-Christian telling me—a Christian leader—I needed to be generous.

Don't misunderstand. My wife and I have been regular givers for all of our married life. We have given a minimum of 10 percent to our church. But this man caused me to look at my attitude toward "giving" and how it related to other areas of my life.

Take Tipping for Instance

I had always resented this American expectation of tipping. But I was suddenly convicted. I remember when the expectation went from 10 percent to 15 percent. I resisted it, until my wife shamed me into it. She would look at the check, then notice what I left on the table and then add to it (she was a former waitress).

Hearing this businessman speak, I suddenly realized that I often gave—or should I say, met my obligations—rather grudgingly. Guess what? I changed my attitude.

Helping Others Make a Living

I now see paying the furnace repairman as an opportunity to help him make a living. I now consider it a privilege to get the oil changed in my car so I can contribute to someone else's economic welfare. And I now see tipping as an opportunity to encourage other people who are attempting to put food on *their* tables.

Witnessing for Christ

Being a generous tipper is also a wonderful opportunity to be a witness for Jesus Christ. You see, I often study my Bible in restaurants. When I do, I make sure I give considerably beyond the 15 percent, just to let my server know that the man who is studying the Bible has been influenced by the Bible.

In one of the restaurants I visit rather regularly, I am entitled to a 10 percent senior discount. When I pay my bill, I graciously receive the discount, but in turn add the 10 percent to the 15 percent tip, allowing me to give my discount back to the server. It is amazing how word has spread among the waitresses.

I now believe that if Christians can't afford to be generous tippers when they eat out, they really can't afford to eat out. Imagine what servers think when they see us bow our heads in prayer before we eat and then leave without being generous. What is worse is a *selfish* Christian who leaves a gospel tract on the table. Don't get me wrong.

It is great to leave a leaflet that explains God's free gift of salvation, but *never* without being generous.

FREE FROM THE LOVE OF MONEY

Mature Christians don't love money. But don't misunderstand. The Scriptures do not teach that "money" per se is evil. Nor do they teach that it is wrong to have lots of money. What they do teach is that it is a serious violation of God's will when we *love it.* That is why Paul said that a mature Christian man is "free," not from money, but "from the love of money."

A RECESSION THAT HIT US ALL

I had an unusual experience in the early 1990s. As many of you may remember—though it is easy to forget when things are going well—we faced a serious economic recession in our country. It began with the oil crisis that was precipitated in the Middle East. In turn, this crisis seriously affected the real estate market. Before long, it flowed over into the banking industry, particularly among savings and loan institutions.

Men Who Lost Millions
Living in Dallas, Texas, I had a close-up view of the effects of this recession. I saw men who had made millions in the oil and real estate market lose everything. I also saw the effects of greed as men used the real estate boom to pad their own pockets—sometimes illegally—and then end up broke or in prison. Even our former governor declared bankruptcy.

This economic crisis affected us all. I saw it affect the churches, including the one I pastor. Giving declined, and some churches couldn't pay salaries and had to lay off some of their staff.

An "Acts 6 Group"
One day we were discussing this economic problem in our church's board meeting. We decided to appoint a special task force to study the situation—a group of several mature men whom we called our "Acts 6 Group." After evaluating the problem for some time, one of the

group's recommendations to the elders was that I—as the senior pastor—deliver a series of messages on what the Bible says about giving.

A New Challenge

Frankly, I had never faced such a challenge before, although I had pastored for many years. To be perfectly honest—and it embarrasses me to admit this now—I had not preached but one or two messages on the subject of giving.

Frankly, I didn't know where to begin. After thinking and praying about the matter, however, I went back to the elders and the special task force with a recommendation of my own. I asked them to join me in a study of everything the Bible says about material possessions and how Christians ought to use them. They agreed, and the process began.

AN AMAZING DISCOVERY

None of us realized what we were tackling when we began our study on giving. We, indeed, studied everything we could find in Scripture related to money and generosity. The study took us six months, meeting once a week for three or four hours every Thursday evening. To our surprise, we discovered that God says more about being generous than any other subject other than Himself.

This should help you understand why I initially mentioned I was embarrassed to admit I hadn't spoken on the topic of money more frequently. How could I have overlooked so much biblical material? After all, as a pastor, I am to teach the **whole counsel** of God.[1]

SHOCKING STATISTICS

We made another very shocking discovery in our research! Statistics reveal that most Christians in America do not include God in their budgets. They consider everything else—their houses, their cars, their clothing, their food, their entertainment allowance—but not God.

One of our elders at that time was the CEO of a large savings and loan institution. One day he commented that he had processed loans for hundreds of Christians and when he did, he always asked for their budgets. "Gene," he said, "I can count on one hand the number of Christians that have God in their budgets."

LEFTOVERS RATHER THAN FIRSTFRUITS

When Christians don't figure God into their budgets, churches get into trouble during an economic crises. If Christians planned their expenditures so they never leave God out of the picture—in the good times and in the rough times—God's work would never suffer. This includes the way credit is used. When Christians borrow money, it should never interfere with their ability to give God their "firstfruits." Sadly, God often gets what is leftover, if anything.[2]

THE SELFISH MAJORITY

Some researchers tell us that the average Christian gives only about 2 percent of his or her income to the Lord. Because approximately 15 percent of the Christian population tithe (give a 10th of their income), this means that the majority of American Christians give next to nothing. This simply indicates that most of us are "lovers of money." Christians as a whole have become materialists, which is a direct violation of the will of God.

Think of it. We are living in the most affluent nation in the world, where the average American has more material blessings than at any moment in history, and yet we are in love with our money. Ron Blue, president of Central American Missions, once said, "Most Christians are tipping, not tithing, with their income to the church. In fact, most Christians tip waitresses more than they tip God at church. At least waitresses get 15 percent."[3]

A MATTER OF PRIORITIES

The issue is: What comes first in our lives? Is it God or money? We can't serve both (see Matt. 6:24). Jesus taught us to "seek first His kingdom and His righteousness; and all these things [the necessities of life] shall be added" to us (v. 33). Jesus was simply teaching that a man who loves money lays up "treasures upon earth" rather than

"treasures in heaven" (vv. 19,20). Jesus also said, "Where your trea-
sure is, there will your heart be also" (v. 21).

People who love money are more earthly minded than heavenly
minded. To them, worldly possessions, activities and benefits are far
more important than eternal values. They are constantly seeking
after more and more. Selfishness and pride take over. This is why the
Scriptures warn:

> Let your character be **free from the love of money**, being
> content with what you have; for He Himself has said, "I will
> never desert you, nor will I ever forsake you" (Heb. 13:5).

AN AGE-OLD PROBLEM

The problem of forgetting God when earthly possessions multiply is
not new. The children of Israel faced this temptation when they
entered the Promised Land. Moses cautioned them ahead of time
that this temptation would come. Note Moses' words of warning in
the book of Deuteronomy:

> "Then it shall come about when the Lord your God brings
> you into the land...to give you, great and splendid cities
> which you did not build, and houses full of all good things
> which you did not fill, and hewn cisterns which you did not
> dig, vineyards and olive trees which you did not plant, and
> you shall eat and be satisfied, **then watch yourself, lest you
> forget the Lord** who brought you from the land of Egypt,
> out of the house of slavery" (Deut. 6:10-12).

Moses added another powerful warning later in this passage when
he cautioned that they would be tempted to say in their hearts, "'**My
power and the strength of my hand made me this wealth**'" (8:17).
Unfortunately, this is exactly what happened.

A TRAGIC EPITAPH

The most tragic words in the Old Testament are recorded in the book
of Judges, which describe what happened once the children of Israel

entered the Promised Land. In spite of Moses' warnings—and after Joshua had died—the Holy Spirit etched these words in the scriptural record, words that in many respects form an epitaph on Israel's tombstone:

> And there arose another generation after them who did not know the Lord, nor yet the work which He had done for Israel. So they forsook the Lord and served Baal and the Ashtaroth (Judg. 2:10,13).

IT HAS HAPPENED AGAIN

"How could this be?" you ask. The facts are, it took only *one generation* for *degeneration* to take place. But stop and think for a moment. Do you realize that is exactly what has happened in our own American society?

No Absolutes

When the Supreme Court of the United States changed the rules and began to make decisions based upon a set of values that contradicted the Hebrew-Christian traditions that guided our nation for our first 200 years, our lives changed dramatically. Everything became relative. We had no absolute standard by which to make judgments regarding morality, crime, rules of government, business ethics, what is taught in our schools and so on. We have done the very same thing Israel did. As we looked about us and saw our prosperity, we concluded: "My power and the strength of my hand made me this wealth." The apostle Paul said it best. In the latter days, "Men will be lovers of self, lovers of money,...lovers of pleasure rather than lovers of God" (2 Tim. 3:2,4).

Cultural Spillover

Unfortunately, this new set of values has flowed over into the Christian community. If we are honest, we will have to admit this is true.

Don't misunderstand. There are exceptions. But when we look, for example, at the giving patterns of Christians at large, we can only conclude one thing: We have become "lovers of money." We are doing what our worldly counterparts do.

What has happened shouldn't surprise us. It is a human tendency that has been verified throughout human history. We can become so wrapped up in the material side of life that we lose spiritual perspective. Money can quickly become an end in itself rather than a means to godly ends.

A STATUS SYMBOL

Accumulating wealth can quickly become a status symbol. We may start out in life having relatively little. But as we accumulate a certain amount of money and material things, we soon discover that we can do more with it than buy food and clothes. We learn that money talks. It attracts friends, gives us power, status and a sense of security.

Again, don't misunderstand. We all need money to exist. It is a cultural necessity. We need it to provide for ourselves and our families. But when we earn money for selfish purposes, we are beginning to build on a shaky foundation. Even friends who are so-called friends because of our money are not friends at all. You will soon discover this is true if you lose your money.

A DEEP PSYCHOLOGICAL NEED

It may surprise you that some Christians have a problem with an inordinate desire for money and material things because they felt deprived as children. They have not been able to have "those things" or "do those things" that everyone else around them has done or is doing.

A Difficult Balance

This is definitely a culturally related problem. Our needs are basically simple. But our culture has complicated what we think or believe we need. This becomes a particular problem for children. They quickly compare themselves with others. If they don't have some of the things their friends have, they actually *feel* deprived, which is a reality to them, not just a figment of their imaginations.

This is a great challenge for parents who want to rear their children to be nonmaterialistic. On the one hand, to give children too much will create problems. But on the other hand, to withhold what is normal also creates problems. If we are not careful, we will create a deepening thirst for material things.

Obsessive-Compulsive Behavior

Let me give you a real-life illustration involving—of all things—chewing gum. I know some parents who decided they weren't going to let their children chew gum. They believed it was a bad habit. Consequently, even if their children asked for gum, they were disciplined. They never kept gum in the house nor would they let the children buy it.

I am sure—if you are perceptive at all—you have already guessed what happened. The children, of course, learned to never ask for chewing gum at home. They developed an insatiable desire to chew gum, however, especially because their friends chewed gum and they saw a lot of gum advertisements on television. And so it became an obsession. Every time the children could get away from their parents, they begged other people for chewing gum, but always spat it out before they got home lest they be punished.

The same thing can happen when children are overly deprived of material things. Children may grow up being materialistic, if not in reality, in their hearts. To resolve this problem takes a great deal of wisdom. We certainly don't want to create the very thing we are trying to avoid.

NOT FOND OF SORDID GAIN

Paul addressed this money issue when he wrote to Titus in Crete and outlined the qualifications for spiritual leaders. He made it clear that men must be chosen who are "not fond of sordid gain" (Titus 1:7). The apostle Peter elaborates on this same requirement for spiritual leaders:

> Shepherd the flock of God among you, exercising oversight not under compulsion, but voluntarily, according to the will of God, and **not for sordid gain**, but with eagerness (1 Pet. 5:2).

The New Testament world was filled with men who had false motives. Paul called them "rebellious men, empty talkers and deceivers," men who were "teaching things they should not teach, **for the sake of sordid gain**" (Titus 1:10,11). Spiritual leaders, of all people, should not be materialistic.

RELIGIOUS FRAUDS TODAY

Unfortunately, the twentieth-century world, like the first-century world, includes religious leaders who take advantage of people. They resort to guilt tactics, white lies, don't-you-feel-sorry-for-me innuendos and other forms of manipulation to get money.

This kind of manipulation is tragic. People are disillusioned. They often generalize and conclude that most Christian leaders are frauds, which is not true.

On the other hand, some religious leaders *are* frauds, and if any Christian man is ever guilty of this kind of behavior, he has completely disqualified himself from Christian leadership, and it is certainly a reflection of immaturity and carnality. He is a "lover of money."

Don't Overreact

Unfortunately, some Christians overreact to these warnings. They conclude that Christian leaders who devote their full time to the ministry should not have as much materially as do their peers. This is a false interpretation of the Scriptures and creates a great deal of difficulty for those who are attempting to serve the Lord.

Double Honor

Paul also addressed this issue in his first letter to Timothy:

> Let the elders who rule well be considered worthy of **double honor**, especially those who work hard at preaching and teaching. For the Scripture says, "You shall not muzzle the ox while he is threshing," and "The laborer is worthy of his wages" (1 Tim. 5:17,18).

Clearly, Paul was speaking about material remuneration. He also made this point clear in the Corinthian letter when he said that those who proclaim the gospel are "to get their living from the gospel" (1 Cor. 9:14).

The Honest Majority

The majority of Christian leaders are honest, hardworking people and, unfortunately, they are also underpaid. Consequently, many live with a constant sense of insecurity, wondering how they are going to pay their bills. Thus, they cannot concentrate as they should on carrying out their ministry.

God never intended for this shortfall to happen. When Christians who are responsible to care for Christian leaders' physical needs fail to do so, they are setting up a temptation for Christian leaders. This neglect can easily become a stumbling block, even to a sincere Christian worker.

A TRAGIC STORY

I had the privilege of sharing in a camp ministry for a week with a doctor who was serving as a medical missionary in Africa. During the course of the week, he related a tragic story. He shared about a man God had used to challenge him to become a medical missionary. This man was also a doctor. He, too, had planned to go to the same hospital in Africa. But he changed his mind and decided to stay in the United States. He became very successful, building a large and prosperous practice. From the world's point of view, he had everything he wanted. But something went wrong. After three unsuccessful marriages, and while still a young man, he committed suicide.

By contrast, the doctor who gave up fame and fortune (from a human point of view) continues to treat hundreds of African patients every week, and sees many of them come to know Jesus Christ as their personal Savior.

Again, Money Is Not the Issue

This story does not put a premium on poverty. Nor is it meant to chide Christian doctors who don't become missionaries and who earn a lot of money. But it does illustrate graphically that to *love money* and the *things money buys* does not in itself make a man happy. It can instead lead to a bitter and tragic end.

Paul issued a solemn warning in his first letter to Timothy:

> But those who want to get rich fall into temptation and a snare and many foolish and harmful desires which plunge men into ruin and destruction. For **the love of money is the**

root of all sorts of evil, and some by longing for it have wandered away from the faith, and pierced themselves with many a pang (6:9,10).

POINTS OF ACTION

The following project is designed to help you evaluate your motives regarding money and material things.

Evaluate Your Priorities

• **Discover what is most important in your life.**
Make a list of those things that are priorities in your life. Try to be completely honest. Write down those things that appear first in your mind.

Establish Biblical Priorities

• **Refocus your priorities in the light of biblical values.**
To do this, ask yourself the following questions: Where is my heart? What motivates me the most? What am I doing with my money? Can I justify my expenditures in the light of eternal values? How much am I giving to the Lord on a regular and systematic basis?

Read carefully the following passages of Scripture to help you rearrange your priorities: Proverbs 15:27; Proverbs 23:4,5; Proverbs 30:7-9; Ecclesiastes 5:10; Matthew 6:19-34; 2 Corinthians 8,9; 1 Timothy 6:6-10.

Follow Biblical Principles

• **Be a generous Christian by applying biblical principles.**
The following are eight biblical principles for giving:

1. Give regularly.
Christians should set aside a certain percentage of their income regularly as they are paid, to help them systematically give to God's work (see 1 Cor. 16:1,2).

2. Plan ahead.

Christians should be joyful, willing givers by planning ahead (see 2 Cor. 9:5).

3. Give proportionately.

Christians are only generous when they are proportional in their giving (see v. 6).

4. Model generosity.

Christians need to be real-life examples of modeling generosity. Considering that the Macedonians gave out of poverty, should Christians not be a model in giving out of plenty? (see 8:1,2).

5. Be accountable.

Christians need to be accountable regarding the way they use—or do not use—their finances to support God's work (see 8:6; 9:3,4).

6. Begin now.

God accepts and honors believers' gifts once they begin to give regularly and systematically, although they may not give proportionately as much as they will eventually once they have their economic lives in order (see 8:12).

7. Give by faith.

God wants us to trust Him for future income and for the proportion that we can give to God's work (see 9:5).

8. Trust God.

God will meet our needs when we put Him first. He will not necessarily give us all we want, but He will take care of us (see v. 8).[4]

Set Goals

• **Set up *specific* goals for your life that are in harmony with biblical principles.**

The following are some additional biblical guidelines:

1. Put God first.

The "love of money" is wrong. We must not value material things above spiritual things. To accumulate money for purely personal gain, prestige and power is sinful.

2. Be honest.

To obtain money in deceitful or dishonest ways is a violation of God's laws.

3. Help others.

Christians are to use their material possessions to care for other Christians who are in need.

4. Be industrious.

Christians are not to be lazy and irresponsible, living off other people. This is sinful (see 2 Thess. 3:10).

THINKING AND GROWING TOGETHER

The following questions are designed for group discussion after reading and studying the content of this chapter:

1. Why do people get unusually uncomfortable when they hear messages on money?
2. How can we keep our motives pure when it comes to accumulating material possessions?
3. When is "enough" enough?
4. What is your greatest temptation regarding money?
5. What biblical principles of giving do you violate the most? Would you be willing to share this with us for prayer?
6. What are your goals for becoming a generous Christian?

SET A GOAL

Write out one goal you'd like to achieve as a result of this study:

_____

_____

_____

_____

Notes

1. The results of this study have been included in two books by Gene A. Getz entitled *A Biblical Theology of Material Possessions* and *Real Prosperity* (Chicago: Moody Press, 1990).
2. For a biblical perspective on debt and when it is inappropriate and unwise, see one of the following in-depth studies of what the Bible teaches about material possessions: Getz, *Material Possessions*, pp. 263-279; and Getz, *Real Prosperity*, pp. 131-142.

3. Gene A. Getz, *The Walk* (Nashville: Broadman and Holman Publishers, 1994), p. 151.
4. For a more in-depth study of these principles, see Getz, *Material Possessions*, pp. 208-211, 213-215, 219-220, 229-232; and Getz, *Real Prosperity*, pp. 46, 87, 118, 120-121, 123.

16

REFLECTING OUR HEAVENLY FATHER

An overseer, then, must be above reproach,
the husband of one wife, temperate, prudent,
respectable, hospitable, able to teach, not addicted
to wine or pugnacious, but gentle, uncontentious,
free from the love of money. He must be one
who manages his own household well, keeping
his children under control with all dignity.
—1 TIMOTHY 3:2-4

MY HEAVENLY DADDY

My children are grown now. But I will never forget overhearing my four- and five-year-old daughters one day having an animated discussion in the living room.

I was standing in the kitchen and my daughters didn't know I was listening. The youngest suddenly had a burst of insight and said to the oldest, "Hey, Renee, God is our heavenly daddy." The oldest—who has always been philosophical—wasn't quite sure how she felt about that comment and so the discussion continued. "But he is," Robyn insisted. "He's our heavenly daddy."

I was startled. It suddenly dawned on me that their image of God was their image of me. What an awesome thought. Needless to say, right there and then I made a deeper commitment to exemplify Jesus Christ for my children to help them develop a correct perspective intellectually and emotionally regarding their heavenly Father.

PROJECTION OR REALITY?

The father image is an important reality—biblically and psychologically. Sigmund Freud first saw the implications, but he drew false conclusions because he didn't believe in the God of the Bible. His presuppositions were naturalistic. Consequently, he concluded that because people seem to need some kind of supernatural support system, the image of God that people have is a projection of their need for a father image. He believed that God existed only in the minds of people, which is a reflection of their insecurity. In other words, God was a mental and emotional projection of their inner needs.

Freud was incorrect regarding his view of God. But he was right in his observations that we do develop certain ideas about God—the God who exists—because of various kinds of experiences with parents, our fathers particularly. After all, we tell our children God is a *heavenly Father.* Like my own daughters, they eventually made the connection. God, who is an eternal Spirit and is invisible to children, gradually takes on the same characteristics in their minds as an earthly father. If a father is kind and loving, so is God—in the child's perceptions. If the father is cold and cruel, so is God.

EMOTIONAL SCARS

I remember sharing Christ with a young woman who had been sexually abused by her father. As always, this horrible experience left this young woman emotionally scarred. Her feelings of resentment were often overwhelming.

As I shared the gospel with her, I explained how she could become a Christian by accepting Jesus Christ as her personal Savior. She was willing to take this step so I began to pray, as I often do, asking her to repeat after me.

I began, "**Heavenly Father,** thank you for sending Jesus Christ to be my Savior."

She was silent. I thought perhaps she had misunderstood what I was asking her to do. "Is there something wrong?" I asked.

Again, she did not respond. Finally, she said, "I can't say that! I mean, I can't say that word."

Suddenly, I understood. She couldn't use the word "father." Earlier, she had poured out her dismal story. The very word "father" brought back horrible memories of sexual abuse that were too painful, too reminiscent of her experience as a child with her own father. Needless to say, as we prayed together, I had to avoid using the word "father" at that moment in her life.

Recently, after a number of years, I talked with this woman again at a special birthday party held in her honor. "Do you remember," I asked, "when you couldn't use the word 'father'?" She smiled and nodded her head. Today, after a number of years of spiritual and emotional healing, she can address God as her "heavenly Father." Her mental and emotional image has changed. She now understands what true fatherhood is all about.

MANAGES HIS OWN HOUSEHOLD WELL

Paul made it clear in his letters to Timothy and Titus that a mark of maturity—or immaturity—in a man is the way he functions as a father in his home. His children particularly will reflect how well he has fulfilled this God-ordained role. If he is mature, Paul told Timothy, a man will be able to keep "his children under control with all dignity" (1 Tim. 3:4). Paul told Titus that this kind of father will have "children who believe" and who are "not accused of dissipation or rebellion" (Titus 1:6).

The Father-Pastor Connection

I know of a church where the main spiritual leader had a home that definitely did not measure up to Paul's specifications in 1 Timothy 3 and Titus 1. He had two married daughters (both claiming to be Christians) who committed adultery, which was well-known in the community. His son was the town drunk and a terrible embarrassment. Yet, this man continued to try to give direction to the church.

Predictably, the results were disastrous. The church experienced continuing problems. The congregation exhibited a lack of trust, gossiping, backbiting and all sorts of carnality.

As I observed this situation, I noticed that this pastor tried to manage the church basically the same way he tried to manage his family. He often ignored problems, pretending they weren't there. When the "ostrich, head-in-the-sand approach" didn't work, he would straddle the fence and not take a stand. Although I know he had convictions, he wouldn't exercise these convictions. He tried to keep everybody happy. By trying to please everyone, he pleased no one. Everyone lost respect for him as a spiritual leader. The correlation between his family and the church was apparent. His family was in a shambles and so was the church.

The True Test

The apostle Paul viewed a well-ordered family as the true test of a man's maturity and ability to lead other Christians. When the whole household is committed to Jesus Christ, you can be sure that this man is spiritually and psychologically mature. But when this is not true—if that man is appointed as a spiritual leader—the church will experience the same problems as his family did. The very weaknesses that made this man a poor husband and father will cause him to be a poor leader in the church. Furthermore, if a man who is not a good leader at home accepts this kind of leadership role, his family members will have less respect for him, which, in turn, will cause greater problems in the home.

A GOAL FOR EVERY CHRISTIAN MAN

Having a well-ordered household should be a goal for every Christian man.

As Husbands

We should love our wives "just as Christ also loved the church" (Eph. 5:25). We should live with them "in an understanding way" and grant them "honor as a fellow heir of the grace of life" (1 Pet. 3:7). Peter warns us that if we don't live this way with our wives, it will affect our prayer lives.

As Fathers

We should never provoke our children to anger but "bring them up in the discipline and instruction of the Lord" (Eph. 6:4). Paul illustrated this concept with a personal illustration from his own ministry. Writing to the Thessalonians, Paul reminded them that he ministered among them as a "father would his own children" (1 Thess. 2:11). He personalized his ministry by "encouraging and imploring each one," which demonstrates how Paul viewed a father's ministry to "each one of...his own children" (v. 11). Christian fathers should not just rear a family, but individual children in that family. Each one is a different personality and needs individualized attention, according to his own "natural bent." This, I believe, is what the proverb means:

> Train up a child in the way he should go, even when he is old he will not depart from it (Prov. 22:6).

SOME SERIOUS MISUNDERSTANDINGS

It is easy to misinterpret what Paul was teaching when he stated that a mature man is "one who manages his own household well, keeping his children under control with all dignity" (1 Tim. 3:4). Consequently, let's look at what Paul doesn't mean.

• **Paul was not specifying that it is necessary to have children to be a spiritual leader in the church.**

Personally, I don't believe Paul was saying a man must be married to be a pastor. If this is what Paul meant, he would have been excluding himself, because it appears he may never have been married. Rather, Paul was simply saying that *if* a man *is married*, and *if* he *has children*, then he should have a well-ordered household. It follows, of course, that if a man becomes a spiritual leader before he has a family, and then fails to measure up to Paul's criteria, he then disqualifies himself from continuing as a spiritual leader in the church.

• **Paul was not referring to younger children.**

Several words are used to describe "children" in the New Testament. The word Paul used in both his letter to Timothy and his letter to Titus is a general word used for "offspring." This word could be used to refer to small children, but the total context indicates that Paul was referring to grown children.

Dissipation or Rebellion

Later in his letter to Timothy, Paul used the same word to refer to "mature children" who are responsible to provide for their mother's material needs (see 5:4). More significantly, when Paul used this word in his letter to Titus, he said that a man selected for spiritual leadership should have "children who believe, not accused of **dissipation or rebellion**" (Titus 1:6). "Dissipation" and "rebellion" refer to a person who is living a riotous and immoral life, characteristics that could only be true of an older offspring.

Eli's Sons

Eli is an Old Testament illustration of what Paul was saying. Both of Eli's sons as grown young men did "not know the Lord" (1 Sam. 2:12). They were both immoral and they "despised the offering of the Lord" (v. 17). They were described by the Lord as "worthless" (v. 12). Consequently, God judged both Eli and his sons. We read that the "sons brought a curse on themselves" and Eli was disciplined by the Lord because "he did not rebuke them" (3:13).

• **Paul was not referring here to normal patterns of child growth and development.**

All small children as well as teenagers go through natural phases of growth. Some people have concluded that when children and youth go through these natural stages and attempt to establish their own identities, they are guilty of the kind of "rebellion" described by Paul in these letters. The facts are that a significant difference exists between these passing phases and the kinds of attitudes and actions to which Paul was referring.

Because of this misinterpretation, some spiritual leaders come down too hard on their own children for the sake of their own reputations. They attempt to get their children to conform to certain behavioral patterns so that they—as spiritual leaders—are not criticized by other Christians in the church.

A Higher Standard Breeds Rebellion

Children resent a higher standard for themselves simply because their parents happen to be spiritual leaders in the church. And they really resent being told they are to be good so their dad looks good. Ultimately, this kind of motivation will backfire. As children grow into adulthood, it may also create the kind of rebellion Paul was talking about in his letters to Timothy and Titus.

Performance Standards Can Be Lethal

A pastor friend of mine overheard his son being reprimanded by another elder in the church. Admonishing this young man, the elder said, "I certainly would expect more from you than that, being the preacher's son."

My friend, a gracious and mature Christian, took the elder aside immediately and lovingly but directly let him know he never wanted that kind of reprimand to happen again.

My friend was not defending his son's inappropriate behavior. Rather, he was concerned that his son not think he was under some kind of performance standard just because he was the "preacher's kid."

"If my son is out of order," my pastor friend said, "come to me and I'll discipline him. Or if he needs immediate discipline and I am not available, don't use my position as a weapon against him."

• **Paul was not speaking of a man who has a perfect family.**

As there is no perfect church, so there is no perfect family. There is no perfect husband or father, just as there is no perfect wife or mother, and certainly there are no perfect children. All Christians have problems in their family lives. Satan will see to that. As long as we are in this world, we will be victims of imperfection.

We should certainly strive to have a family that reflects the life of Jesus Christ. But just as every Christian is in the process of becoming more and more like Jesus Christ, so every family should be in the process of growing spiritually. This is also what Paul had in mind for the Church when he wrote to the Ephesians:

> Until we all attain to the unity of the faith, and of the knowledge of the Son of God, to a mature man, to the measure of the stature which belongs to the fulness of Christ (4:13).

• **Paul was not talking about being a successful businessman.**

Unfortunately, many Christians have made the mistake of judging capabilities for spiritual leadership on the basis of how well a man runs and operates his business, how efficient he is, how smart he is and how much money he makes.

Through the years, I have noticed something that makes a lot of sense. Usually a man who "manages his own household well" will also manage his "business well." But the reverse is not always true. On many occasions, I have observed that men may have well-ordered businesses, but yet their families are falling apart.

What Paul is telling us is that the way a man leads his family is the true test of maturity. Through administrative skill and business acumen, some men have built great financial empires. But when it comes to their family lives, these men aren't able to communicate effectively either with their wives or their children. In some instances, they are so busy running their businesses, they have not taken time to be good husbands and fathers. But in either case, these men certainly would not pass the "spiritual maturity" test as presented by Paul in his pastoral letters.

• **Paul was not talking about how well a man can do church work.**

Some pastors, missionaries and lay leaders are well-known for their achievements in the ministry. They have built large churches, they have led countless numbers to Jesus Christ and they are active in doing the Lord's work. On the surface, they appear to be successful Christian leaders. But sadly, their families have disintegrated.

When this happens, they have often neglected their own wives and children. In some instances, their own sons and daughters grow up rejecting Jesus Christ and resenting Christian work because it has taken their parents away from them.

I have also known children who resent the hypocrisy they see in their parents. They know they are preaching one thing in church and not living up to these truths in their homes.

Wall-to-Wall Experiences

It is relatively easy to fool other people regarding our spirituality. However, we cannot deceive our wives and children. They live with us 24 hours a day, 7 days a week. Their experience with us is "wall to wall." They know us as we really are. When our message to others does not conform to our relationships in the home, we are in serious trouble with our children. We are in danger of driving them away from Jesus Christ—the very One we want them to serve.

• **Paul was not teaching that a spiritual leader should resign if he is not 100 percent successful.**

First of all, not one of us is 100 percent successful. God-fearing families experience many of the same external influences other families do. Our homes are not islands. Even if we do the best job possible in parenting, some children grow up making choices that are out of the will of God.

It Can Happen to Anyone

I know a fellow pastor who discovered that one of his children was living an immoral life. Unfortunately, a lot of people in the church knew about it before he did, but no one told him. They simply criticized him behind his back.

When I met this man, he and his wife were grieving deeply about the situation. They were wondering if they should leave the ministry. As I talked with them, one fact became clear. All of the other children were doing well and were also grieved over their sibling's rebellion. To complicate things, this man had lived in this area for some time and his daughter's behavior had tarnished his reputation.

I suggested that he and his family move to another area and start fresh, where no one knew about his wayward teenager. He followed my recommendation and, at the same time, selectively began to share with a group of mature Christians the need to pray for his child.

Not only has this man developed a successful ministry, but his child is once again living for Jesus Christ. I remember the day the child, then an adult, stood up in church and thanked God publicly for her dad and mom who—though they had rejected her sin—never rejected her.

POINTS OF ACTION

The following project is designed to help you become a good husband and father—to have a "well-ordered household."

Respect Is Earned

• **We cannot demand or force respect and love.**

Fathers who have their "children under control with all dignity" have created this kind of family. This does not mean they have not taught what is "right and wrong," but they have built this teaching on their own consistent walk with Jesus Christ. They have not provoked their "children to anger" (Eph. 6:4). They have not exasperated their children so that they have become discouraged (see Col. 3:21). They have followed the ministry model Paul wrote to the Thessalonians:

> You are witnesses, and so is God, how devoutly and uprightly and blamelessly we behaved toward you believers; just as you know how we were exhorting and encouraging and imploring each one of you **as a father would his own children**, so that you may walk in a manner worthy of the God who calls you into His own kingdom and glory (1 Thess. 2:10-12).

Ask Forgiveness

• **If you have sinned against your children in some way, ask them to forgive you.**

I remember on one occasion my son invited his friend to come home after church. Both of them were about eight years old at the time. Dinner was about ready but they still had time to go out to play. I clearly instructed Kenton to not go far so they could hear me when I called them for dinner.

A few minutes later, I went to the door and called but there was no answer. I walked around the house and called again and again, but there was no answer. Frankly, I became angry. It appeared to be a flagrant act of disobedience. I had made the message clear and repeated it several times, "Don't go far so you can hear me call."

A Bad Judgment

Right there and then I determined what I was going to do. We went ahead and began eating. About 10 minutes later, Kenton and his friend walked into the house. I got up from my chair, marched my son into his own room, closed the door and proceeded to give him a good spanking. Explanations were minimal. After all, I had made my instructions clear. Furthermore, I wasn't in the mood to listen to anything he had to say during the ordeal.

As I emerged from Kenton's room, my wife sensitively took me aside and informed me I had made a bad judgment. What Kenton had tried to explain to me was that his mother had instructed him on an important lesson he needed to learn—that is, to pay attention to his friend and to try to do the things his friend wanted to do while he was visiting in our home.

As events unfolded, his friend had wanted to go down the alley to the creek. Kenton, attempting to follow his mother's instructions, proceeded to do what his friend wanted to do. In his own way, he was trying to practice hospitality, to put his friend's desires first. I found out later that was what he was trying to explain to me, but I wouldn't listen.

I Knew What I Had to Do

Embarrassed and chagrined, I asked Kenton to forgive me for several things. *First,* I had misunderstood him because I wouldn't listen. *Second,* I had embarrassed him in front of his friend, which was probably more painful than the spanking. *Third,* I had allowed my own anger to interfere with good judgment. Had I been wise, I would have discussed the situation with my wife before I ever took action.

As you would expect, Kenton forgave me. In fact, we have discussed this situation several times since then. As we have talked, it has become clear to me that his intentions and motives were right. He had been caught between two authority figures, and his mother's instructions were far more important in his mind at that moment.

A Valuable Lesson

I have learned through the years that it takes effort to understand children. My wife has taught me more about this than anyone. We must listen to our children. We must not become so preoccupied with our own world and our needs that we don't know what is going on in their minds. If we don't know them and understand them, we will not make proper decisions, even in the area of discipline.

Unfortunately, we have all made mistakes. If you have, ask your children to forgive you. You will be amazed at how they will respond. In some instances, the damage is so severe that they may not respond as you had hoped. In these instances, you have done your part. Just keep on loving them, and hopefully some day they will respond to your efforts at making peace with them.

Consult Your Wife

• **Ask your wife to help you evaluate your stature as a husband and father.**

The following are some questions that will help you:

1. How can I become a better husband? What are my strengths? In what areas can I improve?
2. How can I become a better father? What are my strengths? In what areas can I improve?

Consult the Scriptures

• **Carefully study biblical passages that outline how to be a good husband and father.**

I have personally found two passages to be especially helpful. The first has helped me as a husband. The second focuses on being a good father.

Loving My Wife as Christ Loves Me

> Have this attitude in yourselves which was also in Christ Jesus, who, although He existed in the form of God, did not regard equality with God a thing to be grasped, but emptied Himself, taking the form of a bond-servant, and being made in the likeness of men. And being found in appearance as a man, He humbled Himself by becoming obedient to the point of death, even death on a cross (Phil. 2:5-8).

Being a Good Father

> "And you shall love the Lord your God with all your heart and with all your soul and with all your might. And these words, which I am commanding you today, shall be on your heart; and you shall teach them diligently to your sons [children] and shall talk of them when you sit in your house and when you walk by the way and when you lie down and when you rise up. And you shall bind them as a sign on your

hand and they shall be as frontals on your forehead. And you shall write them on the doorposts of your house and on your gates" (Deut. 6:5-9).

Set Goals

• **Set up specific goals for developing a well-ordered household.**

Base these goals first on biblical principles, and then on actual needs that have surfaced during this study. As you set goals, be sure to include your wife in your planning. Pray together about the needs in your household. In some areas, you may also want to include your children in helping you set up these goals. This will help you draw together as a family. It is always easier to be a part of something when you have been a part of the planning.

THINKING AND GROWING TOGETHER

The following questions are designed for group discussion after reading and studying the content of this chapter:

1. What do you believe are the most significant areas most men need to consider to be better husbands and fathers?
2. Can you share some of the steps you have already taken to be a better husband and father?
3. Can you share an experience where you have failed as a husband or a father and then through asking for forgiveness, you have seen significant changes take place in your family relationships?
4. What specific prayer requests do you have for your own family?

SET A GOAL

Write out one goal you'd like to achieve as a result of this study:

_____

_____

_____

_____

17

LOVING
WHAT
IS GOOD

For the overseer must be above reproach as God's
steward, not self-willed, not quick-tempered, not
addicted to wine, not pugnacious, not fond of sordid
*gain, but hospitable, **loving what is good**.*
—TITUS 1:7,8

One Greek word is translated "loving what is good." It is the word *philagathos*. When Paul used this word to describe maturity, he was referring to a man who makes it a priority in his life to fellowship with "good people," to desire "good things" and to participate in activities that reflect the **good** and acceptable and perfect will of God (see Rom. 12:2).

GOOD VERSUS EVIL

Pick up any Bible concordance and look up the words "good" and "evil." Not only are these words used again and again throughout Scripture, but they also often appear as contrasts. We see this contrast before Adam and Eve disobeyed God and introduced sin into the world. God created a tree in the midst of the Garden of Eden called the "tree of the knowledge of **good** and **evil**" (Gen. 2:9). The

Lord told Adam and Eve they could eat of any tree except this tree. God made this message very clear and warned Adam that in the day he disobeyed, he would "surely die" (v. 17).

Unfortunately, our first parents disobeyed God and from that moment forward, they became aware of this great tension in the universe. They knew the difference between "good" and "evil" (3:22). After they disobeyed God, they also "died spiritually," making their tendency to *do evil* far greater than their tendency to *do good*.

Because of Adam and Eve's sin, God introduced His great plan of redemption in Jesus Christ. Without this wonderful plan, all mankind would be doomed to eternal separation from God. Paul made this clear in his letter to the Romans:

> For the wages of sin is death, but the free gift of God is eternal life in Christ Jesus our Lord (Rom. 6:23).

AN INTRIGUING JEWISH LEGEND

An intriguing legend has been written regarding the Creation story. When God was about to create man, He took into His counsel the angels who stood about the throne.

"Don't create him," said the angel of justice, "for if You do, he will commit all kinds of wickedness against his fellow man; he will be hard and cruel and dishonest and unrighteous."

"Don't create him," said the angel of truth, "for he will be false and deceitful to his fellow man—and even to You."

The angel of holiness spoke next. "Don't create him," he warned, "for a man will follow that which is impure in Your sight and dishonor You to Your face."

Then the angel of mercy stepped forward and said, "Create him, our Heavenly Father, for when he sins and turns from the path of right and truth and holiness, I will take him tenderly by the hand, and speak loving words to him and then lead him back to You."[1]

THE NAKED TRUTH

Although this story is fictional, it captures what really happened when Adam and Eve disobeyed God. Their eyes were "opened, and

they knew that they were naked" (Gen. 3:7). They knew the difference between "good" and "evil."

Adam and Eve also introduced sin into the human race (see Rom.
5:12). Consequently, men and women *have* done all kinds of wicked
things against their fellow human beings, just as the legendary "angel
of justice" predicted. As human beings, we *have* become hard and
cruel and dishonest and unrighteous. We *have* become deceitful to
both man and God, and no one can argue against the fact that impurity and immorality have existed throughout history. All of this is the
true story of mankind. It is not fiction.

OVERCOMING EVIL WITH GOOD

But history also tells us there was an "angel of mercy," not in a legendary sense, but in reality. God sent His own Son (often called "the
angel of the Lord" in the Old Testament) to redeem us from our sins
and to make it possible for us to turn from following after unrighteousness and to do what is right and truthful and holy.

A Mark of Christian Maturity
Paul tells us that "loving what is good" is a mark of Christian maturity.
It is possible for every Christian to "overcome evil with good" because
of our relationship with God through our faith in Jesus Christ (12:21).
It is true that "through one man [Adam] sin entered into the world, and
death through sin, and so death spread to all men, because all sinned"
(5:12). But it is also true—thank God—that "through the obedience of
the One [Jesus Christ] the many will be made righteous" (v. 19).

But as Many as Received Him
Don't misunderstand. Salvation is not an automatic gift simply
because Jesus Christ died for the sins of the world. We must receive
that gift by faith. John writes:

> He came to His own, and those who were His own did not
> receive Him. **But as many as received Him,** to them He gave
> the right to become children of God, even to those **who believe
> in His name,** who were born not of blood, nor of the will of
> the flesh, nor of the will of man, but of God (John 1:11-13).

When we receive Jesus Christ as our personal Savior and Lord, we are "born again," "justified" [made righteous] and "we have peace with God through our Lord Jesus Christ" (Rom. 5:1). The moment we take this step of faith, Paul states, "There is therefore now no condemnation for those who are in Christ Jesus. For the law of the Spirit of life in Christ Jesus has set you free from the law of sin and of death" (8:1,2).

OVERCOMING THE POWER OF SIN

Imagine for a moment what happens when a huge Boeing 747 taxis to the end of a runway ready to take off. When this gigantic jumbo jet is loaded with *passengers, cargo and fuel,* its total weight reaches 500 tons.

The Law of Gravity Versus the Law of Aerodynamics

If we have a limited perspective on natural law, we would conclude that the law of gravity states that this huge machine should never leave the ground. But another law can overcome the law of gravity— the law of aerodynamics. When the pilot activates this huge airplane's four great jet engines, the plane will lunge forward, move down the runway, and lift off and climb skyward. In a matter of minutes, what seemingly should never have gotten off the runway is soaring at 40,000 feet. The power generated by those four engines is absolutely mind-boggling.

The Law of Sin Versus the Law of the Spirit

The point is this. Adam and Eve introduced all of us to the "law of sin and of death." This law states that we are forever separated from God. But when God sent Jesus Christ and the Holy Spirit into this world, He activated another law that is greater than the law that keeps us earthbound. It's the "law of the Spirit of life in Christ Jesus." This law sets us "free from the law of sin and death" (v. 2). When we sincerely put our faith in Jesus Christ and receive His gift of eternal life, God's power is activated in our lives, the same power that raised Jesus Christ from the dead and seated Him at God's "right hand in the heavenly places" (Eph. 1:20). When this happens, "even when we were dead in our transgressions" God raised us up with Christ and "seated us with Him in the heavenly places" (2:5,6).

And this power that saved us is also the same power that enables us to live a godly life while still on earth (see 3:14-21). Because of this wonderful plan, we can "love what is good."

SOME SPECIFIC CONTRASTS

Let's evaluate more specifically what Paul meant by "loving what is good" by looking at a paragraph he wrote in his second letter to Timothy. Here we see several significant contrasts:

> But realize this, that in the last days difficult times will come. For men will be **lovers of self, lovers of money,** boastful, arrogant, revilers, disobedient to parents, ungrateful, unholy, unloving, irreconcilable, malicious gossips, without self-control, brutal, **haters of good,** treacherous, reckless, conceited, **lovers of pleasure rather than lovers of God** (3:1-4).

In this paragraph, Paul discussed the positive quality of "loving what is good" by describing a lifestyle that is just the opposite. As we draw closer and closer to the second coming of Jesus Christ, Paul warned that "men will be **lovers of self, lovers of money...haters of good**" and "**lovers of pleasure rather than lovers of God.**"

Paul very crisply, and with four descriptive Greek words, described a person who does *not* love what is good:
- *philautos*   "A lover of oneself"
- *philarguros*   "A lover of money"
- *philedonos*   "A lover of pleasure"
- *aphilagathos* "Haters of good"

Let's look at each of these worldly and carnal qualities more specifically.

LOVERS OF SELF

Paul was certainly not teaching that we shouldn't feel good about ourselves. It is impossible to function as mature men without self-respect and a good self-image. Without a proper view of ourselves, we will not be able to love God and others as we should.

This is an important observation. Some Christians feel guilty when they feel good about themselves. This is definitely false guilt. Of all people in the world, a Christian should have a good self-image. We are God's children. We are heirs together with Christ. We have been redeemed and forgiven of our sins. We were created in God's image to begin with, and though that image was marred by sin, it can be restored. We have the resources to become more and more conformed to the image of Jesus Christ.

Do Nothing from Selfishness or Empty Conceit

What is Paul teaching? A Christian man who loves himself is a victim of the "I," "me" and "mine" syndrome. He is self-involved and self-oriented. His needs are central in all that he does. He is driven by self-interest. In short, he is selfish.

Paul warned against this kind of attitude in his letter to the Philippians:

> Do nothing from selfishness or empty conceit, but with humility of mind let each of you regard one another as more important than himself; do not merely look out for your own personal interests, but also for the interests of others (2:3,4).

A Poetic Metaphor

Sometimes when you're feeling important,
Sometimes when your ego's in bloom,
Sometime when you take it for granted
You're the best qualified in the room;
Sometimes when you feel that your going
Would leave an unfillable hole,
Just follow these simple instructions
And see how they humble your soul.
Take a bucket and fill it with water
Put your hand in it up to the wrist,
Pull it out, and the hole that's remaining
Is the measure of how you'll be missed.
You can splash all you want when you enter,
You may stir up the water galore;
But stop, and you'll find that in no time

It looks quite the same as before.
The moral in this quaint example
Is to do just the best that you can;
Be proud of yourself, but remember
There's no indispensable man.[2]

Although I don't agree in every respect with the "theology" in this poem, I do agree with the principle involved. Though I am important to God and to the Body of Christ, I must not think more highly of myself than I ought to think (see Rom. 12:3). Someone else has said:

The smallest package we have ever seen is a man wrapped up in himself.

LOVERS OF MONEY

As we pointed out in chapter 16, anyone who has a correct perspective on what the Bible teaches knows that Paul was not condemning money per se. Neither did he condemn people who have money. Rather, he was warning people not to *love* money, for "the **love of money** is a root of all sorts of evil" (1 Tim. 6:10).

A Stumbling Block to Unbelievers

When we have money, it is easy to love it. Jesus warned against this very thing, stating that it is often difficult (but not impossible) for rich people to enter the kingdom of God. They have difficulty shifting their affections away from their material possessions and to acknowledge that they need God.

A Temptation to Believers

Accumulating wealth can also create problems for believers. Writing to Timothy, Paul issued a stern warning:

But those who want to get rich fall into temptation and a snare and many foolish and harmful desires which plunge men into ruin and destruction (1 Tim. 6:9).

The late Robert Horton made an insightful observation. He said:

The greatest lesson he learned from life was that people who set their minds and hearts on money are equally disappointed whether they get it or whether they don't.[3]

LOVERS OF PLEASURE

Again, we must understand the positive aspects of this concept. God created our capacity for pleasure. Life would be miserable without it.

The Garden of Eden

God wanted Adam to be happy. That is one reason the Lord created Eve for Adam, and each for the other. He also created a beautiful garden so that Adam and Eve could enjoy all the delectable fruits and vegetables. It wasn't only what they *tasted* that gave pleasure, but what they *saw*—the green trees, the beautiful bushes, and the variety of animals that graced the landscape. God created all of these things for them, and us, to richly enjoy.

The Promised Land

When Israel was ready to cross Jordan, God spoke through Moses, telling His people that they were about to enter "a land flowing with milk and honey" (Deut. 6:3). The Promised Land was to be a place where Israel could experience enjoyment and pleasure.

But the pleasures God created to be "good" became "evil." It began when sin entered the world. We took what God created to be *good* and for His glory and turned it into something that is wrong and sinful. What God designed for marriage, we have used illegitimately. What God designed for sustenance, we have abused. We have made pleasure an end in itself, and we use it in purely selfish, sinful ways that violate the will of God. As millions have discovered, pleasure in itself is a dead-end street. It never satisfies.

PHILOTHEOS—THE KEY TO BALANCE

In the passage we are looking at in Paul's second letter to Timothy, the apostle gave us the key to balance. He contrasts those who love *themselves*, their *money* and *pleasure* with being among those who are "lovers of God" (*philotheos*). It is our love for God that keeps everything in proper perspective.

Which Is the Greatest Commandment?

One day a lawyer came to Jesus, trying to trick Him, and asked Him the following question: "Teacher, which is the great commandment in the Law?" (Matt. 22:36). Jesus' answer explains what Paul had in mind when he contrasts being "lovers of God" with our love for ourselves, our money and pleasure:

> And he said to him, "'You shall love the Lord your God with all your heart and with all your soul, and with all your mind.' This is the great and foremost commandment. The second is like it, 'You shall love your neighbor as yourself.' On these two commandments depend the whole Law and the Prophets" (Matt. 22:37-40).

That Your Joy May Be Full

If I love God as I should, I will live within His will as He has revealed it in the Word of God. Jesus reinforced this concept when He said to the disciples:

> "Just as the Father has loved Me, I have also loved you; abide in My love. If you keep My commandments, you will abide in My love; just as I have kept My Father's commandments, and abide in His love. These things I have spoken to you, that My joy may be in you, and that your joy may be made full" (John 15:9-11).

The only way to true happiness and lasting joy and pleasure that satisfies is to live within the will of God. Then, and only then, all that God has created for us to enjoy will really become enduring.

IN THE LAST DAYS

Paul was describing a pagan mentality in his second letter to Timothy. In essence, he was saying that "in the last days" people will turn away from God. They will not love what is good. They will be openly hostile to Christianity and its values. They will be "haters of good" (3:3).

We cannot read this passage of Scripture without thinking in terms of our society. Today, we live in a culture that is rapidly becoming post-Christian. Without question, people have become "lovers of themselves," "lovers of money" and "lovers of pleasure" rather than "lovers of God." This is a reality, and as Christians we must face that reality. We are living in the midst of a cultural war. Biblical values are no longer sacred—from the White House to the homes in which the average American lives.

To what extent are you allowing your life to conform to the world's attitudes and actions? To what extent are you focusing on yourself, your material possessions and the pleasures of this life? These are the questions every Christian man must ask himself.

LOVING WHAT IS GOOD IS LOVING GOD

The extent to which I love God and reflect that love by doing His will revealed in the Word of God is also the degree to which I "love what is good." Consequently, the real questions I must face are: Do I really love God? How *much* do I really love God?

POINTS OF ACTION

The following project is designed to help you evaluate the extent to which you "love what is good":

Meditate

• Read the following Scriptures and reflect on God's truth, particularly the concept of "loving what is good."

Performing with His Own Hands What Is Good

> Let him who steals steal no longer; but rather let him labor, **performing with his own hands what is good**, in order that he may have something to share with him who has need (Eph. 4:28).

But Only Such a Word as Is Good for Edification

Let no unwholesome word proceed from your mouth, **but only such a word as is good for edification** according to the need of the moment, that it may give grace to those who hear (v. 29).

Equipped for Every Good Work

All Scripture is inspired by God and profitable for teaching, for reproof, for correction, for training in righteousness; that the man of God may be adequate, **equipped for every good work** (2 Tim. 3:16,17).

Bearing Fruit in Every Good Work

For this reason also, since the day we heard of it, we have not ceased to pray for you and to ask that you may be filled with the knowledge of His will in all spiritual wisdom and understanding, so that you may walk in a manner worthy of the Lord, to please Him in all respects, **bearing fruit in every good work** (Col. 1:9,10).

Full of Mercy and Good Fruits

But the wisdom from above is first pure, then peaceable, gentle, reasonable, **full of mercy and good fruits**, unwavering, without hypocrisy (Jas. 3:17).

Evaluate

• **Read the following questions and Scripture verses and evaluate your life to determine the degree to which you are "loving what is good."**
   1. Do I take advantage of opportunities to do good to *all men*—both Christians and non-Christians?

So then, while we have opportunity, **let us do good to all** men, and especially to those who are of the household of the faith (Gal. 6:10).

Remind them to be subject to rulers, to authorities, to be obedient, to be ready for every good deed, to malign no one, to be uncontentious, gentle, showing every consideration for all men (Titus 3:1,2).

2. Am I using my material resources to help others in need?

Now this I say, he who sows sparingly shall also reap sparingly; and he who sows bountifully shall also reap bountifully. Let each one do just as he has purposed in his heart; not grudgingly or under compulsion; for God loves a cheerful giver. And God is able to make all grace abound to you, that always having all sufficiency in everything, you may have an abundance for every good deed (2 Cor. 9:6-8).

3. Do I have a good conscience about my behavior?

This command I entrust to you, Timothy, my son, in accordance with the prophecies previously made concerning you, that by them you may fight the good fight, keeping faith and a good conscience, which some have rejected and suffered shipwreck in regard to their faith (1 Tim. 1:18,19).

4. Am I truly concerned about the unity of the Body of Christ?

Who among you is wise and understanding? Let him show by his good behavior his deeds in the gentleness of wisdom. But if you have bitter jealousy and selfish ambition in your heart, do not be arrogant and so lie against the truth. This wisdom is not that which comes down from above, but is earthly, natural, demonic. For where jealousy and selfish ambition exist, there is disorder and every evil thing. But the wisdom from above is first pure, then peaceable, gentle, reasonable, full of mercy and good fruits, unwavering, without hypocrisy (Jas. 3:13-17).

To sum up, let all be harmonious, sympathetic, brotherly, kindhearted, and humble in spirit; not returning evil for evil, or insult for insult, but giving a blessing instead; for you were called for the very purpose that you might inherit a blessing. "And let him **turn away from evil and do good**; let him seek peace and pursue it" (1 Pet. 3:8,9,11).

Dedicate

• **Present your body to Jesus Christ as a living sacrifice.**

Have you truly presented your *total life* to Jesus Christ without reservation? It is only as you do so that you can discover day by day God's perfect will, "which is **good and acceptable and perfect**" (Rom. 12:2). As you read the verses that follow, dedicate your life to Jesus Christ. Note that to *present your body* is a once-and-for-all event. To *renew your mind* is a process of becoming more and more like Jesus Christ.

I urge you therefore, brethren, by the mercies of God, to present your bodies a living and holy sacrifice, acceptable to God, which is your spiritual service of worship. And do not be conformed to this world, but be transformed by the renewing of your mind, that you may prove what the will of God is, that which is **good and acceptable and perfect** (vv. 1,2).

Trust God

• **Now that you have done your part, trust God to do His.**

When Paul wrote to the Philippians, he said:

For I am confident of this very thing, that **He who began a good work in you** will perfect it until the day of Christ Jesus (1:6).

When the author of Hebrews wrote his letter, he prayed the following prayer:

Now the God of peace, who brought up from the dead the great Shepherd of the sheep through the blood of the eternal covenant, even Jesus our Lord, **equip you in every good thing to do his will**, working in us that which is pleasing in His sight, through Jesus Christ, to whom be the glory for ever and ever. Amen (13:20,21).

THINKING AND GROWING TOGETHER

The following questions are designed for group discussion after reading and studying the content of this chapter:

1. Why is it often difficult for Christian men to "love what is good"?
2. What scriptural statements and paragraphs in this chapter have meant the most to you and why?
3. What aspects of your life would you like to change in order to be able to love God more?
4. Why do we sometimes fail to realize that the degree we love God is the degree to which we "love what is good"?

SET A GOAL

Write out one goal you'd like to achieve as a result of this study:

_____

_____

_____

_____

Notes
1. Paul Lee Tan, *Encyclopedia of 7,700 Illustrations* (Rockville, MD: Assurance Publishers, n.d.), p. 493.
2. Ibid., pp. 261-262, 771.
3. Ibid., p. 830.

18

BEING JUST
AND FAIR

*For the overseer must be above reproach as God's
steward, not self-willed, not quick-tempered, not
addicted to wine, not pugnacious, not fond of sordid
gain, but hospitable, loving what is good, sensible, **just**.*
—TITUS 1:7,8

In November 1515, an Augustinian monk named Martin Luther
began to teach the book of Romans to his students at the University
of Wittenberg. As professor of sacred theology, he labored long and
hard in preparing his lectures. He was captivated and challenged
regarding what Paul stated about justification by faith. "I greatly long
to understand Paul's Epistle to the Romans," he later wrote, "and
nothing stood in the way but that one expression, 'the righteousness
of God,' because I took it to mean that righteousness whereby God is
righteous and deals righteously in punishing the unrighteous."

"I FELT MYSELF TO BE REBORN"

After wrestling in his mind with this concept for a long period of time,
the Holy Spirit eventually penetrated Luther's heart. He suddenly
"grasped the truth that the righteousness of God is that righteousness
whereby, through grace and sheer mercy, He justifies us by faith.
Thereupon," Luther testified, "I felt myself to be reborn and have gone

through open doors into paradise. The whole of Scripture took on a new meaning, and whereas before 'the righteousness of God' had filled me with hate, now it became to me an inexpressibly sweet and greater love. This passage of Paul became to me a gateway to heaven."[1]

TWO BASIC MEANINGS

New Testament writers used the word "just" (*dikaios*) in two basic ways. *First*, "to become just" describes what happens when we are saved. This was Martin Luther's great spiritual discovery. *Second*, "to be just" describes the way we should live after we are saved. Obviously, Paul had the second meaning in mind when he used dikaios to describe a quality of Christian maturity.

More specifically, it seems Paul used the word "just" in his letter to Titus to describe a person who does what is "right" or "fair." In this sense, a "just man" is equitable and impartial. For example, when he makes decisions, they are "just" decisions. Stating it another way, a "just man" is someone who is "righteous" and "upright" in all of his relationships.

THE JUST SHALL LIVE BY FAITH

Luther's experience describes the most foundational way *dikaios* and related words are used by New Testament writers to describe what happens to a person who comes to know Jesus Christ as personal Lord and Savior. Paul stated this clearly in his letter to the Romans, although it took Luther a long time to grasp this truth:

> For I am not ashamed of the gospel of Christ: for it is the power of God unto salvation to everyone that believeth; to the Jew first and also to the Greek. For therein is the right-eousness [*dikaiosune*] of God revealed from faith to faith: as it is written, The just [dikaios] shall live by faith (Rom. 1:16,17, *KJV*; see also Gal. 3:11 and Heb. 10:38).

Positional Righteousness

In Romans 1:16,17, and in many others, Paul was referring to what theologians call "positional righteousness." When we put our faith in

Jesus Christ for salvation, God sees us as being as righteous as Christ Himself. This is the only way any person can ever be saved. Jesus Christ Himself is our righteousness (see 1 Cor. 1:30). This is the great truth that changed Martin Luther's life. In the words of Jesus, he was "born again" (John 3:3). Not only did this great truth in Paul's letter to the Romans change Luther's life, but God also used him to help change the world. "The just shall live by faith" became his clarion call.

This should not surprise us, because Paul used some form of the word dikaios more than 20 times in the first five chapters of Romans to refer to the fact that we are made "righteous" or "just" in God's sight by faith in Jesus Christ.

JUSTIFIED MEN SHOULD BECOME JUST MEN

Once we truly understand and experience God's grace in justifying us and making us "just" or "righteous" in God's sight, it becomes a foundational experience in enabling and challenging us to become "just" in our walk with God and in our relationships with others. It should become a mark of Christian maturity, which is what Paul was referring to in his letter to Titus. Of all people, "justified men" should become "just men."

God dealt with us "justly" not because we deserved it, but because of His love, mercy and grace. This should motivate every Christian to first of all live a just and righteous life before God, and second, to deal justly with others.

Further on in his letter to Titus, Paul encouraged all Christians to demonstrate compassion, sensitivity and concern toward both Christians and non-Christians (see 3:2). Paul made this appeal based on what Jesus Christ has done for us. After stating that we should show **"every consideration for all men"** (3:2), Paul went on to say:

> For we also once were foolish ourselves, disobedient, deceived, enslaved to various lusts and pleasures, spending our life in malice and envy, hateful, hating one another. But when the kindness of God our Savior and His love for mankind appeared, He saved us, not on the basis of deeds which we have done in righteousness, but according to His

mercy, by the washing of regeneration and renewing by the Holy Spirit, whom He poured out upon us richly through Jesus Christ our Savior, that being justified by His grace we might be made heirs according to the hope of eternal life (vv. 3-7).

A CASE OF TERRIBLE INJUSTICE

In October 1982, a young black man named Lenell Geter was sentenced to life in prison for allegedly robbing a fried-chicken restaurant of $615 in Greenville, Texas. Geter was a well-respected engineer and had no police record. Fortunately, after serving 477 days in prison, he was released and eventually exonerated.

Geter had been falsely accused. Both racial prejudice and shoddy police work precipitated this horrible injustice. Those of you who may have watched the exposé on "60 Minutes" will remember the shameful way this case was originally handled.

This kind of injustice has another side. It involves those who are guilty, but never pay the consequences. A Supreme Court justice once said to a man who had appeared before him in one of the lower courts and escaped conviction on the basis of a technicality, "I know that you are guilty and you know it, and I wish you to remember that one day you will stand before a better and wiser Judge and that there you will be dealt with according to justice and not according to law."

JUSTICE AND FAIRNESS

Unfortunately, a lot of *injustice* occurs in this world—we can do little about much of it. In some situations, we must wait for God to set the record straight, even in areas where we believe we have been treated unjustly. We must turn the matter over to the great Judge of the universe. That is why Paul instructed the Roman Christians to never take their "own revenge" but to "leave room for the wrath of God" (12:19).

On the other hand, God gives us opportunities every day to practice justice and to be upright in our dealings with our fellow human beings, especially in our relationships in our immediate families, with our fellow Christians and as we associate with non-Christians who regularly cross our paths.

When Paul wrote to the Colossians and exhorted "masters" to grant to their slaves "justice and fairness, knowing that you too have a Master in heaven" (Col. 4:1), he illustrated what he had in mind when he told Titus that spiritually mature people are "just." The translators of the *Amplified New Testament* captured this meaning when they rendered this concept as being "upright and fair-minded" (Titus 1:8).

Inexcusable, But It Happens

Through the years, I have seen people hurt—desperately hurt—because of self-centered, insensitive and hard-hearted Christians. One of the saddest comments I have ever heard from believers is that they would rather do business with non-Christians than with Christians because Christians, they say, are more unfair, irresponsible and in some cases, more ruthless than non-Christians.

I realize, as most people do, that one bad experience with a Christian can cause someone to generalize about every Christian. I have met believers who have written off Christianity, at least going to church, because they have had one bad experience with a so-called Christian leader. How unfortunate.

A Two-Way Street

We all tend to generalize, to judge "groups" by single encounters. I have met Christians who have "written off" a whole seminary because they have had a bad experience with a single graduate. This in itself reflects injustice, prejudice and unfair judgments. In a sense, "the pot is calling the kettle black." It tells us that a lot of us are immature when it comes to practicing the quality of being "just." It is a two-way street.

But the facts are that it happens, and it is all the more reason to live a righteous and God-fearing life. We must also realize that people simply expect more from people who claim to be followers of Jesus Christ.

A Shining Example

When it comes to being "just" in the way Paul was using this word in his letter to Titus, I can't help but think about Joseph, Mary's husband.

You know the story. Mary was engaged to be married to Joseph, but before they became husband and wife, she became pregnant through the power of the Holy Spirit (see Matt. 1:18). Needless to say, Joseph found himself in an embarrassing predicament. He was engaged—not legally married—and his wife-to-be was with child. Tongues were wagging.

A "Sanctified" Imagination

Try to imagine what was being said:

A friend:	"Joseph, what's with you and Mary? You're in big trouble, my friend. People are talking all over town."
A priest:	"Joseph, you rascal! I want to see you in my office first thing in the morning. You know better than to take advantage of Mary. Furthermore, you've brought disgrace on all of us in Israel."
The parents	"You two ought to be ashamed of yourselves! What do you think we've taught you all these years? What are people going to think of us?"
Joseph and Mary:	"You're really not going to believe this, but..."
The People's Responses:	"Incredible! We've heard of rationalizations before, but this is one of the biggest and boldest we've heard yet! An angel appeared? Angels are sexless! The Holy Spirit? Well, the Holy Spirit only came upon great people like David and some of the other outstanding prophets. You're both crazy if you think you can get by with this one!"

Joseph Was a "Just" Man

Note how Joseph responded, "And Joseph her husband, being a righteous [dikaios] man, and not wanting to disgrace her, desired to put her away secretly" (v. 19).

If we look casually at Joseph's response, we might conclude he was simply embarrassed and trying to save his own reputation. Not so. He was concerned for Mary because he was a *just man*. He understood her plight and the price she was paying to be the mother of the Son of God. He didn't want to expose her to public disgrace.

God Honors Justice

Mercifully, God stepped in and reassured Joseph that their predicament and humiliation were only temporary (see vv. 20,21). The pain they would have to bear, caused by those who were critical because of their ignorance, insensitivity and unbelief, would be well worth it when the angels sang from heaven, "Glory to God in the highest, and on earth peace among men with whom He is pleased" (Luke 2:14). And when the wise men from the East would later bring gifts, lay them at the feet of Jesus and recognize Him as a King, it would be worth it all.

Injustice Today

How many men do you know who have gotten women pregnant out of wedlock and then left them to bear the burden that resulted from a moment of lust and self-indulgence? Or, worse yet, they escaped their responsibilities with "pay offs" and helped the women get abortions.

Don't misunderstand. I am not putting all the blame on men. This kind of sin is a two-way street. But how easy it is to take advantage of someone else and then allow the person to struggle through the problem all alone. That is the ultimate in *unjust* behavior.

May God give us more men like Joseph—upright, just men who are willing to put their own egos behind them and be concerned for others.

THE FALLEN AND HURTING CHRISTIAN

On one occasion, a former student of mine stopped by my office unannounced. It was one of those hectic days. I had been up since 3:30 in the morning working on a writing project. When he arrived, I was just completing a rather heavy meeting in the middle of the afternoon and was about to "crash" and call it quits for the day. Frankly, I didn't feel like *seeing* anyone, let alone *talking* to someone.

Although I hadn't seen this man for years, I recognized his name and invited him into my office, hoping it would only take a few minutes. But God had other plans.

After some small talk, he began to unfold a sad story, one he said he had not intended to tell. After graduation from the school where I taught, he married a girl who was also one of my students. He became a pastor.

A Marital Disaster

From the beginning, his marriage was in trouble. Every story always has two sides, but I believe I heard enough and knew enough to conclude that his report was fairly accurate. His wife became a thorn in his side, a millstone around his neck. She was always hurting other people's feelings in his congregation, creating divisions, gossiping and keeping his own family in a state of confusion. His life as a pastor was filled with embarrassment and heartache. After a number of years, he became so frustrated that he gave up. In anger and resentment, he divorced her and left the ministry.

A Root of Bitterness

When he arrived in my office that day, he had been wandering in the wilderness for nearly three years. He admitted that he had sinned during that time, becoming involved sexually with another woman. In recent months, he had broken off the relationship because he knew it was wrong. He felt helpless, frustrated and rejected by even his closest friends. The people in his former church, to whom he had given his life for many years, had dropped him like a hot potato, although they knew his life had been a living hell. No one reached out to help him.

One day he had stopped to see another pastor he knew well. The pastor was just concluding a counseling session and his secretary called him on the intercom telling him who was waiting. The pastor responded by saying he was too busy, too busy to step out of his office and say hello to a man he definitely knew was hurting.

I Almost Blew It

As this man was relating this story, he suddenly broke down and wept. He wasn't justifying himself. He acknowledged his anger and his bitterness. He confessed his guilt about the fact that he had finally given up and divorced his wife and left the ministry, even though he had been advised by four well-known pastors that he probably didn't have any choice in the matter. "But, Gene," he said through tears, "the man wouldn't even say hello to me!"

My own heart began to quiver. I had almost done the same thing that afternoon. Thank God, the Holy Spirit didn't let me do it, as tired as I was. I sat and listened to his story for more than two hours. I literally felt his pain.

After listening, I suggested some biblical steps for getting his life back in order and in harmony with the will of God. He listened. "I want to help you out," I said. "My time is limited, but I want to help."

We All Need a Listening Ear

I will never forget his response. He looked down and tried to fight the tears. "Gene, what you just said means more to me than anything I've heard for the last three years. Though I may never bother you again and though I may not take your advice totally, I know you care and right now I just need a friend who will listen."

I would be dishonest if I told you it was easy in that moment to be just and upright and caring. It is impossible for me to talk with everyone who wants to share a burden. If I tried, I would probably end up in desperate straights myself. But I thank God I didn't let that one pass me by. And the good news is, the man eventually responded and is now once again walking with the Lord.

POINTS OF ACTION

The following project will help you develop the quality of "being just" in your relationships with others.

A Gift of God

• Make sure you clearly understand Paul's statement that the "just shall live by faith."

Remember that the Word of God uses the term "just" in two ways. The first way involves your salvation experience. The second involves the way you live as a Christian.

Paul described both concepts in two wonderful verses in his letter to the Ephesians:

Your Salvation Experience

> For by grace you have been saved through faith; and that not of yourselves, it is the gift of God; not as a result of works, that no one should boast (2:8,9).

Your Walk with Christ

> For we are His workmanship, created in Christ Jesus for good works, which God prepared beforehand, that we should walk in them (v. 10).

What Paul described in this paragraph contains one of the most critical distinctions in Christian theology. As we have seen illustrated in Martin Luther's life, it is perhaps the one area that Satan has used most frequently to confuse people through the centuries, in spite of the fact that it is one of the clearest teachings in Scripture.

This doctrinal error runs through every major religion in the world, including the offshoots of Christianity that we call "cults" and "isms."

The following are several ways this error is reflected. Check yourself. How well do you understand the salvation experience? All of the following are incorrect.

___ A person can be saved by works.

___ A person can be saved by a mixture of faith and works.

___ A person can be saved by faith and keep himself saved by works.

___ A person can be saved even though he doesn't demonstrate any works.

Unfortunately, some people believe that a simple "profession of faith" results in salvation. One thing is clear from Scripture. We *are* saved by faith, but *true faith* will eventually produce works. James made this point clear when he said, "Even so faith, if it has no works, is dead, being by itself" (2:17).

Saving faith will eventually produce the works of righteousness God planned for our lives. The extent to which we do these works, however, still depends on our commitment to Jesus Christ and our desire to do His will.

Consider Elijah

• Evaluate the extent to which you are living a "righteous" or "just" life as a Christian.

When James used Elijah to illustrate the power of prayer, he used the word dikaios to refer to a Christian who is living a godly life. This is why he exhorted:

> Therefore, confess your sins to one another, and pray for one another, so that you may be healed. The effective prayer of a **righteous** [just] man can accomplish much (5:16).

When New Testament writers used the word "just" in this sense, they meant that we are to live upright, righteous and holy lives as Christians. We are to obey God and keep His commandments. Once we are made righteous (just) by faith in Christ, we are then to reflect Christ's righteous (just) life by the way we live. This is also what Paul meant when he wrote to the Ephesians:

> For you were formerly darkness, but now you are light in the Lord; walk as children of light (for the fruit of the light consists in all goodness and **righteousness** [dikaiosune] and truth), trying to learn what is pleasing to the Lord (5:8-10).

Consult a Friend

• Ask someone you trust to help you evaluate your relationships with others regarding the extent you are just, fair, impartial and equitable.

___ Your relationship with your wife.

___ Your relationship with your children.

___ Your relationship with your neighbors.

___ Your relationship with your fellow employees.

___ Your relationship with others.

THINKING AND GROWING TOGETHER

The following questions are designed for group discussion after reading and studying the content of this chapter:

1. When did you understand what it means to be "justified by faith"? Would you share your salvation experience?
2. Why is it easy to get confused regarding how a person is saved?
3. What experiences have you had (or observed) where people have been treated "unjustly"? How could things have been handled differently?
4. Can you think of relationships where you would like to be treated more "fairly" and "equitably"? Would you share these concerns for prayer?
5. Can you think of relationships where you would like to be more "just" and fair in your dealings with others? Would you share these concerns for prayer?

SET A GOAL

Write out one goal you'd like to achieve as a result of this study:

_____

_____

_____

_____

Note
1. *Luther's Works*, Weimer Edition, Vol. 54, pp. 179ff.

19

LIFTING UP HOLY HANDS

For the overseer must be above reproach
as God's steward, not self-willed, not quick-tempered,
not addicted to wine, not pugnacious, not fond of
sordid gain, but hospitable, loving what is good,
sensible, just, devout [holy].
—TITUS 1:7,8

Several years ago, my wife and I visited Guatemala. One experience left a marked impression on my life.

BLEEDING KNEES

In one small village, one of the missionaries drew our attention to a church that had a long series of steps leading up to a large courtyard. We then noticed people crawling on their hands and knees up the concrete steps through the courtyard and then into the church. Periodically, people went through this routine, although their knees would eventually bleed as they crawled the hundreds of yards over the rough concrete surface.

What would cause people to engage in this kind of religious ritual? They believed that this was a way they could become holy and experience forgiveness for their sins. Although these people were obviously sincere, they were terribly confused. Paul *did* say he wanted "men in every place to pray, **lifting up holy hands**," but nowhere does God say Christians are to have "bleeding knees" to obtain and maintain holiness (1 Tim. 2:8).

NEW TESTAMENT SYNONYMS

At least three Greek words are often translated "holy." Together, these words in their various forms are used approximately 300 times in the New Testament, which demonstrates how important this concept is in God's plan for His children.

The word used most frequently is *hagios*. A second word is *hosios* and the third is *hagnos*. Although this third word is considered a synonym, it is usually translated with the English words "pure" or "chaste."

The Greek word Paul used in writing to Titus to describe an aspect of Christian maturity is hosios. As just stated, Paul used this same word when he wrote to Timothy and said, "Therefore I want the men in every place to pray, **lifting up holy hands**, without wrath and dissension" (1 Tim. 2:8). Paul also used this basic word when he wrote to the Thessalonians, reminding them of the way he and his coworkers lived among these people:

> You are witnesses, and so is God, how **devoutly** [holily] and uprightly and blamelessly we behaved toward you believers (1 Thess. 2:10).

MISPERCEPTIONS

I have already illustrated a serious misperception regarding "holiness" by telling of our experience in Guatemala. We cannot earn holiness by engaging in religious rituals. Neither can we develop it by abusing our bodies. Let's take an in-depth look at some of the other serious misunderstandings regarding this wonderful biblical truth.

Perfectionism

• **Paul was not teaching that Christians can become perfect in this life.**

Most Christians, if they are honest with themselves, will acknowledge they are not living in every respect as Jesus Christ lived. He was the only perfect man who ever lived. He came to earth as the "God-man," and because He was God in the flesh, He never sinned. The apostle John explained this beautifully in the Gospel that bears his name:

> In the beginning was the Word, and the Word was with God, and the **Word was God.** And the Word became flesh, and dwelt among us, and we beheld His glory, glory as of the only begotten from the Father, full of grace and truth (1:1,14).

As Christians, we will not have glorified bodies like Jesus Christ's body until we are transformed into His image when He comes again (see 1 Cor. 15:51-53). This, I believe, is what Paul had in mind when he wrote to the Corinthians:

> For now we see in a mirror dimly, but then face to face; now I know in part, but then I shall know fully just as I also have been fully known (13:12).

Guilt, Self-Deception and Hopelessness

Christians who are are taught that they can become perfect in this life often suffer horrible guilt when they fail. And Christians *do* sin. This is why the New Testament letters continually exhort Christians to renew their minds and to "be transformed" into Christ's image (Rom. 12:2). This was Paul's goal, too. He knew he had not "become perfect" (Phil. 3:12).

This point of view can also cause Christians to rationalize sinful attitudes and actions as being unsinful, which is a form of self-deception and is sin in itself.

Others who take a perfectionistic approach to the Christian life simply give up when they sin. They believe they have failed God and have no real hope. Some also believe they have committed the unpardonable sin, which is a tragic point of view.

A Sad Story

I had a close friend in high school who became a Christian approximately the same time I did. Both of us were sincere people, but theologically confused in certain areas. I thought I had to live a certain way to "keep myself saved." My friend believed that all Christians can have an experience with God that enables them to reach a level of holiness that keeps them from failing God.

Eventually, I learned that my standing before God—my eternal salvation—was not dependent upon my good works as a Christian. What a relief that was. But sadly, my friend experienced moral failure. I remember talking with her one day only to discover that she believed God had given up on her because of her sin. She had lost hope. Nothing I could say seemed to help her understand that God had not forsaken her. Rather, she had forsaken him and didn't believe God would forgive her. Even the story of the prodigal son couldn't reach her. Unfortunately, this same thing happens to some Christians who are taught they can become perfect in this life.

Asceticism

• **Paul was not teaching ascetic practices.**

During the fourth century particularly, hundreds of people sought to escape temptation by punishing their bodies and by living as hermits. They went to incredible extremes to overcome "temptations" and "physical lusts." Saint Esemius wore so many chains that he had to crawl around on his hands and knees. Beserian, a monk, would not give in to his body's desire for rest or sleep. For 40 years, he would not lie down while sleeping.

Christianity and Greek Philosophy

This happened primarily because many of the Greek philosophers taught that the body is evil and the spirit is good. Because our bodies *do* give us a lot of problems that lead us into sinful actions, it was relatively easy for Christians living at that time to synchronize this thinking with Christian theology.

Separation Doesn't Mean Isolation

Asceticism causes Christians to remove themselves from the world and concentrate on themselves. This is a direct contradiction to what Jesus taught. We are to be the "light of the world" (Matt. 5:14). We are to let our "light shine before men" so they may see our good works and glorify our Father who is in heaven (see v. 16). Paul also stated that we are to be in the world, but not part of the world (see 1 Cor. 5:9,10). In other words, it is possible to live in this world and still live a holy life. That is one of the reasons God has left us on earth: to communicate His holiness to those who do not know God.

Self-Denial

• **Paul was not teaching that Christians can become holy by denying themselves what God has created to be normal and natural.**

Today, many people still take vows of chastity, giving up the right to be married. They believe this will make them holy in God's sight.

The Scriptures clearly teach that abstaining from legitimate sexual relations is not a sign of or a means to holiness. Vows of chastity have led to some of the worst forms of sexual immorality. Today, it has demonstrated itself in a groundswell of child abuse. Sadly, innocent people—children particularly—become victims of this false teaching.

Interestingly, Paul stated only one reason for married people to abstain from sexual relations. Writing to the Corinthians, he said:

> Stop depriving one another, except by agreement for a time that you may devote yourselves to prayer, and come together again lest Satan tempt you because of your lack of self-control (7:5).

Legalism

• **Paul was not teaching a legalistic form of Christianity.**

Some Christians believe they can become holy by following a set of rules.

An Emphasis on Externals

I grew up in this kind of religious community where we followed a set of rules. And yet I noticed—even as a young Christian—that these people often reflected jealousy and pride. They were judgmental and prejudiced against people who were not a part of our particular "religious community." They gossiped about one another and were often bitter. In essence, they overlooked those *internal qualities* that are so important to true holiness.

This is exactly what the Pharisees did on many occasions. They set up legalistic rules and then planned ways to circumvent those rules. Jesus condemned this kind of behavior (see Mark 7:9-13).

Religious Rituals

Some Christians believe the degree of holiness they attain is directly related to the amount of time they spend in prayer, Bible study and other forms of religious exercise. This, too, is a form of legalism. As with all people who are attempting to become holy in nonbiblical ways, these people are sincere. Some people spend hours and hours in prayer and meditation. This they believe is a means to holiness and they promote this as the only way to obtain this kind of holiness.

This kind of thinking also contains a serious pragmatic flaw. If holiness can only be obtained and maintained by spending hours in the presence of God, this would mean that ordinary Christians, who have to go to work every day, who have to spend time caring for their families and facing other demands in life, cannot be as holy as those who spend hours in prayer and meditation.

The Peril of the Pendulum

As usually happens, we have also gone to the other extreme and neglected these important aspects of the Christian life. Prayer and Bible study *are* essential to Christian growth and maturity. Every time I complete an extensive time-log study, I am convicted that I am not spending more time with God. The fact still remains that this can become a legalistic activity that doesn't lead to true holiness.

Some Christians also overreact to "legalism" by moving to "license." They take liberties in their lifestyles that definitely violate the will of God. We must beware of the "peril of the pendulum."

A BIBLICAL PERSPECTIVE

Positional Holiness

• **All Christians are perfectly holy in God's sight in terms of their position in Christ.**

All believers are identified as "saints" in the New Testament. The basic word hagios is translated "saints" approximately 60 times. The Corinthians, as sinful and carnal as they were, were also called "saints," or those who "have been sanctified in Christ Jesus" (1 Cor. 1:2). Literally, Paul was calling these people "holy ones" in spite of their worldly lifestyles, which included envy, strife and divisions (see 3:3); pride and arrogance (see v. 21); immorality and drunkenness (see 5:1-6; 11:20,21); and an unwillingness to forgive other Christians (see 6:1,6,8).

Paul also underscored this truth in his letter to the Colossians when he identified these believers "as those who have been chosen of God, holy and beloved" (3:12). God, therefore, sees us as already perfect because of His perfect Son, Jesus Christ. If this were not true, no one could be saved. Theologians often call this great doctrinal truth "positional sanctification." In the mind of God, we are already set apart as His holy people. In His sight, we are already "glorified" (Rom. 8:30). This happens the moment we put our faith in Christ and are saved.

Progressive Holiness

• Becoming holy and Christlike while on this earth is a progressive process that will continue until we are with Jesus Christ in heaven.

This is the great emphasis in the New Testament letters. Again and again we are instructed to become like Christ in His holiness. When writing to the Corinthians who were living such carnal and sinful lives, Paul addressed their sins and urged them to pursue holy lives that reflected Christ's love and the fruit of the Holy Spirit (see 1 Cor. 13:1-13).

Paul's prayer for the Thessalonians summarizes God's plan for believers of all time.

> Now may the God of peace Himself **sanctify you entirely;** and may your spirit and soul and body be preserved complete, without blame at the coming of our Lord Jesus Christ (1 Thess. 5:23).

Theologians often identify this process as "progressive sanctification."

Commitment

• **Becoming holy as God intended involves an act of the will following our conversion to Jesus Christ.**

Again, this is the thrust of many New Testament letters, particularly after the Holy Spirit inspired the authors of these letters to explain our positions in Christ. Paul's letters to the Ephesians and Romans most clearly illustrate this emphasis. For example, in the first three chapters of Ephesians, Paul outlined *our position in Christ*. In the last three chapters, he instructed us to *become like Christ*, "to walk in a manner worthy of the calling with which" we "have been called" (4:1).

We see the same pattern in the letter to the Romans. The first 11 chapters outline in great detail God's mercy in saving us. The remaining chapters describe how we are to live a holy life in view of God's mercies (see 12:1,2).

Walking in the Spirit

• **The degree to which we live holy lives depends upon the extent to which we keep in step with the Holy Spirit and His plan for our lives.**

It is not an accident that the word hagios is used approximately 90 times to identify God's Spirit as "holy." Writing to the Galatians, Paul made this point very specific:

> But I say, **walk by the Spirit**, and you will not carry out the desire of the flesh. For the flesh sets its desire against the Spirit, and the Spirit against the flesh; for these are in opposition to one another, so that you may not do the things that you please (5:16,17).

Every Christian has a choice. Either we are going to "walk by the Spirit" (v. 25) and do what *He* desires, or we will keep in step with the sinful nature and do what *we* desire.

This, too, is a choice. Either we choose to present the members of our bodies "to sin as instruments of unrighteousness," or we choose to present ourselves to God as "alive from the dead" and then yield our body members "as instruments of righteousness to God" (Rom. 6:13). When we choose to yield to God, we have chosen to "walk by the Spirit" and to draw upon His strength and power in order to live holy and righteous lives (see Eph. 3:16-19).

The Fruit of the Spirit

• **A Christian who walks by the Spirit will reflect the "fruit of the Spirit" rather than the "deeds of the flesh."**
   In Galatians 5, Paul outlined the fruit of the Holy Spirit—a true reflection of holiness—and then contrasted this "fruit" with the "deeds of the flesh."

"The Deeds of the Flesh"

Now the deeds of the flesh are evident, which are: immorality, impurity, sensuality, idolatry, sorcery, enmities, strife, jealousy, outbursts of anger, disputes, dissensions, factions, envying, drunkenness, carousing, and things like these (vv. 19-21).

"The Fruit of the Spirit"

But the fruit of the Spirit is love, joy, peace, patience, kindness, goodness, faithfulness, gentleness, self-control (vv. 22,23).

When we "walk in a manner worthy of the calling with which" we "have been called," we will reflect the "fruit of the Spirit" in all of our relationships (Eph. 4:1).

The Spirit and the Word

• **The primary resource that enables us to walk in the Spirit is the Holy Spirit Himself working through the Word of God.**
   The Holy Spirit is the author of Scripture. Men such as Paul and Peter and John were "moved by the Holy Spirit" as they "spoke from God" (2 Pet. 1:21).

Jesus told the apostles this would happen. Alone with His 11 men in the Upper Room (Judas had already left), Jesus said:

> "I have many more things to say to you, but you cannot bear them now. But when He, the **Spirit of truth**, comes, He will guide you into **all the truth**" (John 16:12,13).

That is exactly what happened when the Holy Spirit came. Initially, these men spoke the Word directly as it was revealed. Later, the Holy Spirit led them to write it down, which resulted in what we call the New Testament.

Writing to the Colossians, Paul said:

> Let the **word of Christ** richly dwell within you, with all wisdom teaching and admonishing one another with psalms and hymns and spiritual songs, singing with thankfulness in your hearts to God (3:16).

Because the Holy Spirit is the divine author of Scripture, and because He indwells every believer, He will enable us to live out these truths in our lives, if we yield our lives to Him (see Eph. 3:20,21).

Renewing Our Minds

• **The process of becoming holy is uniquely linked with how we use our minds.**

Paul followed his plea in Romans 12:1 by asking all of us to offer our bodies to God:

> And do not be conformed to this world, but be transformed **by the renewing of your mind**, that you may prove what the will of God is, that which is good and acceptable and perfect (v. 2).

How we use our minds is directly related to whether or not we are living a holy life. This is why Paul concluded his letter to the Philippians by saying:

Finally, brethren, whatever is true, whatever is honorable, whatever is right, whatever is pure, whatever is lovely, whatever is of good repute, if there is any excellence and if anything worthy of praise, **let your mind dwell on these things** (4:8).

Corporate Holiness

• **Although becoming holy is a personal experience, more is said in the New Testament about becoming holy as a corporate experience.**

Out of all the times hagios is used in the New Testament, 78 times it refers to becoming holy as a corporate body and only about 6 times to becoming holy as individual Christians.

Paul beautifully captures this truth in his letter to the Ephesians:

In whom the whole building, being fitted together is growing into a **holy temple** in the Lord; in whom you also are being built together into a dwelling of God in the Spirit (2:21,22).

It is true that each of us has a physical body that is described as the "temple of the Holy Spirit" (1 Cor. 6:19). But all of us *together* are also a temple of the Holy Spirit (see v. 19). God uniquely dwells in the Body of Christ, and it is His will that *together* we reflect the fruit of the Spirit, God's holiness. We need each other. That is why Paul also wrote to the Ephesians:

From whom the whole body, being fitted and held together by that which **every joint supplies**, according to the proper working of **each individual part**, causes the growth of the body for the building up of itself in love (4:16).

A BEAUTIFUL OLD TESTAMENT EXAMPLE

When all is said and done, holiness is still an individual matter. No one else can make the important decisions for us that cause us to grow in Christ and live a holy life.

Joseph's Stand for Righteousness

Joseph stands out in the Old Testament as a classic illustration of what holiness involves. After he was mercilessly sold into slavery by his brothers, God blessed him, and he miraculously became a servant in the household of Potiphar, a man who served Pharaoh as captain of the guard. Potiphar's wife was attracted to Joseph and tried to seduce him. Day after day she tempted him. But Joseph refused to sin against God and his master.

One day, however, all of the other servants were gone. This was her moment. We read that "she caught him by his garment, saying, 'Lie with me!' And he left his garment in her hand and fled, and went outside" (Gen. 39:12).

Joseph's Reflection of God's Holiness

Richard C. Trench, in his book entitled *Synonyms of the New Testament*, traces the origin of the three Greek words *hagios*, *hosios* and *hagnos*. He then uses Joseph as an illustration. He writes that when Joseph was "tempted to sin by his Egyptian mistress," he "approved himself hosios in reverencing those everlasting sanctities of the marriage bond, which God had founded, and which he could not violate without sinning against Him." Furthermore, Trench points out that Joseph "approved himself hagios in that he separated himself from any unholy fellowship with his temptress." And finally, "he approved himself hagnos in that he kept his body pure and undefiled."[1]

Joseph's Model for Christian Men Today

If Joseph could live a holy life in all three dimensions before the law was given at Mount Sinai, before Jesus Christ ever came to earth to model holiness, before the Holy Spirit came to indwell and assist mankind in living a holy life and before the Word of God was revealed in its entirety, how much more should we as Christians be able to live a holy life today? We have *all* of these resources at our disposal.

POINTS OF ACTION

This personal project is designed to help you develop the quality of living a more holy life.

Consult the Epistles

• **Read through the letters that were written to New Testament Christians to determine God's perspective on how to live a holy life.**

To understand holiness and how to live a holy life, we need to look carefully at the letters written to the New Testament churches and to those who were responsible to guide these new and growing bodies of believers—men such as Titus and Timothy.

This does not mean we should ignore teachings regarding holiness in the Gospels and in the book of Acts. However, we must not develop our views of how to live a holy life solely from these beginning sections of the New Testament. If we do, it can lead to some false concepts regarding holiness.

We must remember that the Gospels record the activities of Jesus Christ in laying the foundation for the Church. In the book of Acts, Luke recorded the activities of the apostles and other key New Testament leaders in launching local churches. *But the New Testament letters were written to give us specific instructions on how to live the Christian life.*

Check Yourself

• **As you read, develop a checklist based on exhortations outlined in each New Testament letter.**

The following is an example from Paul's letter to the Ephesians. These are specific exhortations Paul wrote to enable us to live a devout or holy life. As you read through this "checklist," evaluate how you "measure up" to God's expectations. Give yourself a plus (+) where you think you are doing fairly well. Give yourself a check (✓) where you would like to make some significant improvement.

___ "Laying aside falsehood, speak truth, each one of you, with his neighbor" (4:25).

___ "Be angry, and yet do not sin; do not let the sun go down on your anger" (v. 26).

___ "Let him who steals steal no longer; but rather let him labor, performing with his own hands what is good" (v. 28).

___ "Let no unwholesome word proceed from your mouth, but only such a word as is good for edification" (v. 29).

___ "Do not grieve the Holy Spirit of God" (v. 30).

___ "Let all bitterness and wrath and anger and clamor and slander be put away from you, along with all malice" (v. 31).

___ "Be kind to one another, tender-hearted, forgiving each other" (v. 32).

___ "Walk in love, just as Christ also loved you" (5:2).

___ "Do not let immorality or any impurity or greed even be named among you" (v. 3).

___ "There must be no filthiness and silly talk, or coarse jesting, which are not fitting, but rather giving of thanks" (v. 4).

___ "Walk as children of light (for the fruit of the light consists in all goodness and righteousness and truth)" (vv. 8,9).

___ "Do not participate in the unfruitful deeds of darkness, but instead even expose them" (v. 11).

___ "Be careful how you walk, not as unwise men, but as wise, making the most of your time" (vv. 15,16).

___ "Do not be foolish, but understand what the will of the Lord is" (v. 17).

___ "Do not get drunk with wine, for that is dissipation, but be filled with the Spirit" (v. 18).

___ "Be subject to one another in the fear of Christ" (v. 21).

___ "Wives, be subject to your own husbands, as to the Lord" (v. 22).

___ "Husbands, love your wives, just as Christ also loved the church" (v. 25).

___ "Children, obey your parents in the Lord" (6:1).

___ "Fathers, do not provoke your children to anger; but bring them up in the discipline and instruction of the Lord" (v. 4).

___ "Slaves, be obedient to those who are your masters according to the flesh" (v. 5).

___ "Masters, do the same things to them" (v. 9).

___ "Be strong in the Lord, and in the strength of His might" (v. 10).

___ "Put on the full armor of God, that you may be able to stand firm against the schemes of the devil" (v. 11).

___ "Stand firm therefore, having girded your loins with truth" (v. 14).

___ "Put on the breastplate of righteousness" (v. 14).

___ "Shod your feet with the preparation of the gospel of peace" (v. 15).

___ "In addition to all, taking up the shield of faith with which you

will be able to extinguish all the flaming missiles of the evil one"
(v. 16).

___   "And take the helmet of salvation, and the sword of the Spirit,
which is the word of God" (v. 17).

___   "With all prayer and petition pray at all times in the Spirit, and
with this in view, be on the alert with all perseverance and petition for all the saints" (v. 18).

Personalize Paul's Prayers

• **Read through Paul's prayers for New Testament Christians,
which are recorded in his prison Epistles, and personalize them.**
Most of Paul's prayers focus on living a more "holy" or "devout"
Christian life. For example, the following is Paul's prayer(s) for the
Ephesian Christians. To personalize this prayer, simply insert personal pronouns, such as "I," "me" and "my." You can also personalize
these prayers for your group by inserting plural pronouns such as
"us," "we" and "our."

For this reason I too, having heard of the faith in the Lord
Jesus which exists among you, and your love for all the
saints, do not cease giving thanks for you, while making
mention of you in my prayers; that the God of our Lord
Jesus Christ, the Father of glory, may give to you a **spirit
of wisdom and of revelation in the knowledge of Him.** I
pray that the eyes of your heart may be enlightened, so that
you may know what is the **hope of His calling,** what are the
riches of the glory of His inheritance in the saints, and what
is the surpassing **greatness of His power** toward us who
believe. For this reason, I bow my knees before the Father,
from whom every family in heaven and on earth derives its
name, that He would grant you, according to the riches of
His glory, to be **strengthened with power through His
Spirit** in the inner man; so **that Christ may dwell in your
hearts through faith;** and that you, being rooted and
grounded in love, may be able to comprehend with all the
saints what is the breadth and length and height and depth,
and **to know the love of Christ** which surpasses knowl-

edge, that you may be **filled up to all the fulness of God** (1:15-19; 3:14-19).

You will find other prayers in Philippians 1:9-11 and Colossians 1:9-12.

Thinking and Growing Together

The following questions are designed for group discussion after reading and studying the content of this chapter:

1. Why do most people want to "do something" to make themselves acceptable to God?
2. Why do people confuse "salvation by grace through faith" with a "works approach" for salvation?
3. What false approaches have you seen Christians use to try to become holy in God's sight? What are some of the negative results?
4. Would you feel free to share for prayer some of the areas in your life where you struggle the most in terms of reflecting God's holiness? (If the men in your group completed the exercise in the Ephesian letter on pp. 259-261, ask them if they would feel free to share for prayer some of the areas they checked for improvement. As a leader, share first of all from your own life.)

Set a Goal

Write out one goal you'd like to achieve as a result of this study:

_____
_____
_____
_____

Note

1. Richard C. Trench, *Synonyms of the New Testament* (Grand Rapids: William B. Eerdmans Publishing Co., 1948), pp. 333-334.

20

BECOMING A DISCIPLINED MAN

*For the overseer must be above reproach
as God's steward, not self-willed, not quick-
tempered, not addicted to wine, not pugnacious,
not fond of sordid gain, but hospitable, loving
what is good, sensible, just, devout,
self-controlled [disciplined].*
—TITUS 1:7,8

I remember attending a banquet after Tom Landry had coached the Dallas Cowboys to their second Super Bowl victory. During the course of the evening, Coach Landry paid tribute to Roger Staubach who had distinguished himself as one of the best quarterbacks in the NFL.

"There's a reason," Landry shared, "why Roger is so successful. He's a disciplined athlete!" Landry then illustrated his point by sharing with all of us that when the team concluded practice in training camp by running laps around the field, Roger always ran one more lap than anyone else.

Bob St. John, who authored *The Landry Legend*, added to this perspective, "Staubach was a tremendous competitor and also a catalyst, a guy who could turn a game around on individual effort."[1]

TEMPERATE, SELF-CONTROLLED, DISCIPLINED

As Paul concluded his maturity profile in his letter to Titus, he used the word *egkrate*, which is translated "temperate" in the *King James Version*, "self-controlled" in the *New American Standard Bible* and "disciplined" in the *New International Version*.[2] Personally, I prefer the word "disciplined" for several reasons. *First*, its basic concept is used in ancient Greek literature to describe a person who is "strong" and "robust." *Second*, the word itself originally meant "having power over, possessed of." *Third*, Paul used this word in several athletic illustrations to describe the importance of being "disciplined" when living the Christian life.

THE GREEK AND ROMAN GAMES

Greek athletic stadiums were located in several key cities throughout the Roman Empire. Consequently, New Testament writers often used athletic terms and metaphors to illustrate and describe the way Christians are to live their lives for Jesus Christ.

Paul was particularly intrigued with the athletic analogy. This is understandable. He grew up in Tarsus, attended the university there—which at the time was the foremost Greek university in the world, outstripping even the university of Athens in providing students with the best in educational experiences.

Tarsus was also a great center for athletic contests. Though a Jew, Paul grew up understanding Greek and Roman culture, particularly the commitment to develop physical strength and mental concentration in order to engage in vigorous competition in the various Olympic and Isthmian games.

The Foot Race

The Isthmian games, second only to the Olympic games, were held every three years at Corinth. This is apparently why Paul used an athletic metaphor to make a spiritual point in his first letter to the Corinthian Christians. He used a form of this word in his letter to draw a parallel between living a "disciplined Christian life" and being a "disciplined runner":

> Do you not know that those who **run in a race** all run, but

only one receives the prize? Run in such a way that you may win. And everyone who competes in the games exercises **self-control** [self-discipline] in all things (9:24,25).

PREPARATION IS THE KEY

When our daughter Robyn was a student at Baylor University, she decided to compete in her first marathon. She launched into a strict training program, running an average of 6 miles a day and 20 miles every Saturday.

When Robyn was in training, I well remember spending a day mountain climbing with her in Montana. I thought I was in fairly good shape physically, until I tried to keep up with her pace. By midafternoon I was in deep trouble, but fortunately made it down without having to be carried off the mountain on a stretcher. She was prepared. I wasn't.

Robyn continued this regimen for several months. Frankly, I was rather amazed at her commitment and self-discipline. It paid off, because she completed her first race averaging an 8½-minute mile.

What impressed me even more was her physical condition after she had run nonstop for 26 miles. Within five minutes, she was breathing normally and experiencing very little muscular discomfort. Because of her strict training program, she was in excellent physical condition. She not only disciplined herself by running, but also in a number of other ways, including what she ate, getting proper rest and so on.

IN ALL THINGS

In essence, Robyn's story is a modern-day elaboration on the metaphor Paul used in his letter to the Corinthians to illustrate what is involved in living a victorious Christian life. The major point Paul was making is that "everyone who competes in the games exercises self-control [discipline] **in all things**" (v. 25).

And so it is in the Christian life. We cannot reach the goal of becoming mature without being "disciplined in all things." This is why Paul exhorted Timothy:

> Discipline yourself for the purpose of godliness
> (1 Tim. 4:7).

Here Paul used the word *gumnazo*, which means to "exercise vigorously, either the body or the mind." In athletics, both are involved.

Physical Exercise Is Important

Paul definitely believed in physical exercise. So do I. We all know how important it is, particularly in the stress-oriented world we live in today. I have always enjoyed a variety of competitive sports and have participated regularly since my junior high school days. As I have aged, however, I have focused on racquetball to attempt to keep myself in relatively good physical condition.

Racquetball is a great "old man's" sport. It burns up lots of calories, and if you stay in relatively good shape, watch your diet and develop your skills, you can continue to compete at a fairly high level.

My personal goal is to play at least three times a week, and when I fail to maintain this level of exercise, I get lethargic, both physically and mentally. I also find myself getting edgy emotionally, which interferes with my spiritual goals. Stress builds up and I become more emotionally vulnerable in tense situations. This is why every able-bodied man should have some kind of exercise program.

But Spiritual Exercise Should Be a Priority

Physical exercise, when it is done properly, is definitely beneficial (see v. 8). It adds to our physical endurance and it helps us to be more mentally alert and emotionally stable and resilient. There is evidence that it may add months, and perhaps years, to our lives. But, as Paul implies, physical exercise benefits us *only* in this life. On the other hand, maintaining a healthy spiritual life "holds promise for the present life and also for the life to come" (v. 8).

Spirit and Soul and Body

We are integrated beings. This is why Paul prayed for the Thessalonian Christians that they might be sanctified completely, that their "**spirit** and **soul** and **body** be preserved complete, without blame at the coming of our Lord Jesus Christ" (1 Thess. 5:23).

Anyone who has done much counseling is well aware of how these three dimensions interrelate.[3] When we are not functioning well **physically**, it affects both our psychological and our spiritual lives. When we are not functioning well **mentally** and **emotionally** (our psychological dimension), it affects our physical and spiritual lives. And when we are out of God's will **spiritually**, it affects us physically and psychologically.

MAINTAINING PHYSICAL HEALTH

When you feel depressed (normally a psychological problem) and God "seems" far away (a spiritual problem), it is important to determine your physical condition. Are you exercising regularly? Are you getting enough rest? Are you experiencing any chemical imbalances? What about your hormone levels? This is why it is important to get a complete physical examination at least once a year.

"I'm Not Sure God Exists"

I remember a theological student coming to me one day having serious doubts about the existence of God. Here was a man preparing for the ministry, and yet he was having difficulty believing in the most important truth in Christianity.

After listening to him share his thoughts and feelings, I asked him how much sleep he had been getting. He reported that he had been studying night and day trying to unravel and understand some of the mysteries in the Scriptures. At that point, I asked him to do me a favor, to eat a good meal and then to go back to his room and go to bed and sleep as long as he could sleep.

The Doubts Were Gone

Several days later, the same man came back to see me. Guess what? His spiritual doubts were gone, simply because he had overcome his physical and psychological exhaustion.

In many respects, this man was just like Elijah, who after his great victory over the prophets of Baal, wanted to die. His thinking became horribly distorted. He was depressed and disillusioned.

God's prescription for bringing healing to Elijah was in essence what I suggested to this young student. God fed Elijah several good meals and then allowed him to sleep. Several days later, Elijah was a different man (see 1 Kings 19:1-8).[4]

Maintaining Psychological Health

But what if a person is tired all the time, even though he is eating well, exercising regularly and getting plenty of rest? If this ever happens to you, it is important to discover what is on your mind. What kind of stress are you experiencing? Are you repressing any angry feelings rather than dealing with them appropriately?

Psychosomatic Symptoms

This problem can also happen to children. I have seen cases where a child literally wants to die. They become withdrawn, and even ill. In some cases, they develop ulcers. Often the root of the problem is repressed anger. In some instances, they have not been allowed to cry or to express their negative feelings. And the problem is complicated even more when they are told that God is displeased with them when they get angry, which adds more guilt to the angry feelings they have already repressed. The end result is depression and some form of psychosomatic illness, and a distorted view of God.

Maintaining Spiritual Health

It is also true that Christians can experience *all* of the symptoms just mentioned because they are violating God's will. They have lost their appetites, they can't sleep well and they are depressed. They are edgy and impatient. The problem may be that they are experiencing real guilt over their sins, which is affecting both their psychological and physical well-being.

The Price of Deliberate Disobedience

I knew of a Christian man who was committing adultery with a divorced woman. There is no question but that he had a sensitive conscience. In his heart, he wanted to be a strong disciplined Christian. But he knew he was disobeying God. To complicate his guilt, he also knew that he never intended to marry this woman.

The end result of this man's sin was extreme depression—so much so that he couldn't function well on his job. Normally a high-energy person, he lost his desire to achieve. Though he had experienced several other stressful crises in his life, the main cause of his depression seemed to be his sin—living out of the will of God. When he refocused his spiritual life, the dark cloud that shrouded his soul disappeared.

WHICH IS WHICH?

It takes a great deal of wisdom to discern the real cause of a person's problem. This is particularly true because often a fine line exists between all three of these dimensions. Furthermore, these dimensions overlap. For example, a person's problem may indeed be rooted in the *psychological,* or in the *spiritual.* But, the "roots" are also sometimes embedded in both, or in all three. Usually, however, the problem is at least focused in one of these areas.

Whatever the root cause, God wants us to make our relationships with Him a priority. In some respects, this is what Jesus meant when He told us to "seek first His kingdom and His righteousness; and all these things shall be added to you" (Matt. 6:33). Jesus was first and foremost referring specifically to our material needs. What He said, however, can certainly be applied to our psychological happiness and physical well-being. When we keep ourselves in tune spiritually, it goes a long way in maintaining our physical and psychological health.

THE LIFE TO COME

The greatest reward for living a disciplined Christian life leading to godliness will come in eternity. Paul used the same basic athletic metaphor (running the race) when writing to the Philippians, another group of New Testament Christians who would clearly understand this analogy. Paul simply assumed that they would understand the metaphor behind his thoughts when he wrote:

> Not that I have already obtained it, or have already become perfect, but I press on in order that I may lay hold of that

for which also I was laid hold of by Christ Jesus. Brethren,
I do not regard myself as having laid hold of it yet; but one
thing I do: forgetting what lies behind and reaching forward
to **what lies ahead**, I **press on** toward the **goal** for the **prize**
of the upward call of God in Christ Jesus (3:12-14).

THE RACE ISN'T OVER

In this paragraph from Philippians, Paul referred to his own
Christian journey, likening it once again to a foot race. In this
metaphor, Paul placed himself in the race (his personal Christian
experience), but he was still "reaching forward to what lies ahead."
He hadn't reached the "goal" (eternity) and he hadn't received the
"prize" (eternal rewards).

As with any metaphor, this one has various applications, and
inherent in this analogy is another dimension of the Christian life.
The "race itself" is a "training" and "learning" process. The longer
Paul diligently "ran the race," the more mature and stronger he
became in his Christian faith.

BECOMING AN ALL-PRO ATHLETE

Ask any seasoned and successful quarterback in the NFL about his
football experience and he will identify with Paul's analogy. There is
only one way to really "grow" in the position and to become an "all
pro." You have to play the game. A quarterback has to get off the
practice field and compete in regular season games. The more real-
life experience he has competing against other professional athletes,
the better he can read the defense, stay in the pocket as long as necessary and be able to set up and see both his primary and secondary
receivers. And no matter how long he has been playing the position,
he will tell you, if he is honest, there is always more to learn.

So it is in the Christian life. Paul illustrates with his own life in this
letter to the Philippians that no matter how long we have been "running the race," we haven't entered the final meet. And no matter how
much we train, there is still room for improvement. We will not complete "the race" and receive the "victor's crown" until Jesus Christ
takes us home to glory.

CONDITIONING AND CONCENTRATION

We don't really know who wrote the book of Hebrews. But whoever it was, the author—like Paul—had a good grasp of what is involved in participating in an athletic contest. He, too, used the Greek and Roman games to illustrate and describe the disciplines involved in living the Christian life. Thus, we read:

> Therefore, since we have so great a cloud of witnesses surrounding us, let us also **lay aside every encumbrance**, and the sin which so easily entangles us, and **let us run with endurance** the race that is set before us, **fixing our eyes on Jesus**, the author and perfecter of faith (12:1,2).

The author of Hebrews broadens this athletic metaphor by using the word *agona*, a Greek athletic term that refers to a "contest." Consequently, the author could be referring to a "foot race," or to other Greek games involving intense competition and self-discipline, such as fighting wild beasts, boxing, wrestling and throwing the discus.

LAY ASIDE EVERY ENCUMBRANCE

To compete effectively in these games, an athlete had to "lay aside every encumbrance." He must "throw off everything that hinders" *(NIV)*. The Greek word is *ogkon*, which refers to "bulk" and "mass," and which can refer to excessive weight of any kind, including our own body weight.

A Startling Lesson

Most overweight people have difficulty competing effectively in athletic activities that call for quickness, speed and endurance. For example, I love downhill skiing. But I learned a rather startling lesson several years ago. I had allowed myself to put on 10 pounds beyond my normal weight. While skiing, I noticed I had trouble breathing, something that hadn't bothered me before. In fact, at extremely high altitudes where I had skied without any difficulties on previous occasions, I actually thought I was going to hyperventilate. Whereas before I loved to lead the pack down the mountain, I now could hardly keep up. Furthermore, my skills had deteriorated. I couldn't trust my abilities.

And then it suddenly dawned on me why I was having so much trouble. I was overweight. To test my theory, I went on a weight-loss program the next month and then went skiing again. The difference was remarkable. I could breathe again. My endurance was back. I could concentrate and stay in control.

LET US RUN WITH ENDURANCE

The author of Hebrews immediately identified any excessive weight as "the sin which so easily entangles us" (v. 1).

Flagrant Sins

Some sins totally immobilize us spiritually. Paul called them the "deeds of the flesh," acts of "immorality, impurity, sensuality, idolatry, sorcery, enmities, strife, jealousy, outbursts of anger, disputes, dissensions, factions, envyings, drunkenness, carousing, and things like these" (Gal. 5:19-21). This list obviously includes flagrant sins, "encumbrances" that will keep us from running the race "with endurance."

Bad Habits

But what about those "weights" that aren't so noticeable—habits, for example, that we may not consider sin. To be perfectly blunt, are you "10 pounds" overweight in your Christian life? Have you developed habits that keep you from being on the "cutting edge" spiritually— spending too much time watching television, attending movies and reading worthless literature? At the same time, are you neglecting your prayer life, church attendance and Bible reading? To be even more specific, have you developed habits of laziness? Do you lack self-discipline?

"Are these things sinful?" you ask. Obviously, you must be the judge. For me personally, anything that dulls my spiritual appetite and takes my eyes off Jesus Christ needs some careful attention. I just may be "10 pounds" overweight in my Christian life, and it is affecting my "endurance" in running the race that has been set before me.

FIXING OUR EYES ON JESUS

"Fixing our eyes on Jesus" is perhaps the most important lesson in this athletic metaphor. Any runner in the Greek stadium who took his eyes off the goal and either looked at the crowds, or his competitors, would lose valuable time and concentration. So it is in the Christian life. When we get our eyes off the Lord, and onto others, we are in danger of getting sidetracked spiritually.

There's Only One Perfect Man

I remember going through a difficult time in my own life as a young Christian. Several key spiritual leaders I looked up to "let me down." They didn't measure up to my expectations. Unfortunately, the experience became disillusioning—so much so I was tempted to forsake my goal of serving Jesus Christ in full-time ministry. Consequently, I spent a number of months "marking time"—worse yet, "losing time."

But in retrospect, I learned a valuable lesson. I had taken my eyes off Jesus Christ and put them on others. Unfortunately, these men weren't the best examples in the world. But I eventually learned that there is only one perfect man—the man Christ Jesus. He would never let me down.

Modeling the Life of Jesus Christ

Don't misunderstand. We all need Christians we can look up to as examples. That is why Paul told the Corinthians to imitate him as he imitated Jesus Christ (see 1 Cor. 11:1). But we must realize that even the most mature Christians will fail. It is then that we must refocus our eyes on Jesus Christ.

There is another lesson here. Young athletes need models they can look to, men from whom they can learn. You have just seen from Paul's statement that this is part of God's plan for learning to follow Jesus Christ. As a seasoned Christian, then, I must be careful how I live, realizing other Christians are looking to me to learn how to compete effectively. And one of the greatest ways to do this is to demonstrate how to keep our eyes on Jesus Christ and to never get sidetracked because other Christians fail to live up to our expectations.

THE HOMESTRETCH

Paul wrote his last letter while chained in a Roman dungeon. Here, Paul once again used an athletic metaphor to communicate with Timothy, his faithful coworker. Paul knew he was coming into the homestretch in his Christian race. Thus, he wrote, "For I am already being poured out as a drink offering, and the time of my departure has come" (2 Tim. 4:6).

Not too far away from where Paul was chained stood the great Roman coliseum. Sadly, the Roman games had already deteriorated into a spectator sport that involved fights that pitted men against beasts. The blood-hungry crowds were like animals themselves.

I Have Fought the Good Fight

As Paul penned his final letter to Timothy, he certainly visualized in his mind what was happening in this great arena several blocks away. Using athletic language, he wrote:

> I have fought the good **fight,** I have finished the **course, I** have kept the faith; in the future there is laid up for me the **crown** of righteousness, which the Lord, the righteous **Judge,** will **award** to me on that day; and not only to me, but also to all who have loved His appearing (vv. 7,8).

As Timothy read these words, he would clearly grasp what Paul meant. The word for "fight" *(agonizomai)* conjured up an image of Greek boxers who fought with ox-hide gloves interlaced with lead and iron. The battle itself was brutal, but to fail to win was even more tragic. The loser often had his eyes gouged out.

Our Real Competitor Is Satan

Paul's final metaphor underscores the seriousness of the Christian life. We are in a fight against the forces of evil. But Paul had won that fight. He had fought to the finish and he was about to receive the victor's crown. His faith had not failed him.

A PRIZE FIGHT

Paul used the same metaphor in his letter to the Corinthians. In the passage we referred to earlier, he not only made reference to a "foot race," but also to a "boxing match." Note again how often Paul used athletic language:

> And everyone who **competes** in the **games** exercises **self-control** [discipline] in all things. They then do it to receive a **perishable wreath**, but we an imperishable. Therefore I **run** in such a way, as not without **aim**; I **box** in such a way, as not **beating the air**; but I **buffet my body** and make it my slave, lest possibly, after I have preached to others, I myself should be **disqualified** (1 Cor. 9:25-27).

Paul had lived the Christian life victoriously, although he faced horrendous obstacles and powerful enemies, and for several reasons. *First,* he kept his eye on the goal—a face-to-face encounter with Jesus Christ and eternal rewards. He knew what he wanted to achieve. He was not like a boxer swinging wildly and missing his target.

Second, he prepared himself for the battle every moment of every day. He trained diligently. He didn't run out of energy because he was "out of shape" spiritually. He "exercised" himself to godliness.

Third, he competed "according to the rules" (2 Tim. 2:5). He didn't disqualify himself because of penalties.

Fourth, as he entered each battle, he drew on God's strength. He "kept the faith." To use another metaphor, he had "put on the whole armor of God," which enabled him to "be able to stand firm against the schemes of the devil" (Eph. 6:11).

SPIRITUAL DISCIPLINES

Unfortunately, some have interpreted Paul's statement to the Corinthians that he "beat his body" to justify an ascetic approach to life, particularly involving punishing the physical body. As stated in our previous chapter, this is not the way to develop perseverance. Paul did not literally beat his body to bring his passions and temptations under control. The essence of Paul's illustration is that as an athlete diligently exercises and engages in physical training, a Christian must engage in spiritual training. As Christian men particularly, we will never become the men God wants us to be without developing self-discipline in our Christian lives.

Getting Ready

For a couple of years, our son, Kenton, was a member of a Colorado ski team, specializing in downhill racing. Before his team ever went on the mountain, in fact, before the winter snows even came in, every member of the team engaged in a rigorous program of land training—bicycling, weight lifting, running and so on. It was vitally important that all racers be in excellent physical condition before they ever tackled the challenge of developing the mental and physical disciplines it took to develop specific skills on the slopes and to run gates at up to 85 miles per hour.

Our Training Manual

And so it is in the Christian life. We must prepare for those moments in life that call for endurance, intense concentration and effective skills. Fortunately, God has given us a wonderful training manual that outlines how to prepare for every challenge we will face. This manual—the Word of God—also outlines a "game plan" that will not fail. What is more, He guarantees continual victory if we simply obey His instructions and stay on the course He has charted for our lives.

POINTS OF ACTION

In essence, this book is designed to help each of us as Christian men to "discipline" ourselves "for the purpose of godliness" (1 Tim. 4:7). Paul's two profiles in his letters to Timothy and Titus outline for us 20 characteristics or qualities that define what this godliness actually is.

At the end of each chapter in this book, I have outlined several "Points of Action"—steps we can all take to develop these particular qualities in our lives. And now as we come to the end of this study, it is time to reflect back to see how we are doing.

An Opportunity to Evaluate

The following are the 20 characteristics we have studied, followed by a seven-point evaluation scale ranging from **dissatisfaction** to **satisfaction**.

Fill Out the Questionnaire

• Read each question carefully and then circle the number that best represents where you are in your spiritual journey. Be as honest as possible, but don't be too hard on yourself. Give yourself credit where credit is due.

Get Another Point of View

• If you are married, have your spouse fill out this questionnaire before you discuss the questions together. Then compare her scores with your own. If there are discrepancies, discuss why.

Note: If you are single, ask a close friend (of your own sex) to fill out the same survey and follow the same procedures just outlined.

Analyze the Results

• As a result of this process, first highlight your areas of strength. Then highlight areas where you want to grow and mature and become more disciplined.

Reread and Review

• Note the areas where you want to improve. Then go back to the chapters where these qualities are discussed in depth. Reread each chapter and then review the "Points of Action." Once again, set up specific goals you want to achieve in your Christian life.

Determine Your Maturity Quotient

Overall Spiritual Maturity

1. How do you evaluate your overall maturity as a Christian?
   Dissatisfied   1   2   3   4   5   6   7   Satisfied

Above Reproach

2. How do you evaluate your reputation as a Christian both among fellow believers as well as among non-Christians?
   Dissatisfied   1   2   3   4   5   6   7   Satisfied

The Husband of One Wife

3. How do you evaluate your relationship with your wife?
   Dissatisfied   1   2   3   4   5   6   7   Satisfied

Temperate

4. How do you evaluate the degree to which you are maintaining balance in your Christian experience?
   Dissatisfied   1   2   3   4   5   6   7   Satisfied

Prudent

5. How do you evaluate your ability to be wise and discerning?
   Dissatisfied   1   2   3   4   5   6   7   Satisfied

Respectable

6. How satisfied are you with the way your life reflects the life of Jesus Christ?
   Dissatisfied   1   2   3   4   5   6   7   Satisfied

Hospitable

7. How do you evaluate your level of generosity?
   Dissatisfied   1   2   3   4   5   6   7   Satisfied

Able to Teach

8. How do you evaluate your ability to communicate with others who may disagree with you?
   Dissatisfied   1   2   3   4   5   6   7   Satisfied

Not Addicted to Wine

9. To what degree are you satisfied with your ability to control various kinds of obsessions and compulsions?
   Dissatisfied   1   2   3   4   5   6   7   Satisfied

Not Self-Willed

10. How satisfied are you with your ability to relate to other people without being self-centered and controlling?
    Dissatisfied   1   2   3   4   5   6   7   Satisfied

Not Quick-Tempered

11. How satisfied are you with the way you handle anger?
    Dissatisfied   1   2   3   4   5   6   7   Satisfied

Not Pugnacious

12. How satisfied are you with your ability to control any form of verbal or physical abuse?
Dissatisfied   1   2   3   4   5   6   7   Satisfied

Gentle

13. How objective and fair minded are you in your relationships with others?
Dissatisfied   1   2   3   4   5   6   7   Satisfied

Uncontentious

14. How satisfied are you with your ability to avoid arguments?
Dissatisfied   1   2   3   4   5   6   7   Satisfied

Free from the Love of Money

15. How satisfied are you with your ability to be nonmaterialistic?
Dissatisfied   1   2   3   4   5   6   7   Satisfied

One Who Manages His Own Household Well

16. If you are a father, how satisfied are you with your ability to function in this role according to God's plan?
Dissatisfied   1   2   3   4   5   6   7   Satisfied

Loving What Is Good

17. To what degree are you satisfied with your efforts at "overcoming evil with good"?
Dissatisfied   1   2   3   4   5   6   7   Satisfied

Just

18. How satisfied are you with your ability to be just and fair in your relationships with others?
Dissatisfied   1   2   3   4   5   6   7   Satisfied

Devout

19. To what degree are you satisfied with the way your life reflects God's holiness?
Dissatisfied   1   2   3   4   5   6   7   Satisfied

Disciplined
20. How satisfied are you with your ability to live a disciplined Christian life?

Dissatisfied   1   2   3   4   5   6   7   Satisfied

Notes

1. Bob St. John, *The Landry Legend* (Dallas: WORD Inc., 1989), p. 230.
2. Paul concluded this profile by stating that an overseer must hold "fast the faithful word which is in accordance with the teaching, that he may be able both to exhort in sound doctrine and to refute those who contradict" (Titus 1:9). This final statement could certainly be classified as a mark of maturity as well. However, it is really a result of the qualities that Paul had outlined previously. In some respects, it is an outworking of a man who is "self-disciplined" in his Christian life.
3. Opinions differ about what these words mean when we attempt to describe the nature of man. Some people believe the Bible teaches a dichotomist position—that man is basically a "material" and "immaterial" being. They do not distinguish between "soul" and "spirit." Other people believe in a trichotomist approach—that man is composed of three distinguishable parts, "body, soul and spirit." Still others believe in a multichotomist position—that additional words are used to describe the nature of man, such as "heart" and "mind." In trying to understand how people actually function, I have found it helpful to describe human beings as three-dimensional—physical, psychological and spiritual. In this sense, these concepts could correlate with the body (physical), the soul (psychological) and spirit (spiritual).
4. See Gene A. Getz, *Elijah: Remaining Steadfast Through Uncertainty* (Nashville: Broadman & Holman, 1995).

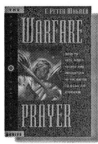 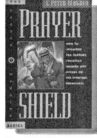  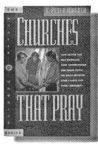
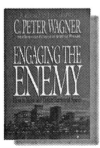  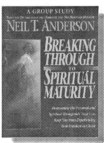 

Continuing Education for Church Leaders.

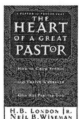